Praise for

The New Royals

"A thoughtful and penetrating look at Queen Elizabeth II and the monarchy going forward by one of the best-connected royal commentators. Katie Nicholl shines an incisive light on the difficulties and opportunities facing the present and future generation of the royal family."
—Andrew Morton

"A unique look back and ahead for the royal family. . . . In the book, [Katie Nicholl] paints this very vivid life and legacy of Queen Elizabeth."
—Al Roker, *The Today Show*

"A cracking book! *The New Royals* is an essential look at what's next for the Crown."
—Piers Morgan

"Katie Nicholl does tremendous work as *Vanity Fair*'s royal correspondent, whether it's a groundbreaking exclusive or a delicious morsel of palace intel. *The New Royals* is more of Katie at her best, gathering string on one of the dynamic family sagas of our time."

—Claire Howorth, executive editor, *Vanity Fair*

"*The New Royals* is a fascinating look at how the Royal House of Windsor is preparing for the next one hundred years of the dynasty. As ever, Katie Nicholl takes viewers on a journey to the very heart of 'the Firm' through meticulous research and compelling interviews with real insiders. It is a must-read for every royal fan."

—Nick Bullen, editor in chief, *True Royalty TV*

THE

New Royals

Also by Katie Nicholl:

Harry and Meghan: Life, Loss, and Love

Kate: The Future Queen

The Making of a Royal Romance

William and Harry: Behind the Palace Walls

THE
New Royals

Queen Elizabeth's Legacy
and the Future of the Crown

Katie Nicholl

hachette
BOOKS
New York

Hachette Books
Hachette Book Group
1290 Avenue of the Americas
New York, NY 10104
HachetteBooks.com
Twitter.com/HachetteBooks
Instagram.com/HachetteBooks

First Trade Paperback Edition: September 2023

Published by Hachette Books, an imprint of Hachette Book Group, Inc. The Hachette Books name and logo is a trademark of the Hachette Book Group.

The Hachette Speakers Bureau provides a wide range of authors for speaking events. To find out more, go to hachettespeakersbureau.com or email HachetteSpeakers@hbgusa.com.

Books by Hachette Books may be purchased in bulk for business, educational, or promotional use. For information, please contact your local bookseller or Hachette Book Group Special Markets Department at: special.markets@hbgusa.com.

The publisher is not responsible for websites (or their content) that are not owned by the publisher.

Editorial production by Christine Marra, Marrathon Production Services. www.marrathoneditorial.org

Set in 11.16-point Goudy Oldstyle

Library of Congress Cataloging-in-Publication Data has been applied for.

ISBNs: 978-0-306-82797-6 (hardcover), 978-0-306-82798-3 (ebook), 978-0-306-82799-0 (trade paperback)

Printed in the United States of America

LSC-C

Printing 3, 2023

For Chris, Matilda, and George.
My everything.

Contents

Preface

All of us who will inherit the legacy of my grandmother's reign and generation need to do all we can to celebrate and learn from her story.

—HRH THE PRINCE OF WALES

Queen Elizabeth II was a record-breaking monarch; her reign of 70 years and 214 days is the longest of any British monarch and the longest recorded of any female head of state in history. Elizabeth II celebrated a lifetime of milestones, surpassing her great-great-grandmother Queen Victoria as the United Kingdom's longest-reigning monarch and becoming the only British sovereign to celebrate a Platinum Jubilee. Her death on September 8, 2022, was a milestone moment too. The Queen was the only monarch most people had known, and despite her age and increasingly frail health, her passing at the age of ninety-six was a great shock.

As Britain entered a period of national mourning and bid farewell to the much-loved monarch in a state funeral, there was a tangible sense of loss and grief, not just for the Queen, but for the bygone era she personified.

The Queen died peacefully at Balmoral Castle in Scotland. At her bedside were her son and heir, Prince Charles, and her daughter, Princess Anne. Protected by the great green forests of the highlands,

Scotland was where the Queen had always been happiest and where she had wanted to die. The moment her heart stopped beating, her son and heir, Charles, the Prince of Wales, became King Charles III.

His accession was marked in a centuries-old tradition with herald trumpets and proclamation ceremonies across the United Kingdom. Because she had died in Scotland, the Queen lay in rest at St. Giles's Cathedral in Edinburgh before her body was flown home to England and transported to the historic Westminster Hall, where she lay in state for four days and five nights. A quarter of a million people filed past her coffin to pay their respects while more than four billion tuned in to watch the television coverage of the funeral, a testimony to the love and respect the late Queen commanded.

Eight months later, on Saturday, May 6, 2023, Charles was crowned at Westminster Abbey, the first king to be crowned since the Queen's father, George VI. Now, once again, Britain has a king and queen. While the coronation had all the pomp and pageantry expected of a great state occasion, it was smaller than the late Queen's and less expensive to stage. One of the hallmarks of Charles's reign is that of a slimmed-down monarchy and an institution that—while funded by the British taxpayer—should not be a financial burden. In an age where the House of Windsor must fight to justify its very existence, deference belongs to the past.

Charles is King in a very different era from his mother's, and to-day, the royal family is at a pivotal point. The landscape of the mon-archy is undergoing a seismic shift under King Charles III and Queen Camilla in a modern society that increasingly questions why the United Kingdom is still beholden to a hereditary monarchy. While the republican movement has yet to gather any real traction in Brit-ain, for now, King Charles, who succeeded his mother as head of the Commonwealth, faces great uncertainty over what this "family of nations" will look like now that the Queen has gone.

His sincere wish is that the Commonwealth can continue to play an important role in a modern era. Closer to home, the King worries about the United Kingdom and keeping England, Northern Ireland, Scotland, and Wales together. Certainly his reign is not without challenges, but he is determined the monarchy should not die out with him or his eldest son, William, now Prince of Wales.

Charles has used the early months of his reign to present himself as a king fit to rule in the twenty-first century. As Prince of Wales, he used his platform to shine a light on the now critical issue of climate change, thus paving the way for him to become Britain's first eco-king. Protecting the planet for future generations is at the heart of the man who is now King.

In his very first address to the nation as monarch, Charles pledged to follow in his mother's footsteps and serve his whole life. In doing so, he quashed decades of speculation that he will abdicate in favor of his son.

Queen Elizabeth II's success and popularity was rooted in her ability to adapt and evolve. Circumstances, family tragedies, and scandals—such as the death of the Princess of Wales, the departure of the Duke and Duchess of Sussex from Britain, and the downfall of her son Prince Andrew—forced her to reinvent the institution of monarchy to secure its future. And yet despite its metamorphosis, the Queen managed to preserve the historic traditions and customs that make the British monarchy so unique.

Charles will try to do the same, but his reign will be short compared to his mother's. Now in his seventies, he will be a transitional king. Nonetheless, he is determined to leave his own legacy.

Fortunately, there is the promise of the popular Prince and Princess of Wales to succeed him and continue the House of Windsor's survival. William knows the future of the monarchy rests on his shoulders while Kate has inherited a title steeped in history and memories of William's mother, Diana. Her great success has been her determination to carve her own role within the royal family while supporting her husband and raising their young family.

William, having learned the lessons of kingship from his grandmother, is proving to be a modern statesman with his father's campaigning spirit and his late mother's empathy. With Kate by his side, and their son Prince George, now second in line to the throne, there is every chance Britain will have a beloved monarchy for decades to come.

The late Queen once said, "I know that the only way to live my life is to try to do what is right, to take the long view, to give of my best in all that the day brings."

That Elizabeth II has given of her best is indisputable. Now she leaves her country with the best of her: a son, grandson, and great-grandson in whom her legacy will live on.

CHAPTER 1

Platinum Queen

I have to be seen to be believed.

—HER MAJESTY THE QUEEN

It was a truly British summer's day, unseasonably wet and chilly with a stiff breeze snapping at Union flags beneath pewter skies. The morning of June 7, 1977, did not augur well for what was supposed to be a day of celebration for the Silver Jubilee of Her Majesty, Queen Elizabeth II. And yet by the time Britain's great national party came to a close that night, it was already being considered a landmark event in the country's history. In every community, it seemed, there had been a coming together for village fêtes and street parties, cucumber sandwiches and coronation chicken, pots of tea and bottles of champagne. The toast raised, be it in a china mug or a crystal glass, was unanimous: "Our Queen!"

Britain was not an especially happy nation at that time, its political life damaged by an energy crisis, a financial crash, and militant trade union clashes. At first, Silver Jubilee plans were almost timidly laid, as if for a party no one might want to attend.

June 6 changed all that. Out of the darkness the Queen appeared in Windsor Great Park to set alight a huge beacon, the signal for others on hilltops across the country to be ignited. Within minutes there was a chain of fire telegraphing love, respect, and congratulations from the four corners of Great Britain back to Her Majesty.

The next day there was a service of thanksgiving in St. Paul's Cathedral. The Queen processed through London in the great gold state coach that had carried her to her coronation twenty-five years earlier. That day there were an estimated one million people on the streets, with half a billion more watching on televisions around the Commonwealth. So in the end it was the party to which everyone received a ticket, an event which renewed the relationship between the monarch and her people and paved the way, with optimism and patriotism, for the next twenty-five years.

Given the tumult of those next decades, it was just as well.

In 1977 there wasn't a whiff of the scandals to come. Lady Diana Spencer was still a schoolgirl, Sarah Ferguson at secretarial college. Arguments over royal finances were not yet raging; society was more deferential. The Queen's Golden Jubilee twenty-five years later would be a more somber affair, coming in 2002 and reflecting a time of great turbulence. The national mood would be more questioning, the country less sure of its feelings toward the royal family. It would take another decade of reinvention by Her Majesty, and the extraordinary uplift of the Diamond Jubilee in 2012, for her to re-earn the popularity once hers by dint of youth, beauty, and majesty. By then longevity and steadfastness would be what counted.

At the end Elizabeth II was the Platinum Queen, her reign had spanned a history-making seventy years and embodied all the resilience and allure of the precious metal after which it was named. No other monarch has ever done what she has done other. The question is, what next for the monument to royalty she built? What next for the dynasty she founded? If hers was the second Elizabethan age, then who will define the years which follow?

———— · ————

PRINCESS ELIZABETH ALEXANDRA MARY was born at 2:40 A.M. on April 21, 1926, at 17 Bruton Street, Mayfair, in the West London home of her maternal grandparents.

"You don't know what a tremendous joy it is . . . to have our little girl," her father Albert, the Duke of York (known to his family as "Bertie"), wrote to his mother, Queen Mary. "We have always wanted a child to make our happiness complete and now that it has happened at last, it seems so wonderful and strange."

The duke was the second son of King George V and Queen Mary. He had fallen in love with the aristocratic Elizabeth Bowes Lyon, a strong, shrewd, and sociable young woman with a natural charm that in widowhood would see her become Britain's beloved Queen Mother. The duke, shyer, more diffident, and with an anxious stammer, was uncharacteristically bold in his single-minded pursuit of her. Believed to have met as children, she caught his eye at a society dance in 1920 and their eventual match, never intended to be that of a king and queen, was to be the making of the modern monarchy.

The arrival of Princess Margaret in August 1930 completed the family, creating the tight unit the duke would nickname "We Four." He chose to replicate his wife's childhood, which had been filled, in her own words, with "fun, kindness, and a marvelous sense of security." His own, at the hands of governesses and tutors behind palace walls, had been melancholic in comparison. He wanted the warm and loving Bowes Lyon model for his own family. When Albert was forced onto the throne just six years after Margaret's birth, he would find both strength and solace in their family structure.

Black and white portraits show then princess Elizabeth's childhood as one of sweet privilege. It can be encapsulated in images of her playing in Y Bwthyn Bach, a thatched cottage in the gardens of Windsor's Royal Lodge, which had been given to the young princess by the people of Wales for her sixth birthday. Home and hearth, nature, horses (her first was a Shetland pony called Peggy, a fourth-birthday present), and dogs (Dookie, her first corgi, arrived in 1933) defined a life still some years distant from the Crown. They would have been the blueprint for the rest of it, if not for the looming abdication crisis.

Upon the death of George V in January 1936, his eldest son, David, became king, reigning as Edward VIII. But he would abdicate after just eleven months, having been told his role forbade him from marrying twice-divorced American Wallis Simpson. It was the gravest constitutional crisis of the modern monarchy. The king's abdication speech, his abandonment of his birthright, his duty, and his country broke the royal family's compact with its people.

Bertie's life changed in a heartbeat. His identity as the Duke of York was stripped from him and he became King George VI, a regnant name chosen to suggest continuity with his father, King George V, whom Elizabeth had called "Grandpa England."

It was a royal footman who broke the news to the little princesses. "Does that mean you will be queen, Lilibet?" asked Margaret, then six, of her ten-year-old sister. "I suppose so," said the princess, her life unimaginably altered by the coronation of her father on May 12, 1937—Britain's third monarch in a year. According to Gyles Brandreth, the friend and biographer of Elizabeth's future husband, Prince Philip: "Least said, soonest mended" was the unstated national policy, as the machinery of monarchy gave the new king's reign a momentum all of its own.

In an early nod to the wily PR arts, which see carefully curated images of the Duke and Duchess of Cambridge and their three children, Prince George, Princess Charlotte, and Prince Louis dominating headlines today, the new king and queen didn't hesitate to use their daughters to promote the idea of a happy family in the palace. Cecil Beaton's dreamy photographs from the era consciously re-create the idealized royal family depicted in artist Franz Xaver Winterhalter's romantic portraits of Queen Victoria, whose extraordinary sixty-three-and-a-half-year reign Elizabeth would eventually eclipse.

In truth, their installment came not a moment too soon, for Britain, rocked by the abdication, was heading to war. Hitler had become chancellor of Germany in 1933 and would invade Poland in 1939. There was financial distress too. The 1929 Wall Street crash gave rise to a global depression, keenly felt in the United Kingdom where Victorian heavy industry—mining, shipbuilding, iron and steel, and textiles—was in decline. In 1936 poverty and hardship were so intense that a crusade of men marched from the north of England to London begging for work, ultimately laying the foundations of the postwar welfare state. All this meant that at the time of George VI's coronation, Britain had never needed the leadership of a good monarch more.

War came on September 3, 1939. Europe was overrun by Hitler's forces. Britain stood alone with George VI and Prime Minister Winston Churchill at its helm. The royals could have taken refuge elsewhere, but the king wouldn't budge. "The children will not leave unless I do. I shall not leave unless their father does, and the king will not leave the country in any circumstances whatever," said his wife, Queen Elizabeth, in a statement to the country after a German bomb hit Buckingham Palace in September 1940.

A month later his daughter Elizabeth made a genuine and heartfelt speech to the children of the Commonwealth in her first public address. "We know," she told them in a radio broadcast, "every one of us, that in the end all will be well . . . And when peace comes, remember it will be for us, the children of today, to make the world of tomorrow a better and happier place."

On her sixteenth birthday in 1942 she received her first military appointment as Colonel of the Regiment of the Grenadier Guards, and attended her first official public engagement to inspect them. Soon she would be signing up herself, joining the Auxiliary Territorial Service (ATS) as Second Subaltern Elizabeth Windsor, and learning how to drive and maintain military vehicles. She knew her way around a Land Rover and late into old age could still be seen driving regularly drove herself around her estates at Sandringham and Balmoral. When at war's end on VE Day, May 8, 1945, the king and queen appeared on the balcony of Buckingham Palace with Churchill, the princess wore the rough khaki ATS uniform she'd earned.

Elizabeth was already a public figure, but her private life held a closely guarded secret: she was in love. The princess fell in love with

Prince Philip of Greece in July 1939, while visiting the Royal Naval College at Dartmouth. She was just thirteen and he was eighteen and, like her, a direct descendent of Queen Victoria. He was as handsome as a Greek god, had excelled at college, graduating as the top cadet of his year, and, recalled the princess's governess Marion Crawford, "showed off a great deal." It was a heady combination: shared roots, military dash, self-confidence, and good looks.

Within a few short years he would be not just Elizabeth's husband but her subject too, kissing his wife at her coronation in Westminster Abbey and pledging "to become your liege man of life and limb, and of earthly worship; and faith and truth I will bear unto you, to live and die, against all manner of folks."

Their relationship began with wartime letters and the impecunious prince—he was without a country or a fortune—calling on Buckingham Palace when his military service permitted. It flourished in the summer of 1946, when they privately agreed their future was together. Their engagement was announced in July 1947, the princess having turned twenty-one in April of that year, and they married on November 20.

In ration book Britain, still grayed by the austerity of the postwar years, a royal wedding, especially that of the lovely young heir to the throne and a decorated war hero, had a romance and potency all of its own. A congregation of two thousand squeezed into Westminster Abbey and two million more tuned in to the BBC's radio broadcast.

Philip was the real deal—he had seen action in the Mediterranean and the Far East; been mentioned in dispatches for bravery and excellent service; and at the close of the Second World War was in Tokyo Bay for the official signing of the Japanese Instrument of Surrender in September 1945. As for the princess Elizabeth, her ATS service and her family's refusal to leave London even after an air raid on the palace saw her held in the highest esteem, in contrast to the Duke and Duchess of Windsor, whose Nazi sympathies had become apparent when they'd visited Hitler's Germany in 1937.

Most significant of all perhaps, with the toxic legacy of the affair between Edward VIII and Wallis Simpson still very recent in British minds, was the sense that Elizabeth and Philip's was a royal marriage that promised, like all the best fairy tales, to end happily ever after.

The bride's dress, the material bought with ration coupons, was by master couturier Norman Hartnell. The gown of ivory duchesse satin was stitched in silver and scattered with crystals and ten thousand seed pearls. Elizabeth chose a design inspired by Botticelli's *Primavera*, symbolizing growth and rebirth following the war. It was an exercise of her soft power, a determination to embody the needs of her nation. Apart from which she looked, according to her bridesmaid, Lady Pamela Hicks, absolutely "knockout."

Philip thought so too, and delighted in his new wife. "Cherish Lilibet? I wonder if that word is enough to express what is in me," he wrote the Queen Mother just after their wedding, fondly using his wife's childhood nickname, now of course the given name of the Duke and Duchess of Sussex's daughter. "Lilibet," he went on, "is the only thing in this world which is absolutely real to me and my ambition is to weld the two of us into a new combined existence."

This they did in the heat and peace of Malta, shielded from public view by fig and olive groves and stubby Aleppo pines. Between 1949 and 1951, Philip was stationed there on naval duty and his wife joined him for extended periods, living the life—almost—of an ordinary military wife. Pictures from the time show her laughing and carefree, dancing at a naval ball. "Magical," confirms Lady Pamela, who went on to become the Queen's lady-in-waiting. "Endless picnics, sunbathing, and waterskiing. It was wonderful for her. The only place that she was able to live the life of a naval officer's wife." Those Maltese days were, Elizabeth would later reveal, among the happiest of her life, even though she had to divide her time between Malta and England, where a young Charles was being cared for by his grandparents and his nanny. It was telling that in 2007, celebrating their diamond wedding anniversary, the Queen and Prince Philip returned to the island where they had been so happy as newlyweds.

Charles Philip Arthur George, their first child and heir to the throne his mother was yet to inherit, was born in Buckingham Palace on November 14, 1948, near enough a honeymoon baby. He would be followed on August 15, 1950, by a sister, Anne Elizabeth Alice Louise, born in Clarence House where the growing family was making its home.

Unusually it would be another decade before the couple completed their quartet of children with Andrew Albert Christian Edward born February 19, 1960, and Edward Antony Richard Louis born March 10, 1964. According to the royal historian Robert Lacey, with whom I spoke, the Queen and Prince Philip's decision to have two more children later in their marriage reflected the Queen's wish to be a more hands-on mother.

"The Queen clearly wanted to be a mother. We know that from the fact that she voluntarily elected to have a second family. I think there's a suggestion she felt—perhaps—she hadn't been there enough the first time 'round. She had Charles and Anne early on in what she thought would be a relatively private and not-too-busy life while her father lived out his full span as king. Then early and unexpectedly, she became Queen, her ultimate calling in life and her divine duty. This was also a woman who had worn a uniform in the Second World War and for whom duty mattered all the more. So family proliferation ended for her in 1952, for the time being.

"I think the decision to have two more children in the 1960s when she had more spare time for being a mother was her acknowledgement of how duty had prevented her being a parent to the full extent she would have liked with Charles and Anne. And it also revealed how the Queen enjoyed parenting more than people have realized. She chose to have four children when her own parents, her sister, and many of her mid-twentieth-century contemporaries just had two."

The Queen did her best to juggle royal duties with being a mother and moved her weekly late-afternoon meeting with Winston Churchill to early evening so she could be with the children for their bath and bedtime routine.

——— ———

By the beginning of the 1950s Britain seemed to be emerging from the social and economic shock of the Second World War. Rationing was starting to ease and the 1951 Festival of Britain was intended to invigorate arts, design, and sport for a generation. But behind this declaration of all that was bright and new, the health of the king was failing. He opened the festival in May of that year, but by September he was having surgery for lung cancer.

On January 31, 1952, King George VI waved Elizabeth and Philip off from London Airport. They were taking his place on a tour to Australia and New Zealand, stopping in Kenya for a romantic break first. It was there at the fabled Treetops Hotel that Philip broke the news to his wife that her father had died in his sleep at Sandringham, aged just fifty-six. On February 6, 1952, Elizabeth returned to Britain as queen. As well as a daughter in mourning, she was now her nation's head of state.

The second Elizabethan age began officially on June 2, 1953—Coronation Day. The rain was torrential, more like January than June, but the route of the procession was crammed with subjects eager to catch a glimpse of their new queen in her gold state coach. Her youth and beauty stood in stark contrast to the ancient ceremony and the archaic language of her vows. The monarch, said Churchill, was "the heir to all our traditions and glories," assuming her position "at a time when tormented mankind stands uncertainly poised between world catastrophe and a golden age." Yet she was so slight, the imperial state crown had to be resized.

At the entrance to Westminster Abbey she turned to the maids of honor carrying her eighteen-foot-long train and asked, "Ready, girls?" She certainly was. *"Vivat Regina Elizabetha"* ("Long Live Queen Elizabeth"), sang the choir as she met her destiny in a gown that incorporated an emblem for every country of the United Kingdom and the Commonwealth—from the Tudor Rose of England to wheat, cotton, and jute for Pakistan.

It was Philip who had urged the palace and the government to televise his wife's coronation, an occasion once considered so sacred it could not be shared beyond the abbey. More than half the population of Britain, 27 million, tuned in, many having bought black and white TV sets for the event. Most appeared to agree with Churchill—Elizabeth was indeed the embodiment of British hopes of a second golden age.

After the majesty and history of the coronation, it was back to the business of royalty for the Queen. In an age when being royal was different from being simply famous, she was stellar. Queen Elizabeth II was a youthful beauty famed for her dainty waist and luminous complexion, both enhanced by the finest couture and gems.

She was a global icon, in the words of contemporary British historian Sir Charles Petrie, "the subject of adulation unparalleled since the days of Louis XIV." Her face was on Britain's stamps and its money and, since the technological advance that had seen the televising of her coronation continued apace, Elizabeth was queen of the airwaves too. She connected with subjects in the farthest corners of her Commonwealth through radio and TV, and she also made a point of going to see them in person. The royal visit became her leitmotif. "I have to be seen to be believed," she once said, and she made sure she was both.

A post-coronation tour with Prince Philip (Charles and Anne were left at home under the care of the royal nanny) included visits to Australia and New Zealand, Bermuda and Jamaica, Fiji, Tonga, and the Cocos Islands, Sri Lanka (then Ceylon), Aden (in Yemen), Uganda, Malta, and Gibraltar. It spanned 174 days between 1953 and 1954 and made history with the Queen's first Christmas broadcast from a foreign country. She recorded her festive good wishes in a strapless evening dress and diamonds at Government House in Auckland, New Zealand.

Her style was copied worldwide. While Kate, Duchess of Cambridge, is now the most emulated royal style influencer, in those heady days the Queen was compared to Grace Kelly; she favored elegant designs by Hardy Amies and Norman Hartnell, who had created her wedding and coronation gowns. She gravitated toward bright block colors and patterns, which meant she could be seen in a crowd, and hats that framed but never covered her face. At night her passion for elaborate embroidery, lace, and fur was given free rein. The Queen was one of the world's sharpest power dressers, her outfits designed to pay homage to another nation by employing a national color or an appropriate motif.

These early years of her reign, the 1950s and 1960s, were a triumph for the new queen, a brilliant ambassador for her country, convenor of the Commonwealth, wife and mother. She took to the role with confidence and professionalism because her father had taught her well and instilled in her the disciplines required for a monarch. She was a woman of great faith, and as head of the Church of England her belief and trust in God would be a source of comfort throughout her long reign. As head of state she was required to undertake constitutional and representational duties but also had a less formal role as "head of nation," acting as a focus for national identity, unity, and pride; giving a sense of stability and continuity; officially recognizing success and excellence; and supporting the ideal of voluntary service.

"These are the functions of monarchy, but above all the dignity and care in which it is carried out is a matter of tone and pitch as much as it is procedures, and more so most of the time," notes historian and constitutional expert Lord Peter Hennessy. "The formal role of the monarchy is to give royal assent to bills, and that's about it. The rest of it is helping set the tone for the nation, being above politics and being head of the Crown services. The commander in chief of the armed forces is the Queen, not the prime minister."

As a serving naval officer who had pledged his allegiance to the Crown, the Duke of Edinburgh would never be her equal. Nonetheless Prince Philip, who died at the age of ninety-nine on April 9, 2021, was a remarkable man. He was born a prince of Greece and Denmark on the dining table of his family home on Corfu, but fled the island in a cradle made out of an old fruit crate when the abdication of the king of Greece in 1922 drove his family out of the country. His mother was diagnosed with schizophrenia when he was eight and his father became peripatetic, living between Paris and Monte Carlo with a mistress. The big sister to whom he was closest was killed in an air crash with her family in 1937. Philip was impoverished, exiled, and, by the age of eleven, perfectly capable of finding his way from one side of Europe to the other alone by train.

In May 1939, six weeks before his eighteenth birthday, he joined the Royal Naval College at Dartmouth. His uncle and British guardian, Lord Louis Mountbatten, helped Philip navigate a new course that carried him, through his marriage to the Queen, into the heart of the British establishment. The problem was that there was no role for him when he got there. He would share the Queen's reign without wearing a crown. He was in her eyes the dearest and most noble of her subjects, his life and work indivisible from her own. He was her consort, confidante, companion, and counsel, but he was obliged to sacrifice his own professional ambitions and any prospect of real privacy to be by her side.

With intelligence and good heart, despite a lot of grumbling and the occasional volcanic outburst, Philip eventually carved a serious position for himself. The Duke stood four-square behind the regiments, corps, and military charities that came into his care. He was patron of more than eight hundred causes and elected himself unofficial ambassador for British trade and industry, especially where science and new technology were concerned. He protected wildlife, green spaces, and woodland. Above all he imbued 10 million young people in over 130 countries with the self-belief and practical skills to achieve the Duke of Edinburgh's Award after founding the scheme in 1956.

But when the Queen first fell in love, neither Philip's pedigree nor his exemplary wartime record made him, in the eyes of British courtiers and the political establishment, the perfect consort. He was, they snobbishly believed, too poor, too brash, and potentially, because of his striking blond looks and athletic physique, a philanderer. "Rough, ill mannered, uneducated, and would probably not be faithful," was the famous and damning summation of one courtier. Yet he was her loyal consort for sixty-nine years and had been her loving husband for even longer—seventy-three years—by the time he died.

"Prince Philip is the only man in the world who treats the Queen simply as another human being," the courtier Lord Charteris, a senior advisor to the Queen, once astutely observed. He also had the knack of pouring her a consoling gin and Dubonnet at the end of a difficult day.

Their children bear her last name—Windsor—not his, Mountbatten. "I'm the only man in the country not allowed to give his name to his children. I'm nothing but a bloody amoeba," Philip spluttered when this was decided in the early 1950s. But in the manner of raising their children he answered to no one. While the Queen was often occupied with affairs of state, the Duke of Edinburgh was a devoted, hands-on father. He was tactile and always up for a bit of tomfoolery. Clarence House often echoed with the sound of laughter and impromptu back-garden games after the arrivals of Charles and Anne.

He believed in robust parenting, which suited Princess Anne, who resembled her father in character and ability. Even when she was tiny she was tough, able, and impatient to succeed, swiftly becoming the apple of his eye. Prince Charles was a gentler and more timid child who lacked the confidence of his tomboy little sister.

Philip's fractured childhood meant he set unusually high standards for resilience in himself and others, and when Charles failed to meet them the Duke could bully and humiliate his sensitive son. According to Jonathan Dimbleby, the Prince of Wales's official biographer, Charles was "easily cowed by the forceful personality of his father . . . When Prince Philip upbraided his son for a deficiency in behavior or attitude, he drew tears to the child's eyes." The author and broadcaster, speaking with the approval of Prince Charles back in 1994, painted a picture of a lonely and isolated child with a disciplinarian father and a detached mother. In later adulthood, however, with their interests more aligned, he grew closer to his parents.

Certainly the teenage prince did not enjoy following in his father's footsteps and going to Gordonstoun, the austere Scottish boarding school where Philip had been head boy. "Charles had neither his father's resilient temperament nor his relative anonymity, and he lacked the physical prowess to command respect. Encumbered by his titles and his status as heir to the throne, he was singled out as a victim from his first day," writes Sally Bedell Smith in her biography of the prince, *Charles: The Misunderstood Prince*.

The consequence of Philip's determination to make a man of his eldest son—his sort of man—was that Charles forged close bonds with supportive women. He depended on a succession of them, beginning with his nannies Helen Lightbody, Mabel Anderson, and Catherine Peebles before he was sent to his first boarding school, aged eight. His beloved grandmother the Queen Mother, and eventually Camilla Parker Bowles would both play a key role supporting him as he emerged from his father's shadow.

The births of Andrew, then Edward, a decade after the arrival of Anne, ended a period of the royal marriage marred by gossip. It centered on 1956 when Philip accepted an invitation to open the Olympic Games in Melbourne. He chose to make the twelve-thousand-mile trip aboard the royal yacht *Britannia*, visiting distant parts of the Empire and Commonwealth en route. The voyage left the Queen alone for four months. The separation was hardly unusual for a naval officer and his wife and had the Queen's blessing. But the royal marriage was always under close scrutiny by the media, and rumors had started to circulate about Philip and Elizabeth. The failing marriage of Philip's friend and private secretary Mike Parker, who was traveling with him, didn't help. Parker's wife filed for divorce while he was overseas with Philip, citing adultery. Whispers soon started to trickle out that the royal marriage was also in trouble, prompting the palace to issue a rare official denial, stating: "It is quite untrue that there is any rift between the Queen and the Duke."

If he was running away from anything, it was perhaps the constraints of palace life. Whatever the truth of those months, the time and space they gave the royal couple rejuvenated their relationship and healed the deep wound Philip felt over his children's surname. Meeting her husband on his way back at Lisbon, the Queen put on a public show of happiness and unity—when Philip boarded her plane, he found his wife and her entire staff wearing false beards, imitating the one she knew he'd grown at sea.

As the Duke celebrated his 1997 golden wedding anniversary with the Queen, he used an honorary gala lunch to pay tribute to his children: "Like all families we went through the full range of the pleasures and tribulations of bringing up children. I am naturally somewhat biased but I think ours have all done rather well under very demanding circumstances and I hope I can be forgiven for feeling proud of them."

It had taken a while to achieve such equilibrium in the family. Although the court year was stable—daily life in Buckingham Palace, Easter court at Windsor, long private summer holidays in Balmoral, and an extended Christmas at Sandringham—the presence of the Queen and Prince Philip was not. Their role as parents was often obliged to come second to their royal duties and crammed diaries. Where parents and children could come together was aboard the royal yacht *Britannia*. They spent happy holidays cruising the remote western isles of Scotland, far beyond the longest-range camera lens. At Balmoral they could also be at their most private, enjoying shooting, stalking, and barbecues on the moors. The Queen was so reluctant to be spotted there that she once dived into some heather when she saw a group of tourists approaching.

Images of Her Majesty off duty, including one of her propped up in bed wearing a triple strand of pearls and lipstick while nursing a newborn Prince Edward, did much to humanize her and modernize her image. So too did the release of unposed studio shots—the outtakes of formal portrait sittings—and holiday snaps from those Balmoral breaks.

But Philip's ambitions in this department were far greater. He believed it was time to sweep away at least some of his wife's royal mystique in the hope of bringing the monarch and her subjects closer together. He wanted to be seen as a royal family more in keeping with the spirit of the age and began by authorizing a groundbreaking documentary, *Royal Family*, broadcast in 1969. It was the first time viewers were permitted inside the palace and was such a ratings success that the BBC estimates 350 million people watched.

The documentary showed the Queen working on her dispatch boxes, watching TV with Andrew and Edward, and dressing the Christmas tree at Windsor. It portrayed the royal couple as parents having tea with Charles and Anne and hosting a private family barbecue at Balmoral. The Windsors were, like everyone else, having sausages.

Philip Bonham-Carter, who granted me a series of exclusive interviews before his sudden death in April 2022, worked as an assistant cameraman on the film. He spent a year with the royals making the documentary, accompanying them on private and official trips, and joining them on holiday at Balmoral and Sandringham, where he captured young Edward and Andrew having a snowball fight.

"I remember the snowball fight and how surreal the whole thing felt," he recalled. "On another occasion we were on *Britannia* on a royal tour. We had been given cabins in the royal area, and it was pretty extraordinary seeing the young Princess Anne and Prince Charles having pillow fights in their rooms. We spent a year, give or take, with the Queen . . . something which had never been done before. At the time the attitude towards the Queen and the royals was totally different to now. As a family they were much more revered then; they were on a pedestal. In those days to have the level of access that we did really was quite unusual.

"We were given absolute access and essentially became part of the Royal Household. Wherever they went, we went . . . Bill [Sir William] Heseltine, who was the Queen's press secretary at the time, was very influential in making it happen and he had a remarkable way of making the Queen relax. Having observed her with many of her private secretaries, including Martin Charteris and Robert Fellowes, the Queen could be quite formal, and she had very formal relationships with her staff, but she was more at ease with Bill and I think that's because he was an Australian. The Queen loves Australians because they're so much more relaxed than we Brits. And I think that's a clue to her character, frankly. She doesn't like stuck-up."

The documentary was a huge hit but it left its audience wanting more. The royals had opened the palace door and it seemed they were now being pressured into putting out a welcome mat too. It was Walter Bagehot, the Victorian constitutional expert who accurately observed of the monarchy: "Its mystery is its life. We must not let daylight in on the magic." Well, they had now. Realizing the documentary had been a mistake, the Queen requested the film never be shown again, and it remains under lock and key in the BBC royal archives—although it was recently leaked on YouTube.

Robert Lacey recalled the impact of the film when it aired: "Everyone thought it was such a step forward, and it seemed the next logical stage after televising the coronation. But we can now see with hindsight how the implications of making the royal family so accessible and everyday hadn't been properly thought through. Maintaining a certain mystique is part of the delicate balance of monarchy and getting that balance right has been the eternal challenge of the queen's reign."

This voracious appetite for news and gossip would lay the foundation for the obsessive public interest in the next generation of royals, notably Diana, Princess of Wales, and then her sons, the Dukes of Cambridge and Sussex, and their spouses. In the seventies however, Britain had to make do with the 1973 marriage of Princess Anne to Captain Mark Phillips and the string of aristocratic girls rumored to be dating Prince Charles, then the most eligible bachelor in the country.

Britain in the early and mid-seventies was a country struggling to find a new international identity in a world where it was being left behind by its industrial competitors. A Tory government was brought down by the combination of an energy crisis, financial crash, and two miners' strikes in two years. And while a Labour administration got the country back to work, it came at the price of galloping inflation and a humiliating bailout from the International Monetary Fund. Racial tensions were rising too. Immigrants from African nations, the Caribbean, and Asia found that Britain's race relations laws did not actually guarantee them equal access to homes or jobs, or protect them from far-right groups such as the National Front. The Select Committee on Race Relations set up in 1968 produced evidence of the inadequacy of government policy in the early seventies, leading to the Race Relations Act 1976.

This then was the unfortunate hinterland to preparations for the Silver Jubilee. Palace planners wondered how much people who'd been living through economic hardship and political turmoil would want to celebrate the seemingly gilded life of the monarch. Yet their fears would be unfounded. This was decades before the internet age but, to borrow a phrase from today's technology, the Silver Jubilee "went viral." The people spoke, and what they said they wanted was their queen.

In the early part of 1977, the Queen and Prince Philip visited thirty-six counties in three months, drawing crowds of up to a million. By the time June came, her jubilee was the defining event in her country's summer calendar. The chain of beacons she lit on the night of June 6 was an accurate depiction of the unity that cemented a fractured country. The coronation spirit was again abroad in the land, with millions enjoying the uncomplicated sense of unity and national pride embodied by the monarch.

It is estimated that on June 7, 1977, 10 million Britons attended 125,000 street parties. In London the roar of the crowds lining the processional route from Buckingham Palace to St. Paul's Cathedral was so immense that the coachmen accompanying the Queen could not hear the hoofbeats of their horses. Five hundred million worldwide watched the spectacle on television.

After that service of thanksgiving, in a speech at the capital's Guildhall, the Queen said: "When I was twenty-one, I pledged my life to the service of our people and asked for God's help to make good that vow. Although that vow was made in my salad days, when I was green in judgment, I do not regret nor retract one word of it."

Very soon Britain would see immense change with the dawn of the Thatcher era and the coming of the eighties, the decade that would change the royal landscape forever with Diana and her wedding to Prince Charles in 1981. The Queen's family would also know personal devastation as Irish terror group the IRA (Irish Republican Army) struck at its heart, murdering Lord Mountbatten as he fished off the coast of Ireland.

But back then in the summer of 1977 it was truly the last of the old days, and Britain was enjoying the uncomplicated innocence of its Silver Jubilee year. This was just as well because once the streets were swept and the bunting furled it would be gone for good.

CHAPTER 2

Highs and Lows

I think those who marry into my family find it increasingly difficult to do so because of the added pressure. The strains and stresses become almost intolerable.

—PRINCE CHARLES

O nly a handful of women in history are famous enough to be known by their first name: Marilyn. Oprah. Diana.

At the dawn of the eighties, Diana Spencer was just another teenager with a feathery bobbed haircut and a fondness for piecrust collars. She epitomized the kind of young woman who would soon be labeled a "Sloane Ranger": moneyed, well bred, and with a bulging Filofax of friends. By the end of the decade she was a princess to the whole world. She had, tragically, only a few more years to live, yet her life and legacy would change the royal family forever.

But it was not just because of the dazzling Diana that this span of time dominated headlines for a generation, the aftershocks of its highs and lows still felt today. The period 1980–1990 encompassed two globe-stoppingly spectacular royal weddings, the birth of five royal babies (including an heir and a spare), one marital breakdown in the separation of Princess Anne and Captain Mark Phillips, and one palace break-in. It was also a time of increasing democratization in terms of the royal family's relationship with the people of Great Britain. This would lead to a painful error of judgment that saw two princes, a princess, and a duchess participate in a slapstick TV game show, an act of reputational self-harm that badly dented the monarchy's dignity.

In short, the eighties breezed in with a youth, energy, and glamour not seen since the earliest days of the Queen and Prince Philip, and blew out in a hurricane of domestic drama. These years rewrote the old rules, asking where the balance lay between royal rights and royal responsibilities, and blurring the boundaries between public figures and private people. The natural consequence was a reshaping of the public's perception of its once untouchable head of state and her extended family. The British people became more curious and more critical, less deferential. Some of them even became republicans.

But let us return to that day in July 1981 when Diana married Charles in a $7,000 dress so vast it swamped her frame, already slimmed by secret bulimia. She had only just turned twenty when she walked down the aisle of St. Paul's Cathedral to meet her groom, twelve years older at the age of thirty-two, and a man who'd already met the great love of his life, Camilla Parker Bowles.

Diana Spencer was born in 1961 on the Queen's Sandringham estate in Norfolk into a family that had historic ties to royalty. In 1975 her father inherited his earldom and took custody of the family seat, Althorp, in Northamptonshire. In 1979 Diana moved into Coleherne Court, an apartment block in London's Earls Court, where she shared an apartment with friends and worked part time as a nursery assistant. Hers was a blameless lifestyle far removed from some of the worldly girls and older women with whom Charles was enjoying a string of discreet liaisons.

She had first met the Prince of Wales when she was sixteen and he was dating her older sister, Sarah. A subsequent encounter at a July 1980 weekend house party and polo match in Sussex opened Charles's eyes to the fact that Diana had grown up gorgeous, and they began a serious courtship. In August of that year she went to Cowes Week to join him aboard the *Britannia*, and then in September to Balmoral to stalk and salmon fish, both big-ticket events for a royal girlfriend.

On paper Diana appeared perfect, since she was both beautiful and aristocratic and had no known romantic (that is to say, sexual) history. The fact that she and Charles had little in common and barely knew each other by the time they were betrothed seemed of less consequence than these credentials. The prince recognized it was an ill-advised match but felt he couldn't back out without damaging Diana's reputation and prospects, such was the frenzy of interest in their romance.

As for Diana, a woman whose childhood security had been destroyed by her parents' bitter divorce—her father was accused of cruelty and her mother of adultery—she believed she would be safe with a man who could never leave her. "She was swept along by the force of it," her friend Dr. James Colthurst told her biographer Tina Brown in *The Diana Chronicles*. "Then when this big machinery of the press and palace took over and made it into this big fairy story, she could give in to it, give over responsibility for it. It was bigger than her." In the 2017 British Channel 4 documentary *Diana: In Her Own Words*, she can be heard on audio telling her voice coach: "It was like a call to duty, really."

It's clear today that Charles hurried into his decision to make Diana his future queen. Given how the union ended, the same mistake would not be repeated with Prince William who courted Kate Middleton for eight years, lived with her, and had two breakups along the way to their 2011 wedding.

Perhaps Charles's choice of Diana reflects the fact that he was emotionally adrift. Camilla had married cavalry officer Andrew Parker Bowles in 1973 and was already the mother of a small son, Tom (born 1974), and a daughter, Laura (born 1978). Then in 1979 Charles lost his beloved great-uncle and mentor, Lord Mountbatten, in a terror bomb planted by the IRA. Mountbatten's boat was blown out of the water with a fifty-pound device in Mullaghmore Bay,

County Sligo, in the west of Ireland, killing him, his teenage grandson, and two others. The murders scorched Britain's soul. The killing of Mountbatten was savage, tactically competent, and politically motivated. It was designed to draw attention to what the IRA called the "continuing occupation" of Northern Ireland by the British. It demonstrated the ongoing risk to the Queen and left Prince Philip speaking of "the great wave of revulsion against this senseless act of terrorism." Nationally it plunged Anglo-Irish relations into an even darker era. On a personal level it left the royal family devastated, particularly Charles, who had lost his closest counselor and confidante.

The gulf between the newly betrothed couple was evident eighteen months later at their official engagement appearance when the BBC reporter conducting the interview asked, "Are you in love?" While a radiant Diana said, "Yes, of course," Charles mused, "Whatever 'in love' means . . ." In *Diana: Her True Story—In Her Own Words*, Andrew Morton's revised twenty-fifth anniversary edition of his original eighties bombshell biography, Diana reflected on his brutal caveat: "That threw me completely. I thought, what a strange answer. It traumatized me."

She famously got cold feet too on the eve of their wedding. "Too late, Duch" (her childhood nickname), her elder sisters Sarah and Jane told her, "your face is already on the tea towels." Actually her name and face were on everything—magazine covers, billboards, the television news, miles of bunting, and every type of souvenir imaginable from teapots to house bricks. Her profile was already as familiar as a classical goddess on a cameo brooch. A full-blown Diana-mania was at work in a besotted Britain.

As for the Queen, she'd seemingly given Diana an early seal of approval at Balmoral when she'd invited her to sit in the royal box to watch the Braemar Highland Games. After the engagement she invited Diana to make her home in the safety of Buckingham Palace. According to Ingrid Seward's 2002 book, *The Queen & Di*, in March 1981 Elizabeth sent a letter to a friend in which she wrote: "I trust that Diana will find living here [in the palace] less of a burden than is expected." The Queen's continuing support for her new daughter-in-law was made very apparent when actress Grace Kelly, married to Prince Rainier of Monaco, died just a year after Diana's wedding to Charles. Aged just twenty-one and still an apprentice to royal life, Diana represented Britain at Princess Grace's official funeral. It was her first solo overseas engagement.

In public and in private Diana always scrupulously observed royal protocols, dropping a deep curtsy to her mother-in-law whenever they met. But her formality did not prevent them from forging a relationship that would, in the words of Andrew Morton, make the monarch "a rather unlikely ally" for Diana when her marriage to Charles first ran into trouble.

The couple's wedding was watched by 750 million people in seventy-four countries around the world and remains one of the most watched programs of all time according to the BBC. (It's tricky to make a comparison to the viewing figures for the weddings of the Duke and Duchess of Cambridge in 2011 and the Duke and Duchess of Sussex in 2018 since both events took place in the internet age, whereas the wedding of Charles and Diana belonged to the era of appointment TV.) What those hundreds of millions witnessed was the last great state occasion of the twentieth century. It starred a fairy-tale princess in a billowing silk taffeta frock with a twenty-five-foot train, the longest in royal history, and a cascading veil made with 152 yards of tulle and ten thousand micro pearls. Charles, in his naval no. 1 ceremonial dress uniform, was her dashing groom. Their wedding was a crowd-pleasing amalgam of old and new, perfect for the 1980s. Charles and Diana marked their first public moments as man and wife with a traditional carriage ride in the 1902 state landau through the streets of London and then sealed it—forever, it was thought—with a protocol-busting kiss on the balcony of Buckingham Palace.

This "wedding of the century" did much to prop up a beleaguered Britain. It was a time of economic volatility in a country which had fallen into a deep recession, with unemployment running at 12.5 percent and inflation having hit a 22 percent peak. Inadequate housing, joblessness, low paid labor, and racial tensions triggered by new stop-and-search laws led to rioting in the Brixton area of London; the Toxteth area of Liverpool; the Handsworth area of Birmingham; the Chapeltown area of Leeds; and the Moss Side area of Manchester through that spring and summer.

The country would be halfway through the eighties before the economic boom that created the yuppie (young upwardly mobile professional) arrived. Yet those early Diana years made Britain, struggling to get a grip on its economy and build a fairer, more just society, feel optimistic about the future.

Her impact was not confined to her native country. Diana's celebrity crossed continents from the second she became a royal girlfriend and ran crazily out of control when she was elevated to Windsor wife. Her star immediately eclipsed her husband's, causing early fractures in their relationship. The diligent, sensitive, and status-conscious Charles found it hard to understand. He could not see that in the new media age, being a royal-born prince and future king was a lesser currency than his wife's megawatt beauty and disposition.

This disparity defined their joint appearances, on display when the Prince of Wales took his new princess to his own principality in October after their wedding. Crowds groaned when it became clear they would see Charles and not Diana, and he was reduced to apologizing, "I'm really sorry, she'll be here in a minute." It was also a major issue on their first official overseas tour, their six-week 1983 visit to Australia and New Zealand. According to Sally Bedell Smith's biography of Charles: "He was embarrassed that the crowds so clearly favored her over him. For her part, Diana was upset by the disproportionate interest in her, especially when she realized it was disturbing Charles. She collapsed under the strain, weeping to her lady-in-waiting and secretly succumbing to bulimia. In letters to friends, Charles described his anguish at the impact all this obsessed and crazed attention was having on his wife."

Diana was the new queen of the walkabout, with a warm heart and a ready joke and a wonderful way with children. As for her legendary style, she grew as a global fashion icon every time she set foot out the door—her hairstyle, gym kit, off-duty outfits, and red-carpet gowns all slavishly copied. She was A-list plus plus plus, the first HRH (Her Royal Highness) to make the transition from royalty into celebrity.

Crucially for the Crown, she had already secured the Windsor dynasty, giving the country a male heir with the arrival of Prince William in 1982. A second son, Harry, followed in 1984 but, says Sally Bedell Smith, his birth revealed not a maturing union between Charles and Diana but a fast-growing gulf. In *Charles: The Misunderstood Prince*, she writes: "Charles was hoping for a girl, as was Diana, until she learned from an ultrasound she was carrying a boy. It was a measure of their distance, of her undercurrent of hostility, that she withheld the result of the test from her husband for her entire pregnancy."

It was a shocking lie by omission, but Diana had her reasons. As we know from Dr. James Colthurst's insightful analysis, her marriage to Charles would never be able to live up to the ideal she had imagined before that long walk down the aisle of St. Paul's Cathedral. Her new role was both suffocating and isolating, the press intrusion and public attention relentless. Camilla Parker Bowles cast a long shadow. On honeymoon aboard the *Britannia*, for an official dinner one night Charles wore gold cufflinks gifted by Camilla and entwined with double C's. At home Camilla was in possession of a chunky gold bracelet inscribed GF—which stood for their nicknames Gladys and Fred—a farewell gift to Camilla from Charles ahead of his wedding. The prince might have ended his sexual relationship with his mistress but he never stopped caring deeply for her, and that was too much for Diana.

The princess's mental decline in the mid- and late eighties was pitiful. As Sally Bedell Smith writes in the prince's biography: "By her own account—in her interviews for the Morton book and her *Panorama* broadcast—she suffered from bulimia, self-mutilation, depression, and acute anxiety. She attempted suicide four or five times. She exhibited signs of paranoia. She was tormented by feelings of emptiness and detachment, she feared abandonment, she had difficulty sustaining relationships, and she kept those closest to her on tenterhooks with her sudden mood swings, explosive rages, and long sulks." Yet she was also "high functioning," capable of "putting on a great show in public" between "dark, private upheavals unfathomable to those around her."

It made it all the harder for Charles to seek help—and to persuade both Diana herself and her adoring, obsessed public that she needed it. This tension is explored in season four of Netflix's *The Crown*, which unstintingly portrays Diana's anguish. The show's depiction of her bulimia means the show carries trigger warnings, which are not unwarranted. In real life, Tina Brown writes in *The Diana Chronicles* that chef Mervyn Wycherley left custard in the fridge for Diana to binge on after official evening appearances, and how Diana's sister Jane Fellowes once spotted penknife cuts on her chest.

Camilla in contrast was an earthy, countryside-loving woman who adored horses, dogs, smoking, and drinking. She was a doughty companion to Charles and remains so today, more than half a century after the couple first met at a Windsor Great Park polo match in 1970. "The Prince could not live up to being a fantasy man. He needed Camilla to make him flesh and blood," writes Sally Bedell Smith.

Sadly, the first phase of their lifelong love affair was mistimed, for Camilla was already in love with Andrew Parker Bowles, a former lover of Princess Anne. When Charles left on an eight-month naval tour without declaring his affections, Camilla accepted Andrew's proposal of marriage and remained his wife until 1995, even though she resumed her role as Charles's mistress in 1986. (In the 1994 documentary *Charles: The Private Man, the Public Role*, the prince told his authorized biographer Jonathan Dimbleby that he had remained faithful to Diana until that year.)

Unsurprisingly the cracks in the Waleses' marriage were beginning to show in public. In May 1986 Diana fainted in public at Expo '86 in Vancouver, possibly because she was so undernourished. Her husband caught her, but her lady-in-waiting Anne Beckwith Smith told Sally Bedell Smith that for the first time, Charles was unsympathetic. "Something had gone from the relationship," she recalled. In her biography, Bedell Smith concludes: "Despite his numerous statements about the meaning of a royal marriage, its importance for the future of the monarchy, and his naive hope that the bonds of duty and children could nurture some sort of love in an arranged union, he had come to the grim conclusion that his marriage to Diana had 'irretrievably broken down.'"

The stage was set for Diana's multiple love affairs, initially her rumored liaison with her close protection officer Barry Mannakee, and then most famously from November 1986 her five-year liaison with Life Guards officer Major James Hewitt. For Charles it would mean the return to Camilla, and for the wider royal family a descent into national soap opera.

By the time the eighties came to a close, it was clear the imminent collapse of the Waleses' marriage amid infidelity on both sides would present the House of Windsor with its gravest challenge since the abdication more than half a century earlier. In July 1986 the marriage of the Queen's second son, Prince Andrew, to Sarah Ferguson and the start of their life together as the Duke and Duchess of York briefly helped distract a country keen to believe in not one, but two royal fairy tales. Ultimately though it was destined to add to the storm damage of the eighties hurricane.

Following the wedding of Charles and Diana, the marriage of Andrew and Sarah was another high point in modern royal history. Prince Andrew, his reputation still aloft following his helicopter heroics during the 1982 Falklands War, had delighted his parents by settling down with his girlfriend. She was a commoner, albeit one whose farming family lived on the fringes of royal society, and the match suggested a House of Windsor that was warm and modern and more accessible than ever before.

Sarah Ferguson was born in 1959 and grew up on her family farm in Hampshire. She was the daughter of Prince Philip's and later Prince Charles's polo manager Major Ronald Ferguson. Her mother, Susan Barrantes, left the UK in 1975 to marry an Argentinian polo player following the collapse of their marriage. "Fergie," as Sarah had always been nicknamed, was very distantly related to Diana, and their mothers had been best friends at school. Denied the chance to have Sarah as her lady-in-waiting, it was Diana who engineered her invitation to the Windsor Castle house party in Ascot Week 1985, where she was seated next to Prince Andrew. Sarah was a far more worldly figure than her friend, having worked a season cooking and cleaning in high-end ski resort accommodation, in PR and publishing, and having enjoyed a three-year relationship with the Irish Formula One tycoon Paddy McNally.

Today we know Prince Andrew as a disgraced figure mired in a sordid international sex scandal. It's easy to forget that back in the eighties he was a military pilot who arrived home from the Falklands War aboard the aircraft carrier HMS *Invincible* to greet the Queen with a red rose between his teeth. He was instantly crowned the "playboy prince," the sexual controversies that would destroy his public standing still far in the future. His new wife was gregarious and confident, a counterpoint to the sometimes diffident Diana. The princess's delight in having a compatriot behind palace walls turned to despair when Fergie's love of riding, skiing, and country pursuits found the kind of favor with senior royals that had eluded her— though she would still struggle to assimilate into royal life. "I couldn't understand it," Diana later admitted to Andrew Morton. "She actually enjoyed being where she was, whereas I was fighting to survive."

In her book *The Diana Chronicles*, Tina Brown describes Sarah Ferguson as having lived "a knockabout life in ski resorts and nightclubs," credits her with "traveling alone to exotic places," and states that "Diana envied Fergie's spontaneous sexuality, her free and easy manner, and the genuine warmth of her relationship with Andrew, which had begun as a bona fide love affair and even after divorce remains an affectionate friendship."

Unsurprisingly then, Sarah's Westminster Abbey wedding to Prince Andrew was a lively and exuberant affair. On the way back to the palace she even gave the crowd a rather unroyal thumbs-up. She wore an ivory duchesse satin frock, which became an icon of flamboyant eighties fashion. It was decorated with bumblebees and thistles from the Ferguson family crest and anchors and waves to symbolize Andrew's naval career. The initials A and S were entwined in silver beading across her seventeen-foot train, and on her head sat a huge crown of gardenias, Andrew's favorite flower, which she removed partway through the ceremony to reveal a brand new diamond floral tiara given to her by the Queen.

The newlyweds shared a Buckingham Palace balcony kiss in an echo of Charles and Diana's, and the Wales and the Yorks were swiftly nicknamed the "Fab Four." Those two marriages, plus the arrival of a new generation of Windsor babies with Andrew and Sarah's daughters—Princess Beatrice in 1988 and Princess Eugenie in 1990—joining William and Harry, gave palace life a veneer of stability.

Yet just as Diana had struggled to cope from the start, so too did Sarah. She found palace life lonely and isolating. Tina Brown writes: "Like Diana in the early days, the Duchess, left alone for weeks on end in the chilly atmosphere of the palace while Andrew was on naval duties, felt utterly at sea in the ordeal of how to become a fit wife for the Queen's second son."

The women, who had been friends long before their respective royal weddings and knew each other from the polo circuit, became allies. The multi-award-winning documentary maker Edward Mirzoeff, who was given unprecedented access during the making of the 1992 documentary *Elizabeth R*, recalled seeing them together at a state reception in Buckingham Palace: "It was a big grand party. Everyone was in the best fig, Diana and Fergie both very glamorous. After about half an hour they must have had a sign it was okay to leave, and I got a glimpse of the two girls running down the corridor outside the state rooms in their ballgowns, shoes off—they'd been released and they were shrieking with laughter. They were kids, really, running away from it all."

This was in 1991 when the Waleses' marriage was effectively over and the Yorks' would soon be souring. Just a year later Fergie would be photographed in circumstances so humiliating—having her toes sucked by her lover—that she would be shunned by her father-in-law, the Duke of Edinburgh, until his death in 2021.

There was something about the arrival of these two young royal brides into British public life that captured the zeitgeist of the eighties, a decade that was brash, bold, and increasingly meritocratic. Brilliance in business or banking or in the embryonic tech industries was as much a golden ticket to the life that a title and inherited wealth once had been, although the cachet of a royal title remained priceless. In 1986 the so-called Big Bang saw the deregulation of the City in London, allowing unimaginably huge sums of money to cascade through the capital. A year earlier Britain's first cell phone call had been made, literally creating a decade of new connections and opportunities. The royal family recognized this vast shift in the economy and society of their country, although some would leverage it more successfully than others.

At one end of the scale was Princess Anne, who declined royal titles for her own children, enabling them to carve a future that if not completely free of royal expectation, bore less of a historic burden. Peter Phillips born 1977, and Zara Phillips (now Zara Tindall following her marriage to British rugby star Mike Tindall) born 1981, were plain "Master" and "Miss." It was an appropriate choice for a mother who made her country's equestrian Olympic team on her own merits and who in public life had been known to fix her own tiara in place.

In 2020 Princess Anne sat down with me for an exclusive interview in *Vanity Fair* and spoke about that radical decision. She told me: "I think it was probably easier for them, and I think most people would argue there are downsides to having titles. So I think that was probably the right thing to do." Zara agreed with her mother's decision, in 2015 telling the *Times* newspaper in a rare interview: "I'm very lucky that both my parents decided to not use the title and we grew up and did all the things that gave us the opportunity to do."

At the other end of the spectrum was Prince Edward, whose eagerness to embrace the new social mores of the eighties did incalculable damage to his wider family. The youngest child, he had not found his feet either in his career or private life. (That said, when he did marry in 1999 he would become the only one of the Queen's four children to enjoy enduring love first time around, and he and his wife Sophie, Countess of Wessex, have proved to be stalwart working royals.)

Edward enrolled in the training course for Britain's elite Royal Marines but quit in January 1987, just four months in. His mother, the head of the armed forces, was displeased, his grandmother felt it a dereliction of duty, and his siblings were horrified, according to royal author Ingrid Seward in her book *My Husband and I: The Inside Story of 70 Years of Royal Marriage*. Only his father, Philip, was sympathetic, knowing better than anyone the physical and mental demands of such a life. It was speculated that Edward would instead forge a civilian career in the arts world, which had captivated him as a Cambridge undergraduate. It must have been tempting to start with something splashy that he thought would be successful, thus justifying his decision to dump a military role.

His first project was novel but far from being a success, it was a disaster. Edward persuaded his mother, against the advice of courtiers, to let the family participate in *The Grand Knockout Tournament*, a competition quickly nicknamed "*It's a Royal Knockout*." It was modeled on an internationally successful TV franchise which saw teams of competitors, often dressed in cumbersome foam costumes, pitted against each other in absurd games involving greasy poles, rolling logs, water cannons, and custard pies. And so it was that in June 1987 Prince Edward, Princess Anne, and the Duke and Duchess of York laced themselves into olde English fancy dress and cavorted through the tackiest game show on the planet, alongside television celebrities, magicians, singers, and sports stars in aid of various charities.

Rewatching it today it's impossible not to cringe. In one brief broadcast the young royals did away with centuries of tradition and much of the mystery and majesty of the Crown. They ridiculed their own institution and in doing so gave permission for everyone else to do the same. Historian Ben Pimlott would describe it as "a critical moment in the altering image of British royalty" in his 1996 book, *The Queen: A Biography of Elizabeth II*. He was right: the debacle did have a real-world cost. What, the people of Great Britain started to wonder, was so special about the royals if they could be seen on screen dressed as giant vegetables and tossing foam hams at each other? With this growing sense of modernity and informality there seemed to be little that set them apart from the man in the street, raising the twin questions of status and cold hard cash.

Charles Anson was the Queen's press secretary from 1990 to 1997. He has also been a senior diplomat, and a spokesman for two British prime ministers, and he has had a top-flight communications career in the commercial realm. It means he sees things from multiple perspectives: royal, political, and economic. He told me: "*It's a Royal Knockout* was a turning point. It stepped dangerously over the line of royal dignity and made a lot more of the private dimension, which in turn made it more difficult afterwards to distinguish between public duty and private life."

Anson also believed the game show gave renewed vigor to the debate about the size and cost of the royal family as a taxpayer-funded institution. Later in the nineties this led to the creation of the palace's Way Ahead Group, a strategic gathering of Royal Household officials designed to protect the monarchy into the future, partly by ensuring the family was seen to offer value for money while keeping its dignity and neutrality. The group's roots can be traced directly back to the tournament and to the aspirations of the younger members of the royal family and their spouses.

Anson added: "That was a bit of a turning point. Suddenly people are thinking, hang on, we've got this much wider royal family and it doesn't make sense. And then there was the debate that has gone on, and will always go on, about how much the monarchy costs and the size of it. . . . There was a feeling, certainly, post the eighties that it would be a good thing in the modern world to reduce the amount of flank available to be fired on by the media and public opinion."

Anson and his fellow courtiers were not against modernizing in principle; they were simply counseling caution. Princess Margaret and Princess Anne had nailed it with their decisions not to take HRH titles for their children. Charles and Diana were looking increasingly adept too. "Prince Charles and Diana introduced a more informal and different way of doing things. Through his involvement with the Prince's Trust you see Prince Charles in the East End of London helping young people who have not had the best start in life and who need a leg up," said Anson. "He is hands-on and marvelous. On Diana's side, informality was a thoroughly traveled course. She had a great gift for being able to carry out public engagements in a stylish and formal way, but with informal touches, bending down to talk to a child or making a joke or being inclusive. She was emotionally intuitive and the Queen was happy with that. She's the first to understand the royal family is made up of individuals who want to do things in their own style."

Naturally the Queen expected their efforts to enhance the institution, not set it up for ridicule. After the tournament Edward faced the media and asked for their opinion. An uncomfortable silence followed and he stormed out in a huff. "Sir Prat-A-Lot," read one crushing tabloid headline above a picture of him in a Tudor hat the following day. Edward made the royals look like buffoons rather than people worthy of homage and ermine and financial handouts from the government. Along with the freakish public interest in Diana and the new national pastime of ridiculing the Duchess of York (cruelly referred to as the "Duchess of Pork" while she struggled with her weight), the debacle marked the death of royal deference.

It's hard now, in the age of the internet, to understand the power of the British press, particularly its tabloid newspapers. Back in the eighties its influence could move the UK's money markets and open and close the door to Number 10 Downing Street. In the circulation wars of that decade Diana was the heaviest weapon of them all. Pictures of the princess in her gym kit, at the shops, cuddling her sons, out to lunch, dancing, wearing a different tiara—they were all front-page news. An exclusive nugget of gossip from a driver, a baggage handler, a waiter, or a seamstress would be enough to win Britain's newspaper battle—until the next snatched image or exclusive story from a royal insider.

It was inevitable that the Queen got caught up in it all. With the endless revelations and the intense scrutiny of her family, questions started to be asked about her own skills as a parent. Had Elizabeth been a cold and uninvolved mother? Had she let the Crown come between her and her children? Was the fact that she'd had two more babies, Andrew and Edward, a full ten years after having her first pair, Charles and Anne, an acknowledgment that she hadn't done a great job in the beginning? The notion that the royals were not an ideal family, but a dysfunctional one, started to gain traction.

The monarch, who followed her mother's dictum of "Never complain, never explain," had already seen one of the most private parts of her life—her marital sleeping arrangements—become the subject of national debate. That was in 1982 when a break-in at the palace revealed the Queen and Prince Philip had separate bedrooms. When intruder Michael Fagan scaled the fourteen-foot wall around Buckingham Palace one July morning and wandered around royal apartments before discovering the Queen alone in bed, the country's first response was "Where the hell were the police?" while the second was "And what about Prince Philip?"

Coincidentally it was separate rooms, which when revealed in the press confirmed to the public what courtiers and the royal family already knew: the Waleses' marriage was over in all but name. The couple were visiting Portugal in February 1987 and demanded to sleep apart. By 1988 when Patrick Jephson, Diana's new equerry, took up his post, the marriage was in his words "largely a sham" in which the couple's advisors had to agree on rendezvous points so they could arrive for public appearances looking like a team.

By then Diana's relationship with James Hewitt was so much part of her daily life that she was even photographed with him alongside Prince Charles at a 1987 reception at Guards Polo Club in Windsor. Charles meanwhile was deeply in love with Camilla, their liaison beginning to be guessed at outside of his loyal circle; notably in 1989 they were photographed swimming and sunbathing together on holiday in Turkey, despite having taken several friends and even Camilla's husband, Andrew Parker Bowles, along as "cover." Both affairs were set to detonate in the decade to come.

The nineties would bring the Queen lower than at any other point in her reign. Her annus horribilis in 1992 saw the collapse of the marriages of Charles and Andrew, Anne's divorce, and the fire at Windsor Castle. It was a decade of scandals including Camillagate in

1992–1993, in which a leaked late-night phone call between Charles and Camilla revealed the heir to the throne wondering if he might be reincarnated as a Tampax so he could live in his mistress's knickers. Andrew Morton's book *Diana: Her True Story* was read by a stunned world in 1992, and the princess gave her BBC *Panorama* interview in 1995. Finally there was her tragic death in Paris in 1997.

The eighties had promised much to the monarch: marriages, more grandchildren—the securing of her dynasty, no less. Instead there was treachery and turmoil, and the bright patriotism that had been in evidence since her 1977 Silver Jubilee was starting to look very tarnished indeed.

CHAPTER 3

Decade Horribilis

I sometimes wonder how future generations will judge the
events of this tumultuous year. I dare say that history will
take a slightly more moderate view than that of some contemporary commentators.

—HER MAJESTY THE QUEEN

They say a picture is worth a thousand words and if there was one
image that captured the reality of royal life in the nineties, it
was the inferno that destroyed the ancient fortress of Windsor Castle
in November 1992. It represented the damage done to the monarchy
by the War of the Waleses and the split of the Duke and Duchess of
York, the divorce of Princess Anne, and the constant swirl of tabloid
scandal.

The Queen understood better than anyone the consequences:
Elizabeth II was only on the throne because of a marital crisis in the
monarchy. Britain in the nineties might not be so forgiving, so quick
to move on if contemporary troubles were allowed to engulf the institution. Respect and affection, she acknowledged, now had to be
earned. The age of deference was over.

It was in this decade that the Queen confided her deepest fears to her late cousin Lady Elizabeth Anson, who granted me a series of exclusive interviews that have not been published until now. Lady Elizabeth was no relation to the Queen's former press secretary Charles Anson. Her mother was a niece of the Queen Mother, and she grew up with Elizabeth. A professional party planner by trade, she was entrusted with organizing Charles and Diana's post-wedding party, the Queen's eightieth birthday party at the Ritz, a celebration to mark the fiftieth anniversary of her coronation, and the Queen and Prince Philip's seventieth wedding anniversary dinner. She often hosted intimate dinner parties for the Queen and the Duke of Edinburgh at her London house, and the two women spoke on the phone very regularly until Lady Elizabeth's death in November 2020 at the age of seventy-nine, following a spell of ill health. During one of our many conversations, Lady Elizabeth recalled how the Queen once told her: "I don't worry about myself, I worry about the future." Her words reflected her fears for her monarchical legacy, such was the state of her family.

We might have a better understanding of this turbulent chapter in royal history and its devastating impact on the monarchy but for one scandalous and until now unknown fact: the BBC lost countless hours of priceless historical footage from the early nineties documentary *Elizabeth R*. Shot in the run-up to the Queen's Ruby Jubilee in 1992, the documentary was filmed when the War of the Waleses was at its bitter height, the Yorks' marriage was dying, and Camilla Parker Bowles was already a non-negotiable part of Charles's life. What clues the footage might have offered to the Queen's mood or state of mind we will never know because Edward Mirzoeff, the only director to ever be granted the privilege of a sit-down interview with the Queen, confirmed to me it has been lost from the BBC's royal archives:

"We had quite incredible access to the Queen over a period of about a year and we kept every single frame because there was so much footage which didn't make the final cut but was actually interesting and important," recalls Mirzoeff. "It was essentially wonderful historical footage which was kept under lock and key in a place called the royal archives, which is supposedly the most secure place in the whole of the BBC.

"Everything was signed off with strict instructions not to touch the rushes, and then it was discovered that they had all been deleted. The palace was deeply shocked and we couldn't believe it. I don't know why or how it happened; the BBC never explained. There were investigations but no answers. Possibly it was an anti-royalist or an overzealous librarian who wanted to be tidy and couldn't see the point of keeping stuff which was not going to be used, but this material was irreplaceable. There were conversations of all kinds and some extraordinary moments that we had filmed, such as Mrs. Thatcher coming to the palace after announcing her resignation. Everybody's seen the pictures of her in tears in the car going to the palace but no one saw her actually there with the Queen. She was obviously very moved by the occasion and reluctant to be filmed too much, and the Queen was perfectly happy with that but there was some footage and that was a moment of history. It's very sad that so much has been lost."

Nineteen ninety-two was the year in which the Latin phrase *annus horribilis* would pass out of textbooks and into everyday speech after the Queen used it to describe the disasters of the previous twelve months. The event was a speech at London's Guildhall marking the fortieth anniversary of her accession to the throne. But far from being a celebratory occasion, the monarch's face was wan and tired against her somber black hat and coat. "Nineteen ninety-two is not a year on which I shall look back with undiluted pleasure," she admitted.

The decade began happily enough. There was the arrival of Princess Eugenie, the Queen's sixth grandchild and the second daughter of the Duke and Duchess of York. Then the monarch celebrated her Ruby Jubilee, marking the occasion with *Elizabeth R*, which aired on Accession Day, February 6, and was a blockbuster TV moment.

Director Edward Mirzoeff was given unrivaled access to the Queen at home and at work, the cameras were allowed to capture her at family gatherings, on a state visit to the United States, and preparing for a banquet at Windsor Castle. "The idea was to do a film to reveal the working life of a constitutional monarch and the day-to-day activities of our Queen. What she actually does, why she's there, the reasons for having her, and I think *Elizabeth R* went some way towards doing that," Mirzoeff told me. "What I was equally interested in doing, though I never mentioned this to them at the time, was a portrait of the monarch as a human being who actually has a personality of her own and a sense of humor, someone who has a private life as well as a public life.

"You don't interview the Queen under any circumstances, but I thought, 'Wouldn't it be nice if we could just hear her voice?' and so I suggested we did a voice recording where no questions were asked. We would just allow her to talk. And to my astonishment, they agreed. What I can't actually describe well enough is the sense of this large, cluttered drawing room she was in, sitting on a sofa, with me beside her and the sound recordist behind the sofa so he couldn't be seen. It was early evening in November and the light was going down and there was an extraordinary atmosphere as I sat down with the Queen. I couldn't question her, but I could say, 'Do you remember, Ma'am . . . ?' and allow her to talk about sequences we had filmed, investitures, for example. And so she just spoke her thoughts, which we hardly edited. What she said was what was in the film. I thought that gave you a greater sense of what she was like than almost anything else.

"Listening to the words, you get the person, and it was the most extraordinary experience. We went back to the cutting room, laid the soundtrack on some of the film, and everything suddenly came alive. We thought, this is absolutely wonderful."

Half the country watched the documentary, delighted to catch a glimpse of the Queen, who finally appeared at ease in front of the camera. According to Mirzoeff, she relaxed sufficiently for her sense of fun to shine through: "There was an occasion in Windsor when one of the lights that we were using scorched a curtain. You'd have thought she might have got into a state about it. In fact, she thought it was amusing.

"She's got this wonderful, very, very dry sense of humor which I don't think people have appreciated before and, to a certain extent, still don't because it isn't obvious. She's not cracking jokes like she's a comedian but she has a lightness about her and enjoys things and she sees the funny side of life. She's extremely observant and notices things that nobody else sees, then comments on them afterwards and really rather wittily. She sees people's mistakes, the gaffes they make. She loves things going wrong. But of course when your life is as regulated as hers and there's nothing that can go wrong, it's wonderful when something does."

Philip Bonham-Carter, who had worked on the *Royal Family* documentary and was subsequently a cameraman on *Elizabeth R*, recalled his memories of working with the royal family. He remembered the Queen's on-screen confidence as she mingled with world leaders at a Commonwealth heads of government meeting in Zimbabwe. She was, according to Bonham-Carter, so comfortable in the presence of the cameras that she allowed a hidden microphone to be placed in a bouquet of flowers she was carrying, so that she could be heard meeting with people and speaking to the crowds on various walkabouts. Charles Anson, who was press officer at the time, recalls the Queen being complicit on the understanding that her subjects, if they were captured by the microphone, would not be reflected in any negative way.

Bonham-Carter believed the Queen was happy with the final cut of the film, which they watched together with the Duke of Edinburgh. According to Charles Anson, "When Eddie [Edward Mirzoeff] asked the Queen's private secretary if she was happy with the film he was told: 'You'll know if she's happy if you're invited to stay for tea.'"

While the Queen rarely expressed displeasure, aides who worked closely with her refer to "the stare." According to one former member of the Household: "You'd know if you were out of favor or if the Queen didn't like something because of what we called 'the stare,' which was a long and withering look from Her Majesty delivered in total silence and that would fix you for what felt like an eternity. I remember we were at Holyrood with the Queen on one occasion when her then deputy press secretary Geoff Crawford said teasingly, in that disarming Aussie way of his, that he always knew when the Queen was slightly irritated or bored. She asked, 'How exactly do you know that?' and Geoff replied, 'It's that stare,' prompting the Queen to roar with laughter."

Fortunately there was no stare, but there was an invite to tea for the producer and his crew. According to Bonham-Carter: "The only negative remark the Queen made about the film was 'I thought I worked harder than that.' Perhaps she felt she had made it all look too easy! What really came across during filming was the Queen's sense of humor and enjoyment of life. I have never seen the Queen more relaxed than she was after a dine-and-sleep dinner held at Windsor Castle. It was so good to see her thoroughly enjoying entertaining her guests as she showed them around the castle library. It felt such a relief from her endless responsibilities and duties as the monarch and the many challenges she faced."

Elizabeth faced many challenges before the year was over. Just a month after the film was broadcast in March 1992, the Duke and Duchess of York announced their separation. The Yorks' relationship had been too strained by the lengthy absences demanded by the duke's naval career. At first Sarah was enormously popular both with the royal family and the general public. She was outgoing and warm, funny, and clearly in love with her prince but struggled when left to adapt to palace life alone. This was to become a familiar pattern. Diana also complained that she felt isolated and unsupported when she married Charles, and more recently Meghan the Duchess of Sussex has spoken publicly about the challenges of marrying a prince and bearing the burden of public scrutiny and palace politics.

Sarah was formally separated from Andrew when in August 1992 paparazzi pictures emerged of her topless, having her foot sucked by her "financial advisor" John Bryan, as they holidayed together in the South of France. Fergie was at Balmoral when they were published, temporarily back in the family fold for the royals' extended Highland holiday. She fled the castle, and it is to her credit that years of

diligent co-parenting of Beatrice and Eugenie have given the embattled York family a sense of cohesion.

But all of this was a sideshow to the main event: the collapse
of the marriage of the Prince and Princess of Wales. In February
1992 the semi-detached royal couple flew to India for an official visit
where the media-savvy Diana was photographed alone before the Taj
Mahal, the world's greatest monument to love. The symbolism was
unmistakable: the magical marriage was finished.

In June that symbolism was translated into hard fact with the
publication of Andrew Morton's book *Diana: Her True Story*. It doc-
umented the day she claimed to have flung herself down the stairs at
Sandringham while pregnant with William, her self-harm, her bulimia, and the agonizing end of the royal marriage.

"It was hugely controversial because for the first time the fairy-
tale princess and the fairy-tale life people thought she was living
exploded," Morton told me. "Here was the princess talking about
bulimia and Camilla Parker Bowles for the very first time. It was a cry
for help. Diana wanted her story out because she was sick of living a
lie. She felt that she was being misrepresented as a happily married
princess, a decorous adornment to the handsome prince, when she
was actually dying inside.

"She was living alone at Kensington Palace while her husband
was at Highgrove with Camilla, effectively living as a married couple. The book was the truth, but at first people didn't want to believe
it. It was met with total horror and denial. I was attacked by everyone
from the palace to Fleet Street to the general public because people
didn't want to believe it was true. The establishment was desperate
to undermine what I had written, rival royal reporters tried to knock
it down, and the pressure was on us to prove the book was authentic.

"Of course I had all the tapes of Diana [she had taped answers to
questions and smuggled them to Morton via her old friend Dr. James
Colthurst] so I knew it was authentic, but we'd given her deniabil-
ity so that she could say she had nothing to do with it. The game
changer was when Diana was seen visiting Carolyn Bartholomew [an
old friend], who was quoted in the book talking about Diana's school

days. That was the moment people realized Diana was aware of what was in the book and didn't have a problem with it."

Then in August 1992 came the royal sex scandal nicknamed "Squidgygate," the publication of details of a 1989 phone conversation between Diana and her old friend and lover James Gilbey. In it she called Gilbey "darling" and he called her "Squidgy." He discussed his sexual pleasure; she told him she didn't want to get pregnant. As well as this suggestion of adultery by the wife of the future king, there were banalities about TV soaps and horoscope readings and the refrain common to all frustrated daughters-in-law: "Bloody hell, the things I have done for this fucking family."

Shortly after that, in November 1992 (with a second crushing installment in January 1993), came Camillagate—another leaked conversation, this one between Charles and Camilla, also illicitly recorded back in 1989. It involved phone sex, double entendres, and Charles's puerile joke about being reincarnated as "a Tampax." It made him a global laughingstock and raised humiliating questions about his suitability for the throne.

To the Queen it must have felt as if the palace walls were metaphorically coming down. Then on November 20, 1992, they literally did. If Buckingham Palace was Her Majesty's headquarters then it is Windsor Castle which was her. It's impossible to overstate her distress when it was consumed by fire.

The blaze was sparked by a restorer's lamp that set light to a curtain. It ripped through 115 rooms and raged for fifteen hours, causing damage estimated at between $23 million and $33.5 million, figures which would be almost double today. Very little was lost because much of the art and artifacts had been removed for safekeeping prior to the restoration work. Nine principal state rooms were destroyed and a hundred more severely damaged. More than half were restored as original; there were new designs for others including St. George's Hall and the Queen's private chapel, personally approved by the monarch. The rebuild was completed in November 1997.

Royal author and historical advisor to *The Crown* Robert Lacey has pointed out the terrible parallels between the destruction of the Queen's home and the smoking ruins of the House of Windsor at the close of 1992: "The Windsor fire symbolized everything that had recently gone wrong with the royal family. There was an inescapable symmetry between the collapse of the castle and the collapse of three of the Queen's children's marriages."

The castle's repair bill set light to a second fire. At the height of a lengthy recession, the country stalked by redundancy and home repossession, the public purse was expected to pay. The prevailing mood, captured by commentator Janet Daley in Britain's *Times* newspaper, was "when the castle stands, it's theirs, when it burns down, it's ours." Her Majesty ultimately paid $1.7 million toward the restoration herself, and a further 70 percent was funded by opening Buckingham Palace to the public for the first time. It was a shrewd business move, and today roughly 500,000 annual visitors pass through the wrought-iron gates. The palace is public and does not belong to the monarch. All nineteen state rooms can today be explored as well as the world-famous picture gallery, and as of 2021 the gardens are also accessible to the public for ten weeks during the summer. With reports that Charles plans to occupy just a wing of the building long term, Buckingham Palace has the potential to be an even bigger moneymaker.

On December 9 of that already bleak year came the separation of the Prince and Princess of Wales. Announced by then prime minister John Major, it was no surprise but still an almighty shock.

The royal split was followed three days later by a royal wedding: Princess Anne's second, to Vice Admiral Sir Timothy Laurence in Crathie Kirk, the royal family's place of worship when they are in Balmoral. Photographs of the day show the happy couple with just thirty guests in an intimate Scottish celebration—the bride carrying a posy of lucky white heather being serenaded by bagpipes to the delight of family members including her children, the Queen and Prince Philip, and the Queen Mother. It was a rare moment of good cheer in what had been a terrible year.

Despite the emotional battering she'd taken, it was still a surprise when the Queen made a plea for clemency during her "annus horribilus" speech on November 24. "I sometimes wonder how future generations will judge the events of this tumultuous year," she told her Guildhall audience. "I daresay that history will take a slightly more moderate view than that of some contemporary commentators. . . . There can be no doubt, of course, that criticism is good for people and institutions that are part of public life. No institution—City, monarchy, whatever—should expect to be free from the scrutiny of those who give it their loyalty and support, not to mention those who don't. But we are all part of the same fabric of our national society and that scrutiny, by one part of another, can be just as effective if it is made with a touch of gentleness, good humor, and understanding."

It was a rare hint that beneath her royal armor lay a woman with a demanding 24-7 job and a lot of family problems.

Charles Anson told me how the Queen coped at the time. "What keeps the Queen going is that she has a very strong discipline, a very strong commitment to her role as sovereign, and a huge amount of experience. Quite simply, she is able to carry on. She genuinely likes her work and finds it fulfilling over and above the call of duty. Plus she absorbs setbacks and does not let them interfere with what she's going to do next. I think she has very strong buffers in that respect. I remember being with the Queen for a state visit to France in 1992, and we were in Paris and the Queen was about to enter the Hotel de Ville to address an audience of six hundred or more VIPs. I had to consult her on something urgent just as she was about to speak but she did not demur. She listened to me without impatience, gave me the answer, and continued without pause to the podium with Jacques Chirac, who was then mayor of Paris, and who introduced her. She was so calm and accessible even at a moment when she probably didn't want to be disturbed." She needed every bit of that famous focus to face what was coming.

Secretly Diana was about to take the greatest gamble of all: she was planning to speak on prime-time television, giving a bare-knuckle fight of an interview to the BBC's flagship documentary program *Panorama*.

Today we know that disgraced reporter Martin Bashir used a variety of dirty tricks to persuade Diana to talk, including fabricating invoices to make her believe courtiers of unimpeachable integrity were on a snoopers' payroll. But Diana was also keen to retaliate against the pro-Charles documentary *Charles: The Private Man, the Public Role*, which had aired in June 1994.

Diana effortlessly upstaged her estranged husband on the night of its broadcast by wearing a sexy black Christina Stambolian cocktail frock—instantly dubbed the "revenge dress"—to a fund-raiser in London's Kensington Gardens. The brouhaha over the frock briefly eclipsed the fact that that program was a PR disaster for the prince, who had been widely criticized for admitting his own adultery and discussing his failed marriage on prime-time television.

The princess was determined hers would be a triumph, and on November 5, 1995, she sat down with Bashir in conditions of utmost secrecy in her apartment in Kensington Palace. By November 20 the program was ready for broadcast, drawing a record-breaking audience of 23 million. It was nothing less than a missile into the heart of the royal family. While Diana did not criticize the Queen (who according to Charles Anson did not watch), she was damning of Charles's ability to wear the crown, remarking, "It's a very demanding role, being Prince of Wales . . . being king would be a little bit more suffocating. And because I know the character, I would think the top job, as I call it, would bring enormous limitations to him, and I don't know whether he could adapt to that."

She wore her plain gold wedding band and her watch, a dark blazer and modest white top. Her blue eyes were heavily lined, her lips glossed. Peering out from beneath that famous fringe, she told her story with humanity, sadness, and occasional wit. A tabloid opinion poll would show 92 percent of the public thought she'd made the right decision to speak out, and even a poll commissioned for the more upmarket *Sunday Times* gave an approval rating of 67 percent.

The princess herself would come to regret it according to her friend Rose Monkton, because of the damage it did to William and Harry.

Her lines on her marriage were brutal—when referring to Camilla Parker Bowles she said, "There were three of us in the marriage so it was a bit crowded," and admitted of James Hewitt, "I adored him. Yes, I was in love with him." It was also the moment she floated the idea she could be "a queen of people's hearts," the phrase which would become her epitaph.

Finally, she seized the opportunity to demand clarity from Charles's lawyers, saying, "I await my husband's decision of which way we are all going to go."

It wouldn't take long. Just a few days before Christmas 1995 the Queen, who was hurt and concerned about the situation, wrote to Diana asking her to agree to an early divorce from Charles "in the best interests of the country." The archbishop of Canterbury and the prime minister were both in concord. The split was finalized on July 15, 1996, in Court No. 1 at Somerset House in London with neither of the warring spouses present. They were one mile, fifteen years, and an epoch of royal history away from their glorious wedding day in St. Paul's Cathedral.

Charles Anson observes: "There have been divorces within the royal family but in this case the divorce had constitutional significance because the Prince of Wales is heir to the throne and the Princess was Queen Presumptive. It was a major setback because part of the stability of the monarchy is the stability of these personal relationships, especially when they are in the direct line of succession at the core of the monarchy."

The Waleses' divorce initially promised a new and different chapter. What it brought was tragedy. Unmoored from the royal family, Diana was eager to build a new world of work and friends. And so in July 1997 she accepted an invitation from Harrods owner Mohamed al-Fayed to bring William and Harry for a holiday to his family compound in the South of France. Within weeks Diana would be on a romantic cruise alone with al-Fayed's playboy son, Dodi, embarking on an impetuous affair which would lead to their tragic deaths in Paris on the last day of August as they fled media pursuit.

At 4:00 A.M. on August 31, 1997, there was a power surge as the news of their fatal car crash in a tunnel beneath the Pont de l'Alma filtered back to Britain. All those who heard it first started waking everyone else up. This nationwide sense of devastation and discombobulation was felt nowhere more keenly than at Balmoral, where Charles was distraught, according to his biographer Sally Bedell Smith. He paced the grounds waiting for the dawn. He woke William first at 7:15 A.M., then took him to Harry's bedroom so they could break the news together. Harry would later reflect on the BBC documentary *Diana: 7 Days*, which marked the twentieth anniversary of the princess's death: "One of the hardest things for a parent to have to do is to tell your children that the other parent has died. But he was there for us, and he tried to do his best to make sure we were protected and looked after."

In the hours which followed, the Queen made her decisions as a grandmother rather than as monarch. She decided to protect Diana's boys, keeping them at Balmoral within the tight private circle of the family. What little normality was left in their lives would, she decreed, continue. William and Harry went stalking with Prince Philip to keep them away from the rolling television coverage. The Queen stayed on the estate to care for them. It may have been the best thing for William and Harry, but in hindsight the damage it did to her and to the institution of the monarchy was incalculable. It looked like she didn't care. Over time the public came to understand the Queen's dilemma: her public duties versus her concerns for her son and grandchildren—William and Harry were still so young and having to process immeasurable grief.

Charles Anson says: "Balmoral feels a very distant place in a crisis. You just don't have a feel in that peaceful landscape of a crisis going on within your own country. Had the Queen and Prince Philip been at Windsor when that dreadful accident happened, there would have been more of a frisson of public grief and anxiety. I think it would have been a case of 'Hang on, people are really upset about this.' In any case, I think there was a deep sense of shock. The Queen, very much a family woman, was absolutely wanting to protect those two boys whilst the Prince of Wales had to go to Paris and come back with the Princess."

A decade later Lord Luce, the Queen's former lord chamberlain, in an interview with the writer Matthew d'Ancona of the *Spectator* magazine, pointed out that the legitimacy of the monarchy depended upon public consent as well as heredity. "What you cannot do is to pull up the drawbridge and hide behind the moat," he acknowledged. "You have got to remain in touch." When Diana died the Queen appeared remote to her subjects, and it cost her dearly.

It was September 5 before she returned to London, made a palace gates walkabout, and spoke live to the nation: "We have all felt those emotions in these last few days. So what I say to you now as your Queen and as a grandmother, I say from the heart. I want to pay tribute to Diana myself. She was an exceptional and gifted human being. In good times and bad, she never lost her capacity to smile and laugh, to inspire others with her warmth and kindness. I admired and respected her for her energy and commitment to others, especially for her devotion to her two boys."

They of course walked behind their mother's coffin at her funeral the following day, creating the enduring image of a ceremony that stilled the country. Harry would later articulate the horror. William would say it was the hardest thing he ever did: "I felt like she [Diana] was walking beside us to get us through it." Diana's life was celebrated and mourned by tolling bells and breaking hearts until she was taken home to her family seat, Althorp, and buried on an island called the Oval in the middle of a lake.

The months immediately afterward were a time of reconciliation between Charles and the public. Plans to introduce Camilla Parker Bowles into public life and pave the way for her and the prince to step out officially as a couple were immediately put on ice. Charles's priority was his sons. He demonstrated his paternal care for William and Harry, making sure he was there for them as much as he could be, and he was encouraged by the warmth of his reception as he resumed public life.

Her Majesty had done much to placate the country with her address, but she recognized a shift in public mood and was alarmed. Speaking to the *Spectator* magazine, Penny Russell-Smith, former deputy press secretary at Buckingham Palace, observed: "For the first year or so after the Princess's death, there was a lot of long, hard thinking and self-criticism going on, to see what could and should be changed, and to make sure that what was changed was done for the right reasons."

In November of that year, in a speech to mark her golden wedding anniversary, the Queen acknowledged that the monarchy only survives through public support. She told Prime Minister Tony Blair and an audience at London's Guildhall: "Despite the huge constitutional difference between a hereditary monarchy and an elected government, in reality the gulf is not so wide. They are complementary institutions, each with its own role to play. And each, in its different way, exists only with the support and consent of the people. That consent, or the lack of it, is expressed for you, Prime Minister, through the ballot box. It is a tough, even brutal system but at least the message is a clear one for all to read.

"For us, a Royal Family, however, the message is often harder to read, obscured as it can be by deference, rhetoric or the conflicting currents of public opinion. But read it we must. I have done my best, with Prince Philip's constant love and help, to interpret it correctly through the years of our marriage and of my reign as your Queen. And we shall, as a family, try together to do so in the future."

It sounded as if she was promising never to misread the mood of the country quite so badly again. There would be no family crisis to rival it until the drama of Megxit more than twenty years later.

When the clocks ticked down to midnight on December 31, 1999, ushering in the new millennium, the Queen was in London's Millennium Dome, arms linked with Prince Philip, singing "Auld Lang Syne." The year 2000 was shaping up to be a time of growth and optimism. Tony Blair was in Downing Street and Bill Clinton was in the White House, the events of 9/11 and the subsequent wars in Afghanistan and Iraq were still to come. The millennium year was the peak of the economic cycle for the world's wealthiest countries. Capitalism was winning. Globalization was galloping. Life felt good.

By then the Queen had been on the throne for half a century. She was aging and so were her mother and her sister, who would die within weeks of each other in 2002. First was the princess Margaret, who succumbed to complications from a stroke in February 2002, aged just seventy-one. A little more than a month later at the end of March, Britain's beloved Queen Mother died, having reached the age of 101. The only surviving member of George VI's "We Four" was Elizabeth.

The Queen Mother had been at the heart of the British royal family since her wedding to the then Duke of York, later King George VI, in 1923. This however was the Queen's Golden Jubilee year and she was compelled to think about the future as much as the past. Celebrations to mark the occasion had first been mooted with little expectation, given all that had gone wrong in the previous decade.

Charles Anson, who returned to the palace as communications advisor to the Queen's Golden Jubilee weekend, says: "When it comes to celebration of the monarchy, the Queen is rather modest by nature, so she would not be pushing for major celebrations unless that was what the public wanted. And what you saw at the end of 2001 and beginning of 2002 was a monarchy that had been through a pretty major convulsion with the death of Diana and a media that was very active in following the royal family, and particularly interested in setbacks as well as successes. Nearly five years after Diana, there was a feeling that we needed to get the balance right.

"In the end it played out rather well for the palace because people were very keen to celebrate the Golden Jubilee. Jubilees are a time-honored way of looking at your own country, your own history, through the mirror of the monarchy. The interest grew from the media debate: look, are people really interested in celebrating this jubilee? Is it important? And the public reacted and said, 'Yes, we are interested. This is about our history. This is about our monarchy.'"

Charles Anson also believes the deaths of Princess Margaret and the Queen Mother focused British minds on the monarch and her lifetime of service: "I think people looked up and said, hang on, the Queen's been on the throne for fifty years and I've not really noticed it. I've noticed the Prince of Wales and Diana, and this, that, and the other, but not thought much about the contribution the Queen has made, the significance of her public service for fifty years, to her own country, and fifty-five countries in the Commonwealth, and also being queen of fifteen other realms.

"Here is this monarch who was going about her business in a modest way. Not expecting people to automatically appreciate it, but obviously being glad if they did. She embodied the idea of continuity and a very settled way in an often unsettled world. She was this thread of continuity through our national life, but also through the lives of people in other countries who admired the monarchy or liked the British spirit or appreciated the understated ways of the Queen. Some of these were British qualities, some of these were qualities of the monarchy, but they all came together and made for a really remarkable celebration which was, of course, focused around the Queen and the royal family, but was also about our own history from the Second World War through postwar austerity and on to the Swinging Sixties and the seventies, the eighties, and the nineties, up to 2002. And the Queen had been there all that time."

With this spirit prevailing, the Golden Jubilee was a royal success, with the Queen crisscrossing the Commonwealth visiting Jamaica, Australia, New Zealand, and finally Canada on a forty-thousand-mile odyssey. At home in the UK she toured seventy cities and towns in fifty counties and then presided over four days of national celebrations in June. Says Charles Anson: "The public got behind the royal family once again, wanting that traditional monarchy, the pageantry, the sense of history, the sense of another Elizabethan age. There was all of that feeling as well as the emotional allegiance. It was all back, despite Diana's death. If you'd come down from Mars in 2002 and looked at those crowds of over a million people in the Mall, you'd think this organization has not had a problem for at least a hundred years."

In case anyone wondered if these half-century celebrations were some kind of swan song, the Queen made it plain she was not slowing down or bowing out. In an address to both Houses of Parliament on April 30, 2002, she said: "I would like to thank people everywhere for the loyalty, support, and inspiration you have given me over these fifty unforgettable years. I would like to express my pride in our past and my confidence in our future. I would like above all to declare my resolve to continue, with the support of my family, to serve the people of this great nation of ours to the best of my ability through the changing times ahead."

She had put behind her a decade of despair and disaster and was now looking forward. It was clear her subjects still wanted a royal family emblematic of their better selves at the head of a country they could be proud of. Robert Lacey explains: "If we go back in history, Prince Albert and Queen Victoria came up with this idea of the royals being a 'representative' figurehead family that would seek to reflect and exemplify the shared values of society. In the nineteenth century's age of democratic revolution, Britain's nonelected monarchy developed this justification for its existence that fitted well with the age of photography and the developing of mass media—and that idea has stood the test of time. Some critics scoff, of course, and while they are entitled to their point of view, they have failed to make much headway in Britain's current democratic consensus.

"An act of Parliament could abolish the monarchy tomorrow, as it was abolished in the seventeenth century for more than a decade before its restoration in 1660. But the modern acceptance and enjoyment of the institution seems to have become a pretty established cultural reality. If we, the British people, our political leaders, and most of our media didn't choose to respond to the monarchy in the way that we do, and if taxpayers weren't prepared to cough up the money on a regular basis, then it wouldn't be happening."

Charles Anson was part of the discussions about the Way Ahead Group, which was instrumental in orchestrating this shift. He explains: "The Way Ahead group started post-1992, the annus horribilis. It was a case of making sure the monarchy remained relevant.

The way it survives is to be seen by up-and-coming generations because the worst thing for a monarchy is not hostility, but indifference. It's better to be disliked and have a debate about that because there's room then for improvement. The feeling after 1992 was that this was a society in a state of change, so the senior [Royal] Household advisors at the palace needed to ask if the Queen and her family were touching all the points that they should. It was important the royal family were seen to be active across the nation in a broader way.

"Very quickly we formed a nucleus group of senior advisors and called on government departments, the voluntary sector, and others for suggestions as to where people might benefit from a royal visit or a royal message." Anson adds that in the end the group's work became so embedded as part of royal strategy that "it didn't come to an end; it just got absorbed into the system."

One of its most significant decisions in the nineties had been to resolve the royal income tax issue, with the Queen agreeing to pay from 1993 onward. That decision protected the family from criticism on the financial front. But the Way Ahead Group had another, harder battle to fight.

As Robert Lacey points out: "If you're looking for one problem or set of problems in the reign of Elizabeth II, they all come down to Charles—and specifically to his infatuation and love for one woman, who was not his wife. In 1998 when Charles was trying to persuade his mother to be more accommodating of Camilla, the Queen described her as 'that wicked woman.' Those damning words were reported in distress by Prince Charles himself."

Yet Camilla had always been, in the words of one of Prince Charles's former aides, "non-negotiable." Plans to introduce her to a hostile public and an apparently unyielding extended family had been mothballed in the wake of Diana's death. Now it was time to advance them once more. The marriage of the Prince of Wales to the woman he'd always loved was finally about to become a reality.

CHAPTER 4

Operation Mrs. PB

It was horrid. It was a deeply unpleasant time and I wouldn't want to put my worst enemy through it. I couldn't have survived it without my family.

—Camilla, Duchess of Cornwall

When Charles admitted adultery in his TV interview with Jonathan Dimbleby in 1994, he insisted he had been faithful to Diana when he took his wedding vows and remained so until their marriage "became irretrievably broken down, us both having tried." In the two-and-a-half-hour documentary *Charles: The Private Man, The Public Role*, he confirmed what many of his family and close friends already knew. Camilla, he told Dimbleby, was "a great friend of mine. She's been a friend for a very long time, and will continue to be for a very long time."

Of the end of his marriage to Diana he said this: "It is a deeply regrettable thing to happen but unfortunately, in this case, it has happened. It is the last possible thing that I ever wanted." He did not, he reiterated, go into marriage "with the intention of this happening or in any way in a cynical frame of mind, and I have, on the whole, tried to get it right, I have tried to do the right thing by everybody. It would be nice if it could be over and done with. It has happened and that is that." It was more open and honest than Charles had ever been before. There was only one problem with his candor: it raised more questions than it answered. When exactly had his marriage to Diana collapsed? When had his love for Camilla been reignited? Would the Prince and Princess of Wales now be divorcing? Who would then become his queen? And the thorniest issue of all, how was a public still enamored of Diana supposed to get to know and like the woman famously nicknamed "the Rottweiler"?

———— · ————

BY THE MID-NINETIES Charles and Camilla were conducting their love affair behind closed doors, careful not to be photographed together. The prince divided his time between St. James's Palace and Highgrove, where he could be close to his mistress. Diana was based at Kensington Palace, while William and Harry bounced between all three Households and school.

With their father the young princes spent time at the royal estates and enjoyed country pursuits such as shooting and stalking. It was free-range fun but it could be formal. Diana's protection officer Ken Wharfe remembers seeing the boys "in Turnbull and Asser suits because Charles wouldn't allow them to wear jeans and trainers at breakfast. He had an almost Victorian attitude to things like that." As for their new nanny Tiggy Legge-Bourke, she famously gave her charges "fresh air, an air rifle, and a horse." With their mother, by contrast, they went to the cinema and to restaurants, grabbed the occasional burger at McDonald's, played tennis, and had fun at theme parks.

There is no doubt William's and Harry's lives improved after their parents' separation, since the official split freed them from the arguments and tensions which had blighted the preceding years. But the boys were still at the mercy of salacious tabloid headlines about their parents' love lives—as were Camilla's children, Laura and Tom Parker Bowles, who were old enough to understand the humiliation of the Camillagate tape.

When Charles called the Parker Bowleses' family home, Laura would often answer the phone and tell the future king exactly what she thought of him. "Of all the children in this tangle, Laura and William seemed the most vulnerable," says a long-standing family friend. "Laura was furious with Charles in the early days and blamed him for what had happened. When he called the house, if Laura answered she'd tell Charles to f*** off."

This is hardly surprising, for the relentless scrutiny of their mother meant that paparazzi outside the Parker Bowles family home was the norm. Tom, a food writer and critic, recalled in an interview with Geordie Greig for the *Mail on Sunday*'s *You* magazine in May 2017 how the family became prisoners in their own house: "We used to keep binoculars in my mother's bathroom and one of us would look out every morning to see how many paparazzi were hiding in the bushes. We could tell by the flash of sun on their camera lenses. At the peak, there would be half a dozen hiding outside."

According to one family friend the other children's anguish helped William gain a sense of perspective in relation to his parents' marriage: "It was probably quite good for William to see how the breakdown affected other people, not just him and his family," the source told me. "He had a tendency to think it was only him who was suffering when in fact there were many people in pain."

His cousins Beatrice and Eugenie, to whom he has always been close, were at this time watching their own parents' marriage come to a close. The Duke and Duchess of York's divorce was finalized in 1996 after a four-year separation. Yet this other royal couple, despite the tabloid scandals caused by Sarah Ferguson's unwise holiday pictures, had maintained a rock-solid friendship and the ability to co-parent in harmony while carving out new lives and other relationships for themselves.

For Charles and Diana the situation was very different. Charles, desperate to avoid confrontation, knew not to push his sons and did what he could to keep the peace with Diana. While it would be some years before William and Harry accepted Camilla, according to Diana's former private secretary Patrick Jephson, the princess herself came to terms with her husband's mistress in the final year of her life. Jephson told me: "I don't think Diana ever stopped loving Charles and because of that she wanted him to be happy even if that meant him being with Camilla. Diana, very much to her credit, recognized the reality of the situation and was big enough to see that, no matter how badly she had been treated by Camilla, she was not going to repay her in the same coin."

But even though Diana was mellowing, Camilla remained stuck in the shadows. Getting her into the daylight was the job given to PR genius Mark Bolland who was appointed to Charles's top-tier team in 1996. "Operation Mrs. PB" was a big part of his job description, even if it didn't appear officially on any contract of employment.

"At this stage there was absolutely no talk of marriage or Camilla being queen; it was more 'Can we actually just spend some more time together? Can we go to the theater together? Can we do private things together and not live in fear of terrible headlines? Can we try and have a normal relationship, whatever that means in this extraordinary context?'" according to Mark Bolland.

Even that was a tough task. The War of the Waleses had resulted in a toxic working culture at the palace for which the only cure was a cull of senior staff. Bolland remembers: "In order for this to work, I had quite a strong view that anybody there who'd been a part of anti-Diana operations had to go."

First out the door was Commander Richard Aylard, the prince's private secretary who had allowed his boss to admit to adultery on TV. Aylard's replacement, Sir Stephen Lamport, worked closely with Bolland on what they'd identified as the three key issues now facing Charles: the rehabilitation of his own public image, the introduction of Camilla, and keeping William and Harry out of the media spotlight. Operation Mrs. PB was underway.

Diana's death in August 1997 stopped plans in their tracks, and once again Camilla slipped back into the shadows. She had made putting Charles first in her life, and the slow outing of their relationship would not resume until Charles's fiftieth birthday celebration in November 1998, where she was de facto his guest of honor. The Queen stayed away, unwilling to sanction her son's new relationship, although it would not be too much longer before even Her Majesty was won over by the charm offensive.

Sally Bedell Smith believes the Highgrove party was the first night Camilla slept at Charles's house with William and Harry under the same roof. William had met his father's mistress in June 1998, just before his sixteenth birthday and less than a year after his mother's death. Having finished his exams, the young prince was home from Eton and with Camilla now a regular guest at St. James's Palace, it seemed advisable to introduce them. The meeting went smoothly, although Camilla was so nervous she reportedly needed a stiff gin and tonic afterward. The story was broken by the tabloid the *Sun* and, most unusually, the palace made a point of confirming its accuracy: "Yes, Prince William and Mrs. Parker Bowles have met. Meetings between the children and Mrs. Parker Bowles are a private family matter which we are not prepared to discuss, and we hope for their sakes the media will now leave this very personal matter alone." Of course the media had no intention of doing any such thing and revealed details of Harry's meeting with Camilla, which took place at Highgrove a few weeks later.

William had met Camilla for both tea and lunch since that first meeting, realizing that with their shared love of the countryside, dogs, and Scotland they had plenty in common. He was on hand to make sure the meeting with Harry, who was fourteen at the time, went without any hitches—a gesture of support which must have delighted his father.

According to Patrick Jephson, Charles's aides were quick to capitalize on the new relationship between Camilla, William, and Harry to secure her public acceptance.

Unsavory as this might have been, it worked. Camilla began to be referred to as Charles's companion rather than his mistress, and stories appeared in newspapers about her philanthropic work with the

Royal Osteoporosis Society, of which she was patron. (She became a supporter of the charity after losing her mother Rosalind to the disease in 1994.) Her approval ratings were climbing. The nation was still divided over whether or not the prince should marry Mrs. Parker Bowles—just 40 percent believed they should wed—but an encouraging 60 percent said they thought Camilla had a positive influence on Charles. The men behind Operation Mrs. PB gambled that the time was right for the couple's first official outing.

This extraordinary spectacle, coming after Charles's birthday party where Camilla was his guest, was staged at the Ritz Hotel in London to celebrate the fiftieth birthday of Camilla's sister Annabel Elliot. It was January 28, 1999. Charles and Camilla arrived separately but left together, stepping into a barrage of flashguns and screams and whoops from the waiting crowd. News networks screened the images around the world, with early bulletins across the United States interrupting their programming to show live pictures. CNN had a film crew there to capture the moment for its global audience, while the Associated Press reported: "The romance, once the worst-kept secret in Britain, is out in the open." Within weeks they were seen quietly everywhere: on a hunting field, in the West End watching a play, at a Rachmaninoff concert.

Next up was a "family" holiday to Greece in August 1999. It had been William's idea to invite Camilla, Tom, and Laura on their holiday yacht *The Alexander*. By now Laura and William got along well, and both William and Harry enjoyed Tom's company. William and Harry saw how happy Camilla made their father and according to Lady Elizabeth Anson: "The boys behaved marvelously with Camilla. They accepted her because they knew it would make their father happier and all of their lives easier."

That's not to say there weren't bumps along the way, particularly with Harry, described by Diana as the "naughty one." When he joined his elder brother at Eton in September 1998, he quickly settled in and then assumed the role of class joker. The jokes were practical, traditional, and played on masters rather than fellow pupils—Harry might balance a book on a door so it fell on a teacher as they walked in. A friend remembers: "The more invincible he realized he was, the more he played up."

By the end of his second year, the young prince was heading for the bottom of the class in almost every subject. At home he was too busy partying to catch up. With a busy work schedule and Camilla now very much a priority in his private diary, Charles placed too much trust in William and Harry to look after themselves.

"I think one of the challenges was that he wasn't present enough because he was so busy," says one of his former aides. "The boys wanted their independence and they probably had a bit too much of it. Often when they wanted to speak to their father, he wasn't around, and because he didn't carry a cell phone with him they would get frustrated that they couldn't get hold of him. If they needed him they'd end up calling his protection officers so they could talk to him, which wasn't ideal. They wanted to speak to their dad, but Charles doesn't do calls on the hoof or texting; he likes to make time for considered conversations."

Charles came to depend on other families such as the Legge-Bourkes and the Van Cutsems, with whom William and Harry forged such a deep connection that they remain friends to this day. The princes' former master of the Household, the late Sir Malcolm Ross, explained to me: "Charles relied on others to help him. They were friends he trusted implicitly. They had safe houses where the boys were protected and looked after."

Lady Elizabeth Anson concurred: "There were various people who helped and Tiggy, their nanny, was one of them. She was a jolly hockey sticks type of a girl who made their life as fun as possible and the boys spent many weekends with the Legge-Bourkes and also with the Van Cutsems. The Van Cutsem boys were like brothers to William and Harry, and their mother, Emilie, like a surrogate mother. At Highgrove on weekends the boys could be at a loose end because Charles wasn't always around."

Given this, it was inevitable that William and Harry would start pushing their boundaries. They created a den in the cellar at Highgrove, styled it "Club H," and held discos for a band of friends who came to be known as the "Glosse Posse"—the well-connected social set in Gloucestershire. Charles had banned smoking and drinking alcohol in Club H, but by the summer of 2001 Harry was smoking Marlboro Reds regularly and getting drunk on pints and chasers bought by well-meaning friends at the Rattlebone Inn, a sixteenth-century pub in a nearby village. Those who knew turned a blind eye, but when an aide recognized the unmistakable smell of marijuana emanating from Club H, the young prince was busted.

Harry was given a furious dressing down by his father, which led to him falling out with William properly for the very first time. Harry resented taking the flack when William had also been drinking at the Rattlebone Inn. Nonetheless, it was Harry's excesses exposed in print in January 2002 that led to a fulsome apology and stories of a goodwill visit to a drug rehabilitation center called Featherstone Lodge in South London. This chastening experience would not prevent future debacles—the time in 2005 he wore a Nazi costume to a fancy dress party or his legendary 2012 trip to Las Vegas that ended in strip billiards—but it did encourage him to think about philanthropy, introducing him to the idea that he could help others to help themselves.

The boys were growing up and it was time for both to pivot away from the protective quadrangles of Eton. For Harry, whose gifts lay not in the classroom but out on exercise with the school's Combined Cadet Force, the CCF, it was an easy decision. He would trade university for Sandhurst, the UK's prestigious Royal Military Academy. For William who would one day be king, life was not so simple.

William was eighteen years old and desperate to escape his title and destiny, just for a year. His father vetoed his wish to spend his gap year in South America playing polo but offered him a solution—a military exercise in Belize with the Welsh Guards, a holiday on the remote island of Rodrigues off the coast of Mauritius, and then a ten-week trip volunteering in Chile with Operation Raleigh. To William's delight he found his companions on that trip, all strangers, to be fiercely loyal and protective, so much so that one night as they sat around a campfire high in the mountains, he confided: "You're all so lucky. I don't have much choice about my future. One day I will be king, and to be honest I am not much interested in that at the moment."

By then he already knew his A-level results were good enough for a place to study art history at St. Andrew's University. After that he would go to Sandhurst to prepare for his role as the head of the British Armed Forces and then, inexorably, a life of public service beckoned. He was right in what he said to his fellow Operation Raleigh volunteers: he didn't have a lot of choice.

———.———.

CHARLES TURNED TO CAMILLA, who had navigated her own children's teenage years, for advice. She told him to carve out more time for the boys, but she never got so involved that she could be considered to be interfering. She was keen not to put a neatly shod foot wrong because by then the M-word—"marriage"—was no longer forbidden. She was being accepted both by Charles's family and the British people. Operation Mrs. PB was working. Patrick Harrison was Charles's press secretary at the time. He reflects: "The genius of what Mark did was that he summed the whole thing up in one word: non-negotiable. That is it; and that was the strategy."

The Queen could not completely embrace the idea of Camilla until after her own mother's death in 2002. Although the Queen Mother adored Charles, she did not believe his marrying his mistress would be good for the monarchy. To her it had echoes of the abdication. With her passing there was a sense the issue could be addressed. The Queen dispatched her trusted aide, Keeper of the Privy Purse Michael Peat, from Buckingham Palace to St. James's Palace to sort out both Charles's byzantine household and the formalizing of his relationship with Camilla.

During Bolland's and Lamport's tenures the brief had been to make the couple's relationship acceptable to the public. By 2002 it was about putting a ring on it.

In the UK, the early part of the new millennium was a time of cultural advance, a boom for teen pop and hip-hop, and the dawn of modern reality television shows such as *Big Brother*. It saw the birth of the gaming phenomenon and of a hurry-up lifestyle powered by a cell phone, usually a Nokia. Life felt younger and more carefree and families were increasingly acknowledged as coming in all shapes and sizes. Same-sex marriage was still more than a decade away, but the idea of two middle-aged divorcees saying "I do" suddenly felt like no big deal.

The Queen had attended a sixtieth birthday party hosted by Charles and Camilla for King Constantine of Greece in 2000. But it was Her Majesty's invitation to Camilla to join the royals at a concert and garden party at Buckingham Palace to celebrate the 2002 Golden Jubilee, which was seen as an official end to any hostilities.

It is significant that this was the year the Queen and her senior courtiers would draw up a list of reforms signaling a modernizing of the monarchy. It was by now more than thirty years since Charles's 1969 investiture as Prince of Wales, and more than forty since he was given the title in 1958. It had been a long apprenticeship and he was no nearer to the "top job," yet his mother was keen for him to become more familiar with it, so he began receiving state papers from cabinet and ministerial meetings. He was also asked to carry out investitures on the Queen's behalf. Other reforms included moves toward ending male primogeniture, where a younger son could leapfrog an older daughter in the line of succession. This resulted in the Succession to the Crown Act of 2013 which allows the Queen's great-granddaughter, Princess Charlotte of Cambridge, to take her place in the queue for the throne. The same act ended the provision by which royals who married Roman Catholics were disqualified from the line of succession.

It was an image overhaul, quietly launching the concept of Charles as a shadow king and making the monarchy appear more up to date; the kind of institution in which two people, both with failed marriages behind them, could wed. By then most people thought the heir to the throne should get a move on. According to Patrick Harrison:

"There was a feeling of 'Come on, sir, do it!' Not just amongst us, but also amongst some of the public and even the media."

By the end of 2004, the path to the altar for Charles and Camilla had been cleared with the radical suggestion of a civil ceremony followed by a church service of prayer and dedication. The Queen gave her permission over the Christmas holidays and William and Harry added their blessing. It was just before the New Year in Birkhall, now his Scottish home, that Charles asked Camilla to marry him, presenting her with a 1930s Art Deco–style ring of platinum and diamonds which had belonged to the Queen Mother. Given how much Charles adored his grandmother, it was fitting that he had chosen it for Camilla and very romantic considering they planned to announce their engagement on Valentine's Day 2005. According to Sally Bedell Smith, Camilla told a friend it was just "two old people getting hitched" and that is pretty much how the country reacted: cheerful, relieved, unalarmed.

However, news of the engagement leaked on February 10, 2005. The wedding was set for April 8 at Windsor Castle. Clarence House preempted any controversy over whether Camilla would become the second Princess of Wales (her rightful title as spouse to the Prince of Wales) by announcing she would be known as "HRH the Duchess of Cornwall" after her marriage. As the monarch's eldest son, Prince Charles automatically assumed the titles Duke of Cornwall, Duke of Rothesay, Earl of Carrick, Baron of Renfrew, Lord of the Isles, and Prince and Great Steward of Scotland. Camilla didn't want to step into Diana's shoes as the next Princess of Wales, the title which would be given to the Duchess of Cambridge when William became the next Prince of Wales. Besides, there would likely have been a public backlash. It was eight years since Diana's death, but emotions still ran high.

In keeping with the dramas of their thirty-five-year love affair, the run-up to the ceremony was far from straightforward. First there had to be a last-minute change of venue after it was ruled a civil ceremony could not take place at Windsor Castle because members of the public could then, under British law, get married there too.

Charles and Camilla would have to marry at Windsor's beautiful old Guildhall and then return to the castle for the religious service.

Next was a late change of date when Pope John Paul II died and the Vatican announced his funeral, which demanded attendance by heads of state, would take place on the day of the wedding. Charles and Camilla's nuptials were pushed back to April 9, coincidentally the day of Britain's best-known steeplechase, the Grand National. It had descended into such farce that Sir Malcolm Ross was dispatched from Buckingham Palace to the prince's Household at Clarence House because in his words: "The wheels were falling off."

In the end though, it went perfectly. Charles made Camilla his legal wife at the Guildhall, watched by just twenty-eight close family and friends, with Camilla's son Tom and Prince William acting as witnesses. At the end of the twenty-minute ceremony according to Sir Malcolm Ross: "A great cheer went up from inside the registry."

Camilla looked both elegant and appropriate in an eggshell pale dress by Anna Valentine, who would become her go-to designer, and a wide-brimmed Philip Treacy hat. For the ceremony in St. George's Chapel she upped her game. Her floor-length porcelain-blue gown was topped with a hand-painted and embroidered shantung coat, also by Anna Valentine. Philip Treacy made her a half halo of pale-gold ostrich feathers. She looked stunning, as if she'd grown into her new role overnight.

The blessing in St. George's Chapel was an emotionally charged affair conducted by the archbishop of Canterbury and observed by the Queen and the Duke of Edinburgh. When the happy couple emerged onto the chapel's historic steps—as the newly wed Edward and Sophie had before them in 1999 and as Harry and Meghan would in 2018—the spring sun burst through the clouds, bathing the wedding party in light and warmth. After so many years apart it was an auspicious start to their new married life together.

"We honestly didn't know until the day exactly how it was going to land. We did, of course, plan for all kinds of eventualities," recalls Patrick Harrison. "We were prepared for everything. My biggest concern was the public reaction. We couldn't predict whether someone was going to protest in some way, such as throw an egg, or boo. But they didn't. It was a joyous occasion. Even the weather held out and we had bright sunshine, so I do think God up there was blessing it."

Above all, it was a jolly family day. It says a lot about the prevailing lightness of mood that according to Lady Elizabeth Anson: "At a lunch after Charles and Camilla's civil ceremony, Harry got everyone to put a bet on what the Queen would be wearing later. It was green, cream, or yellow. Harry said green; he was quite sure of it. . . . He went and put a bet on it. But when she turned up she was wearing cream. She said, 'I had to, otherwise it would have been insider trading.'"

Charles gave a touching speech in which he thanked the Queen for hosting the reception in Windsor's Waterloo Chamber and paid tribute to "my darling Camilla, who has stood with me through thick and thin and whose precious optimism and humor have seen me through."

But it was the Queen's words which brought a lump to the throat. Laying to rest the ghosts of the past, she had two important announcements to make. The first was that Hedgehunter had won the Grand National and the second was that she was delighted to be welcoming her son and his bride to the "winners enclosure."

Referencing two of the most formidable fences on the Grand National course, the Queen said of Charles and Camilla: "They have overcome Becher's Brook and the Chair and all kinds of other terrible obstacles. They have come through, and I'm very proud and wish them well. My son is home and dry with the woman he loves."

It was an unusually sentimental speech from the monarch and it captured the visceral sense of relief the couple had, in their fifties, been able to make their enduring love official. Camilla, who had been in the pews of St. Paul's Cathedral as a spectator when Charles wed Diana, was now his bride. There was none of the national euphoria which characterized that amazing July day back in 1981, but there was an overwhelming sense of good cheer and good wishes to a middle-aged couple whom most people thought had earned the right to be together.

"I just can't believe it," Camilla told the broadcaster Melvyn Bragg, one of the guests at the reception. And it was indeed the unlikely outcome to an affair that had survived two marriages and the death of Diana, and attracted the wrath of the public and the monarch. It had made a royal outsider the second most senior female HRH in the land after the Queen. As for Prince Philip, "at least it's settled, and that's good," he'd told his friend and biographer Gyles Brandreth just a few days earlier.

For Camilla it was both a personal and professional departure. She was fifty-seven when she committed herself to Charles and by extension a life of service to crown and country. For a woman who had never had a full-time job, this was quite a shift in gear. Not only was she expected to be by Charles's side on domestic and overseas engagements, but she had to look the part too.

There were ladies-in-waiting, protection officers, and private secretaries. Her days brimmed with royal commitments and charity invitations as she built a portfolio of patronages reflecting her interest in literacy and the arts, her love of animals, and her determination to support the elderly and the vulnerable. She started to travel long haul with Charles, beginning with a March 2006 trip in furnace-like temperatures to Delhi, Rajasthan, Jodhpur, and Jaipur in India. In addition there were dress and hat fittings, appointments with her facialist, and long sessions in the hairdresser's chair having youthful blond highlights painted into her trademark shaggy bob. Anna Valentine, who had designed her wedding outfits, went to work on Camilla's official wardrobe, eventually creating a signature style today as recognizable as the Queen's and the Queen Mother's.

Camilla has become synonymous with tailored skirt suits in a palette of neutrals, pastels, and navy. And for evening and state occasions she likes heavily embroidered gowns, often in ivory or champagne shades which flatter her skin tone and increasingly blond hair. From the earliest days of their marriage Camilla always made it clear her role was to support Charles, not upstage him. Far from feeling threatened by his wife as he had done at the height of Diana-mania, the prince was relaxed and reenergized by Camilla's companionship.

"The duchess was absolutely wonderful right from the start, completely open and totally driven by one thing: supporting the Prince of Wales. That was her number one aim in life and it still is. And you can see how much the prince enjoys and values having the duchess with him," says Patrick Harrison. "If you're a member of the royal family, as well as your professional advisors around you, you also need someone you can share reflections and funny moments with . . . you need someone to bounce off, someone who loves you and is by your side."

The prince's newfound happiness and confidence began to thaw frosty relations with the British and international media. Charles hoped interviews would now focus on his work rather than his personal life. When he sat down with CBS just ahead of his first official visit to the United States in a decade, in November 2005, it was to discuss his town planning experiment: the model village of Poundbury in Dorset, today home to forty-two hundred people. But the interview on October 27, 2005, with 60 *Minutes* correspondent Steve Kroft was also illuminating in that he answered, with good grace, a question about how he would define his job: "I would list it as worrying about this country and its inhabitants. That's my particular duty. I find myself born into this particular position and I'm determined to make the most of it and to do whatever I can to help. I hope I leave things behind a little bit better than I found them."

His answer was endearing in its honesty and hopefulness, a far cry from the bruising encounters that had flattened his spirits and sense of self in the nineties.

Fast-forward a decade and the prince was a fully-fledged small-screen star, appearing alongside youth TV presenters Ant and Dec on a documentary celebrating the thirtieth anniversary of his charity the Prince's Trust. Charles set the trust up in 1976 with his $9,000 severance pay from the Royal Navy, to help young people from underprivileged backgrounds stay in education or receive professional training. By September 2020 it had helped give one million youngsters in the UK a sense of security and purpose, and it now operates in nineteen countries.

"When the Prince of Wales started the trust he hit on an idea that nobody had really thought of, which was investing in young people," reflects group chief executive of the Prince's Trust, Dame Martina Milburn, whom I interviewed about the work of the trust. "It seems so obvious now, but the prince was really ahead of his time with the trust. He genuinely has a great passion for young people fulfilling their potential. I know the thing he really worries about is young people who feel they don't have a future. Twenty years ago one of only a handful of organizations that would help young Black kids was the Prince's Trust because none of the banks would give them the time of day. People like Jay Kelly, Idris Elba, or Marvin Rees, the mayor in Bristol, all say, 'If it wasn't for the Prince's Trust, I wouldn't be here.' That's extraordinary."

Charles was keen to show off the trust's achievements and allowed the irreverent TV duo Ant and Dec to tail him for a year, filming in Clarence House, St. James's Palace, and Kensington Palace. They captured the Duchess of Cornwall and William and Harry talking about him onscreen too. The result was a triumph, showing him as a happily married husband and devoted dad—hardworking, passionate, cheerful, and amused. Suddenly he was relatable in a way he had not been throughout the War of the Waleses and in the aftermath of Diana's death. "It was," says Patrick Harrison, who helped set up the interview, "about breaking down barriers."

In the main Camilla stayed away from the cameras other than when she was with Charles. Like the Queen Mother, one of the most successful female consorts in recent royal history, she wants to be the support act rather than the star. Occasionally with Charles's encouragement she has stepped into the limelight, such as on April 21, 2006, when the couple co-hosted the Queen's eightieth birthday at Kew Gardens. Camilla dazzled in diamonds and a yellow-gold gown as she took her place alongside the monarch, inevitably raising questions about whether she herself would ever be queen.

At the time of her wedding to Charles, Clarence House said Camilla would be styled "princess consort" when Charles took the throne, but in February 2022 the Queen said it was her "sincere wish" for Camilla to be known as "queen consort," which is her consti-tutional right. "We didn't speculate at the time because it wasn't appropriate," according to Patrick Harrison. "When you have a long-serving and very much loved queen, to start talking about an-other queen isn't quite right." Nonetheless those closest to Charles say it was always his intention for Camilla to be queen and now, after many years of loyal and devoted service to the Crown, the vast ma-jority of the public support her title.

King Charles III and Queen Camilla may not be as youthful and attractive as the new prince and princess of Wales, William and Kate, but they do have the advantage of decades of experience in their royal roles promising continuity, stability, and tradition.

His reign will be far shorter than the Queen's, and Charles no doubt feels the time pressure to have an impact. And of course there's the inescapable fact that the next are already megastars in the royal firmament.

CHAPTER 5

A Modern Royal Romance

> When I first met Kate I knew there was something very special about her.
>
> —PRINCE WILLIAM

The candlelit table at Bordorgan Home Farm was beautifully set with linen napkins and polished silverware. Taking pride of place on a silver platter was Kate's specialty, lemon-infused chicken served with roasted potatoes and organic vegetables. It was just the two of them, as it often was, but Kate cooked supper every evening so she could hear William's stories of the search and rescue missions he'd carried out, saving sailors in distress at sea or hikers in inaccessible areas, flying out of RAF Valley with No. 22 Squadron.

There were no protection officers inside the white-washed five-bedroom farmhouse set on a remote bay on the island of Anglesey, Wales. William's security team had their own living quarters nearby, affording the couple the same privacy they'd enjoyed at St. Andrews University where they'd met as freshmen in 2001.

Kate had first been introduced to William pre-matriculation through their mutual friend Emilia D'Erlanger (now godmother to

Prince George) who was part of the Gloucestershire set in which they both socialized. They'd been reunited at the Scottish seaside university, both studying history of art. They got along well and when William had a wobble over his course, which he wasn't enjoying, it was Kate who helped him switch to geography rather than quit. By the second year, their friendship had blossomed into romance behind the closed doors of 13a Hope Street, the smart student townhouse they rented with two friends.

William had seen Kate in a different light when she'd sashayed down the catwalk in a see-through dress for a charity fashion show at the start of their second year. "Wow, Kate's hot," he'd exclaimed to a male friend, and later that night he made a pass at her during the after-party. Kate, who was dating someone else at the time, rejected William's advances, but several months later she found herself single and willing to give the prince a second chance. William loved her breezy confidence as much as her looks, and the fact that she treated him just like anyone else. Indeed when a friend told Kate she was lucky to be dating the prince, she retorted: "He's lucky to be going out with me!"

Thanks to the loyalty of close friends and a pact between the palace and the media after Diana's death to protect her sons until they became working royals by not using paparazzi shots of them, the romance stayed a secret for several months. "Our aim was to create a framework of safety and privacy for William," says former Clarence House press secretary Patrick Harrison who oversaw the agreement. "We were determined it wouldn't be open season while he was at university. We wanted him to have as normal a student life as possible. Obviously, we could see it was a serious relationship with Kate and we didn't want to do anything that would seem like we were nudging it in one direction or another, or giving it more emphasis or less emphasis. That would have been entirely wrong and I think we were always very conscious of that."

The couple were careful not to flaunt their love affair, but when paparazzo Jason Fraser photographed them embracing on the slopes of Klosters in April 2004, the secret was out. Kate became one of the most famous women in the world overnight.

William had dated before. He'd fallen for Jecca Craig, whose parents owned a 55,000-acre game reserve in the foothills of Mount Kenya. She'd had pride of place at his June 2003 twenty-first birthday party at Windsor Castle. Before Jecca, William had spent the summer of 2001 with Arabella Musgrave, the eighteen-year-old daughter of a well-connected polo family and full member of the Glosse Posse. But there was no doubting Kate was different. Their courtship would last eight years and be tested by two breakups over William's reluctance to commit too hastily. The tabloids might have nicknamed her "Waity Katy" but as their engagement interview would make clear, it had been the couple's choice to ensure the future Queen understood what she was taking on. It was as much an apprenticeship as it was a love affair, and Kate's willingness to accommodate her boyfriend's royal duties and military training suggested she had what it took for a lifetime of duty to crown and country.

In an interview with journalist Tom Bradby that aired on the BBC, speaking about Kate and her parents, Michael and Carole Middleton, William said: "I really want to make sure they have the best guidance and the chance to see what life has been like or what life is like in the family, and that's . . . why I have been waiting this long. I wanted to give her a chance to see in, and to back out if she needed to, before it all got too much. I just wanted to give her the best chance to settle in and to see what happens on the other side."

William also revealed that the couple, who seemed very much in love, had promised themselves to each other long before they made their commitment public: "We've talked about today for a while; we've talked about this happening so Kate wasn't in the dark at all. We were planning it for at least a year, if not longer; it was just finding the right time. I had my military career and I really wanted to concentrate on my flying and I couldn't have done this if I was still doing my training, so I've got that out of the way and Kate's in a good place in terms of work and where she wants to be and we both just decided now was a really good time."

William trusted his girlfriend enough to propose with his mother's iconic sapphire engagement ring. Kate had chosen a dark-blue wraparound dress by designer Issa clearly designed to amplify the legendary gem which William said was "my way of keeping [Diana] close to it all." But he was adamant Kate would be a different sort of Princess of Wales. "There's no pressure. . . . It is about carving your own future. No one is trying to fill my mother's shoes; what she did was fantastic. It's about making your own future and your own destiny and Kate will do a very good job of that."

Those who knew Kate could see from the start she would make a perfect royal bride, someone who was discreet and loyal but also confident and self-assured, with a core of steel that would serve her well in the role ahead. "I've never heard a critical word said about her," says Patrick Harrison. "She was welcomed from the moment she arrived and didn't put a foot wrong. She was always keen to listen to advice and try to get it right. This was her approach from the outset."

Perhaps that was no surprise, for Kate came from a self-made family in which doing your best was applauded and expected. Her father, Mike, had been a flight dispatcher; her mother, Carole, a flight attendant. They made their fortune when Carole—at home with Kate, her younger sister Pippa, and their little brother James—launched a kitchen table company selling party supplies and grew it into a multimillion-dollar enterprise. The family traded up to a substantial country home in rural Berkshire and later added an apartment in London's Chelsea neighborhood. They were able to educate their children at one of the UK's top independent schools, Marlborough College in Wiltshire. Collectively and individually, the Middletons were famous for three things: their excellent manners, their self-discipline, and their closeness to each other.

Kate was no snob. She'd worked as a deckhand on a boat during her summer holidays and as a waitress while at university; she'd raised money for charity and pitched in with marketing and photography for the family business. She was sporty and well traveled, an accomplished cook, and threw excellent dinner parties. Her happy family gave her emotional stability and a robust sense of identity. By the time she was voted prettiest girl in her university year, she was indeed real-life princess material. It helped that Charles and Camilla liked her from the outset.

That said, it had taken a serious breakup—their second—in spring 2007 for William to be certain she was "the one." As a serving officer with the Blues and Royals regiment of the Household Cavalry, he was posted to Bovington barracks in Dorset for five months' training. There he enjoyed army life and some of the freedoms it entailed. Kate, who was living at her parents' flat in Chelsea and working as an accessories buyer for the High Street chain Jigsaw, wasn't impressed when William came back to the capital on weekends and preferred to go out clubbing rather than spend time with her.

There had been reports in the tabloids of him flirting with other girls. She wanted William's commitment and wasn't prepared to be made a fool of. But William felt it was all getting too serious too quickly, that he was being hemmed in by the relationship. He knew the monarchy could not afford to see his parents' history repeated; he was irked by the media and public scrutiny of his love life, which had seen Kate besieged by the world's press on her twenty-fifth birthday on January 9 that year, hoping for an engagement announcement. It was simply too intense for them both, and as William told one friend: "The fun has gone out of it." The outcome was a brief separation in April 2007 and the occasional unwise bachelor evening downing beer and sambuca in a provincial nightclub.

Kate meanwhile refused to be the downcast ex. She embarked on a mission to show William what he was missing, partying at some of his favorite London nightclubs with his friends and showing off her athletic physique in eye-catching minidresses and thigh-high boots. Within weeks they were reunited at a party at William's barracks, where according to one eyewitness they were "all over each other."

The breakup, Kate later reflected in their engagement interview, had been a challenge but ultimately made her stronger. It also made William realize what he was set to lose and what exactly Kate had to offer. She had slipped seamlessly into royal life and her family had embraced her royal boyfriend, who would later acknowledge: "Mike and Carole have been really loving and caring and really fun and have been really welcoming towards me, so I've felt really a part of the [Middleton] family." Although he wasn't going to be pressured into marriage, neither was William going to let true love slip away.

On June 24, 2007, I broke the news on the front page of the *Mail on Sunday* newspaper that the royal couple were back together. Days later Kate was spotted sitting a couple of rows behind William at the Concert for Diana at Wembley Stadium. The July 1, 2007, event (Diana's birthday) marked the tenth anniversary of the death of the Princess of Wales. Kate's presence and her inclusion in William's commemoration of his mother was hugely significant. It confirmed what I had told the world: she and William were back together and this time for good.

Seated on a sofa at Clarence House, excited if a little nervous, the couple would address the rocky times in their relationship with a disarming candor in their engagement interview. William, rather formal in a dark-blue suit, claret tie, and pocket kerchief, said, "We both were very young . . . trying to find our own way. We were growing up." Kate added, "You find out things about yourself that maybe you hadn't realized. I think you can get quite consumed by a relationship when you are younger and I really valued that time for me as well."

Following their reunion, the couple had discussed their long-term future on a make-or-break holiday to the Seychelles in August 2007. William assured Kate they would be together although he needed to complete his military attachments, not just to the Blues and Royals but also to the navy and the RAF. It meant long periods of separation but that secret agreement would sustain them. William learned to fly at RAF Cranwell in Lincolnshire, and when Charles presented him with his wings in April 2008, Kate was there to watch. The following month, May 2008, she was formally introduced to the Queen at the wedding of William's cousin Peter Phillips, both occasions clear indicators of the growing seriousness of the relationship.

William remembered: "[The Queen had] wanted to meet Kate for a while, so it was very nice for her to come over and say hello and have a little chat." "Very friendly," is how the Duchess of Cambridge recalled her initial encounter with the approving monarch.

Kate was also present when in June that year William was made the one-thousandth Knight of the Garter, a personal gift from his grandmother and an immense privilege, according to the late Sir Malcolm Ross: "It was no coincidence that the Queen made William the one-thousandth Knight of the Garter. There was a lot of speculation it might be Tony Blair but the Queen wanted it to be William. She made quite a point of putting her grandson center stage."

Kate and Harry stifled giggles as they watched William, wearing a blue velvet cape, tights, and ostrich plumed hat, join other Knights of the Garter in a procession between Windsor Castle and St. George's Chapel. It was a kind of anointing, a role steeped in loyalty and service to the sovereign that traced its roots back to Edward III in the fourteenth century. In making her grandson one of the current rank of twenty-four knights, and the youngest by quite some margin, the Queen was announcing his arrival in the top tier of royalty.

But he was still some way from being a full-time working royal. In September 2008 the Blues and Royals lieutenant announced he would be transferring his service from the army to the RAF to train as a search and rescue pilot early in 2009: "I now want to build on the experience and training I have received to serve operationally—especially because, for good reasons, I was not able to deploy to Afghanistan this year with D Squadron of the Household Cavalry Regiment.

"The time I spent with the RAF earlier this year made me realize how much I love flying," William explained in a press statement. "Joining search and rescue is a perfect opportunity for me to serve in the forces operationally while contributing to a vital part of the country's Emergency Services."

Unlike Harry, who served two tours in Afghanistan with the British Army, William, being a direct heir to the throne, was forbidden to go to war. He had relished the excitement of a naval secondment aboard the Type 23 frigate HMS *Iron Duke*—in July 2008 he helped seize $49 million worth of cocaine in the Caribbean—but his appetite for adventure was not sated. He wanted to be on a front line, even if he could never be in combat. His decision however did not meet with universal approval in the media, which labeled him a "reluctant figurehead."

Crucially for the prince, however, his grandmother saw the value in military service for the man who would one day be head of the British Armed Forces. Patrick Harrison comments: "William and those around him felt this was not a sprint; there was no need to rush into doing five hundred royal duties a year. His search and rescue work was incredibly important to him, as was Harry's military service. Harry didn't want to do it for five minutes and then tick the box. He wanted to do it properly and over a considered length of time. William was the same. He knew that royal duties would form the rest of his life and that's something he fully accepts, but he realized that he had this opportunity to do something he wouldn't ever be able to do again."

Two years later in September 2010, Flight Lieutenant William Wales was a fully qualified search and rescue pilot.

Although William was in the RAF and Harry was serving in the army, their paths crossed, and the brothers found themselves training and living together at RAF Shawbury in Shropshire, where they gave a rare TV interview about their lives. There was plenty of competition about who had the better job, as well as friendly banter about their roster of household chores. "Bearing in mind I cook—I feed him every day—I think he's done very well," said William. "Harry does the washing up but then he leaves most of it in the sink. I do a fair bit of tidying up after him. He snores a lot too. He keeps me up all night long."

"They'll think we share a bed now," groaned Harry. He vowed it would be the "last time we'll live together."

"It's been emotional," agreed William drily, their hearty joshing of one another making it seem, back in June 2009, impossible the brothers would ever fall out.

They were very much a team. Earlier, in January 2009, Charles had agreed his sons should have their own office at St. James's Palace to oversee their public, military, and charitable activities. He would finance it through the Duchy of Cornwall, the 130,000 acres of land and assets worth more than $1.2 billion, which historically accompany the title Prince of Wales and provide the holder with a private income. The Queen backed the plan and the young princes started down the road to independence under the stewardship of their private secretary Jamie Lowther-Pinkerton, head of the new joint Household for Prince William and Prince Harry.

Lowther-Pinkerton was a former British Army officer who had served in the Special Air Service and been an equerry to the Queen Mother. Capable and shrewd, he was an excellent pick and remains close to William; he is godfather to Prince George, and his son Billy was a page at William and Kate's wedding.

The princes' new office was bolstered by Miguel Head, a former Ministry of Defence press officer well liked by both brothers, who was appointed to the communications role. Personal Private Secretary Helen Asprey took control of their private diaries and attended to everything from their clothes shopping to Christmas gift wrapping.

The young royals adopted new cyphers too. William's, like his grandmother's and father's, was red, a W topped with a coronet. Harry's, an H topped by a coronet, was blue, a similar shade to the one used by his mother Diana. And with that they had in effect joined what their grandfather the Duke of Edinburgh called "the Firm."

One of their first moves was to consolidate within one organization the growing number of charities they supported. In this their grandfather Prince Philip was their role model. When I interviewed Princess Anne in 2020 for *Vanity Fair*, she told me: "My father was very keen on trying to persuade various charities who were close together in terms of what they were doing to put themselves together and pool their resources and manpower. And it has happened in some areas. . . . In this day and age, there are more and more charities appearing. You've got to be quite smart about how you engage with them and what they're going to do."

The Foundation of Prince William and Prince Harry sprang into life in September 2009, enabling them to leverage their public profiles and better focus on the causes they cared about.

William was starting to lay out his own philanthropic vision and, interestingly, to demonstrate a working culture closer to his mother's than his father's. Charles likes to micromanage and take a deep dive into every element of his many endeavors. Diana believed the royals should do "less but better," according to a former aide who explained: "William saw his father take on an enormous amount and watched him get more and more frustrated because he couldn't make change happen in all the areas he really cared about. Charles would work so hard, and it would wind him up terribly. I think William's view was 'Can't you be a bit more like Granny and just do what you need to do and calm down a bit.' Diana managed to get attention for the issues she cared about without being at her desk morning, noon, and night. . . . From an early age he was aware of surrounding himself with good people, not spreading himself too thinly, and being very focused. He would do what he needed to do to make something work, but he wouldn't drive himself into the ground surrounded by huge piles of work like his father."

William, who had already earmarked homelessness and conservation as key areas of interest, admitted as much. "I've been trying to take the best bits of both of their [Charles's and Diana's] charitable lives and trying to amalgamate them," he explained at a charities forum in 2009. "My grandmother inspires me, obviously; I think she has done a fantastic job."

There was one tricky issue for him to confront—that of any suggested future role in the Prince's Trust. William was reluctant to take on a project so closely identified with his. "Charles had wanted William to take over the Prince's Trust, which has done such incredible things, but William wasn't interested," according to one of Charles's most senior aides. "I think Charles was disappointed, but he understood William wanted to do his own thing in the same way that [Charles] had wanted to create his own organization as a young man."

Meanwhile the young princes' foundation was a success from the outset, and William and Harry were an impressive double act. Their first joint charity venture, the Concert for Diana at Wembley, made more than $1.2 million for good causes, and it was obvious the foundation was the brothers' way of following in their mother's philanthropic footsteps.

"The big question was, what would have the biggest impact?" says a former aide. "Jamie Lowther-Pinkerton was incredibly strong on this. When he was planning what kind of roles they were going to have, the decision was made early on and collectively that it wasn't going to be a charity model like Her Majesty the Queen's or the Prince of Wales's. The feeling was William and Harry didn't need to be patron of every charity they worked with. What they did was to bring over forty charities together under one umbrella in order to share resources, knowledge, and ideas, which meant they were able to have a bigger impact."

It was a novel concept and consolidating their causes was a success, allowing the brothers to embrace their own areas of interest without spreading themselves too thinly. William earmarked conservation, and today this is at the center of his Earthshot Prize, the most prestigious global environmental prize in history and a campaign, which he hopes will be his legacy. Harry focused on military initiatives and veterans' communities, building toward the Invictus Games, which would be inaugurated in 2014.

There was overlap and occasionally conflict. "They have both been passionate conservationists for a very long time and inevitably they both wanted to champion those issues. The idea that only one of them could spearhead something would sometimes cause a little bit of tension and we'd have to work things through," explains a former aide. "Ultimately Prince William ended up working closely with the charity Tusk and concentrating on the illegal wildlife trade work, while Harry did important conservation projects in Africa and led on military projects. There were times when it worked to have them together but when you're growing and wanting to establish yourself, there are things you want to own."

Harry was also still deeply involved with his Lesotho-based charity Sentebale, which he co-founded in Diana's memory with Lesotho's Prince Seeiso. Harry had spent part of his 2004 gap year in the country and been deeply moved by the plight of children orphaned by AIDS. Sentebale cares for children trapped in extreme poverty or orphaned by the HIV/AIDS epidemic and was the recipient of the princes' first joint overseas visit.

I accompanied "Team Wales," as the royal brothers were nicknamed, on their trip to Lesotho in 2010 and remember being struck not only by their closeness but also by the respect they had for each other and how well they worked together. William had always maintained he did not want to be an "ornamental royal," echoing Diana who famously did not want to "just be a name on a letterhead." "There is a time and a place for shaking people's hands and being at an engagement but I think there's an awful lot more from actually doing stuff," William has said. "You could just turn up and open things—and don't get me wrong, there's always a good reason to do that—but it's about bringing some other things into it as well."

With the help of their new office and their new foundation, both he and Harry were able to enact this idea of dynamic charity. For William it meant a night sleeping rough in temperatures of 24 degrees under a bridge in London to raise awareness for the homeless charity Centrepoint. For Harry it meant taking his brother to Lesotho to see Sentebale's work first hand.

The Queen supported both of her grandsons in their endeavors. In 2016 she famously joined Harry in a sketch with President Barack Obama and former First Lady Michelle Obama. As they warned Harry, "Careful what you wish for!" while laying down the American Invictus team's challenge to the UK, a US serviceman dropped the mic and said, "Boom!" "Oh really . . . please," responded Her Majesty, utterly deadpan. "Boom!" added Prince Harry, dropping the mic himself with a smug grin as the footage faded out. The gag went viral, echoing the monarch's success when she was a Bond Girl to Daniel Craig's 007 at the opening of the London 2012 Olympics. A lover of the game charades and known in private as a first-class mimic, the

Queen, who enjoyed acting onstage in her youth, apparently only needed to be asked once when her private secretary inquired if she would be up for the sketch. "She agreed on the spot; she thought it was a wonderful idea," according to a former aide.

Her approach to William's role was different, more serious. She was keen to help him develop a connection with the countries and realms he would one day rule. So in January 2010, just days after he qualified as a helicopter pilot, she sent him to New Zealand and Australia on his first overseas tour on her behalf. It was a delicate mission because it raised questions about Her Majesty passing the baton and about the popularity of Charles and Camilla, who had enjoyed a lukewarm reception on a 2009 tour of Canada. The palace rebutted any suggestion the Crown might skip a generation—but William's raised profile indicated he was already being groomed for kingship.

This was a fresh and modern royal visit with more by way of barbecues, beer, and banter than white-tie formality, and it was a huge success. William, in corduroys, sneakers, and open-neck shirts, drew impressive crowds and charmed both nations with easygoing walkabouts.

By the time he returned to the UK it was apparent he was succeeding where his father had not—carving a successful career in the armed forces while juggling royal duties and holding on to the woman he loved. The determined and headstrong temperament that had earned him the nickname "Basher Wills" as a child stood him in good stead, making him stick fast to his idea of the life he wanted.

The announcement that William and Kate were making things official would follow later that year, the engagement news revealed by Clarence House at 11:00 A.M. on November 16, 2010. It was also announced on Clarence House's new Twitter feed, launched a month earlier. The Queen would make world headlines by sending her first tweet in 2014. She signed it, of course, "Elizabeth R.")

Speaking to guests at a Windsor Castle reception later that day, the Queen declared: "It is brilliant news. It has taken them a long time," a sentiment shared by Charles who on a trip to Devon told waiting media: "They've been practicing long enough!"

Michael and Carole Middleton made it clear they felt they were gaining a son. "We all think he [William] is wonderful and we are extremely fond of him," they said, speaking from the drive of their Berkshire home, Michael clutching some handwritten notes.

Fifty miles away in London the media scrambled to document this happy moment in royal history. "I remember sitting in a café in Southwest London when the call came through from the palace that I had to get to St. James for a shoot that afternoon," says royal photographer Chris Jackson, who has captured royal life for nearly two decades. "That was the moment everything changed. Maybe at the time I didn't realize just how much, but I do remember it was very exciting to be a part of it."

The press conference at St. James's Palace ahead of the official photo opportunity was a comparatively intimate engagement. I shared a bone-china cup of tea with the new royal fiancée, who told me she preferred to be called Catherine, not Kate, and confided she was anxious about her forthcoming appointment with the world's photographers. This was of course the day the world learned William had proposed with his mother's sapphire engagement ring.

The royal couple began their official life together with a mini-tour of the four countries in the UK, starting in February 2011. Their first engagement was naming a lifeboat close to their home in Wales. Next they went back to St. Andrews, the town synonymous with their romance, and then in March they traveled to Northern Ireland and in April, Lancashire. Kate resembled Diana insomuch as she was warm and responsive to the crowds, her outfits sold out within hours, and she seemed the very epitome of a young and glamorous royal bride. Where this relationship differed was that it was a definite double act: Kate never eclipsed William; they were two halves of the same whole. It was apparent she saw herself as William's partner, something which was crucial in her role as wife to the future king.

From behind his lens Chris Jackson observes: "Kate has always been very natural and very real in front of the camera; she's low-key and that has stood her in good stead within the royal family. As a couple, she and William have a great synergy which comes across in the pictures. Even in high-pressured situations or with a heavy workload, they gel well together." It was so different to the tours on which an upset Charles was an also-ran to the worshipped Diana.

Kate was keen to learn the ropes from those who really understood the inner workings of royal life. A Buckingham Palace aide remembers: "There were many times after the engagement when she came to Buckingham Palace and spoke to the Queen's ladies-in-waiting, who are Her Majesty's closest confidantes, and her private secretaries for advice and guidance. She would often come to the press office at Buckingham Palace to meet with aides there and show an interest in what we did, which was lovely. What struck me was that she was not afraid to ask for help. She wanted to know what it was like attending a state banquet, what it was like to do a walkabout and a regional tour, and what to do when you stayed on the royal train. It was all new to her and she was very open to speaking to everyone from the least senior to most senior members of palace staff."

In addition Kate had her own sensible, loving family to lean on in private. Michael and Carole Middleton's dignity and discretion in the run-up to the royal wedding made them more popular than ever at Buckingham Palace. As Robert Lacey, the historical advisor to *The Crown* puts it: "The Middletons have blended into the royal family as in-laws in a way that the Spencers never did. People have commented on how Prince Harry's rebellion against royal life was shaped by the determined personality of his older wife. Well, William's way of life has also been shaped by his own older wife—along with the family that goes with her." The palace, guided by William, was determined to repay the Middletons' support by keeping them more involved and better informed than had been previously common for any other royal in-laws.

In planning her wedding Kate had one overriding goal: it had to be a romantic affair, not the starchy ceremony of an heir to the throne. That meant Kate asking florist Shane Connolly to create an avenue of maple trees in Westminster Abbey, it meant the Queen giving the young couple Buckingham Palace for their wedding-night party, and it meant William ripping up the 777-name guest list written by courtiers because neither he nor Kate knew anyone on it. "Get rid of it. Start from your friends and then we'll add those we need to in due course. It's your day," the Queen told him.

She did, however, overrule her grandson on his wedding outfit, he would later reveal: "I wanted to decide what I wore for the wedding. I was given a categorical 'No.' . . . You don't always get what you want, put it that way. But I knew perfectly well that it was for the best. That 'no' is a very good 'no,' so you just do as you are told!" He had wanted to wear his Household Cavalry blue frock coat but was told to wear the red tunic of the Irish Guards of which he is colonel, instead.

Similarly just a month before the wedding the monarch asked her grandson to fly to Christchurch in New Zealand, which had been devastated by an earthquake, to represent her. Traveling to the other side of the world so close to his big day must have been daunting, and when he got back the Queen wrote to congratulate him. "When you get a letter from her or a bit of praise, it goes a long way . . . mainly because there's such gravitas behind those words," he said. It was another example of how Kate and William's life even on the eve of their wedding could not completely be lived on their own terms, although it was clear the palace machine, under the command of the Queen, was doing its best.

The day itself, April 29, 2011, was a blend of state pageantry and familial celebration. William even managed to joke about it. "We're supposed to have just a small family affair," the prince whispered to Michael Middleton when he arrived at the altar of Westminster Abbey with Kate on his arm. She looked stunning in a Sarah Burton dress of ivory and white satin with French Chantilly and English Cluny lace, its corseted bodice giving way to a cascading skirt designed to echo an opening flower. Her hair, left loose in a demi-chignon, was held in place by the Halo tiara, originally commissioned by George VI for the Queen Mother and given to the Queen as an eighteenth-birthday present. She looked regal, classical, happy, and composed. The whole country was jubilant. William had finally got his girl, and there were not one but two Buckingham Palace balcony kisses to prove it.

According to Lady Elizabeth Anson who was a wedding guest and was also involved in planning a pre-wedding reception for the foreign royals and dignitaries who had made the guest list: "William and Catherine achieved something that was ordinary in an extraordinary setting. The atmosphere in the abbey was unique; it was like a family wedding in a very large church. The trees broke it up and when you were standing at the altar it felt like a very small space, as if they were surrounded by their family and friends. The wedding had the most amazing feel, so happy."

Later that day William would drive the new Mrs. Wales, as he would jokingly refer to her, back to Clarence House in his father's Aston Martin Volante, which Harry had decorated with a "JU5T WED" registration plate and red, white, and blue ribbons. He'd also added trailing red and silver heart- and star-shaped balloons and others marked with a multicolored W and C. And it would all close with a disco in the throne room, at which Harry stage-dived into the arms of friends after one too many cocktails, ending long after William and Catherine had gone to bed.

Royal life was changing, and how.

Patrick Harrison, who coordinated all of the broadcast media and social media coverage of the wedding, reflects: "William was being allowed to pursue his own life, his own friendships and relationships whilst still having enough of an awareness of his future roles and responsibilities. He fiercely defends his private life and his ability to make his own decisions, but he also is very respectful and cognizant of the institution of which ultimately he'll be the head. I think you see that in the wedding.

"William and Kate were not required to have a full-fat official diplomatic event. If they had been, they may have felt constrained by it, that they had lost control of their own wedding. As it was, they were very involved in everything: the choice of music, the arrangements for the evening reception, and so on. They felt very much that it was their day and, because of that, they felt so comfortable in the knowledge that it was their wedding, they were very happy to share all the joy of it with the public."

Married life didn't change the newlyweds; they didn't even have a honeymoon straight away. William went back to work flying Sea King helicopters while Kate was photographed grocery shopping at their local supermarket in Anglesey days later. She had embraced life as a military wife, getting to know some of the other RAF wives and spending her spare time learning about photography. The Queen had gifted them Apartment 1A at Kensington Palace as their official London residence, but it needed an extensive refurbishment. They were happiest on the island where William could do his job undisturbed and Kate could work on the photography skills she would eventually use to chronicle the lives of the children who would soon follow their wedding.

It was a peaceful, joyful chapter of their life with direct parallels to the Queen's extended stays in Malta with the Duke of Edinburgh when she was still just a princess and he was an ambitious naval officer posted to the Mediterranean. Those lengthy visits were cut short by the King's declining health. William and Kate, however, had time on their side.

They did have some significant royal duties, such as a tour of Canada in July of that year. It was their first overseas trip together and their introduction to a Commonwealth country where they may perhaps one day reign as king and queen, so it was important for establishing a close and meaningful connection between the Cambridges and the Canadians who turned out in their thousands.

Patrick Harrison who helped coordinate the tour and accompanied the newlyweds remembers: "William was very concerned to make sure that Kate was okay the whole time. He was considerate of her and really looked after her but of course she did brilliantly herself. It was an incredibly successful tour and they seemed to sail through it. They were both involved in the itinerary and made it absolutely clear that, yes, of course, we'll do the suits and the shaking hands but can we please make it as active as possible? It opened up some new opportunities and possibilities for us, like a dragon boat race and playing hockey on an official engagement, and that was fantastic. Our feeling at the palace was it was all part of the general direction . . . of an institution that was engaging well with populations around the world and working hard and, in William and Kate's case, picking up the royal mantle very smoothly."

By the end of 2011 the House of Windsor was looking to the future, having acquired a thoroughly modern princess who had known her prince for a decade, and having just hosted a royal wedding, which had banked a huge amount of global goodwill.

Kate was popular within the family too. What had impressed the Queen was her assimilation into royal life. Charles liked Kate from the outset and was impressed by her knowledge of art history. He felt his sons had no interest in culture and was delighted that he and Kate shared a passion and that she enjoyed their regular private viewings of the Royal Collection.

Perhaps though it is the verdict of the two other great royal consorts of modern times, the Duke of Edinburgh and the Duchess of Cornwall, which count. Royal biographer Ingrid Seward says Prince Philip thoroughly approved of Kate, something William acknowledged after the Duke's death when he wrote in a public message: "I will always be grateful that my wife had so many years to get to know my grandfather and for the kindness he showed her."

As for Camilla, "It's wicked!'" was her joyful and decidedly nonregal response to the press following the news that Kate had finally agreed to marry into the Firm, with the two women growing even closer in the years that have followed.

Finally, to the public the newlyweds were ordinary enough to be relatable yet sufficiently regal to hold aloft the dreams of a nation. The Queen headed for her Diamond Jubilee in 2012, safe in the knowledge that she had a stellar line of succession. According to one courtier, the eighty-five-year-old monarch had been "practically skipping with joy" before she left Buckingham Palace for Westminster Abbey for the royal wedding. Her delight in this new dynamic was not misplaced: William and Catherine Wales, the Duke and Duchess of Cambridge, were going to be great.

CHAPTER 6

Annus Mirabilis

I rededicate myself to the service of our great country and its
people now and in the years to come.

—HER MAJESTY THE QUEEN

The weather was laughably bad, all leaden skies and lashing rain,
but the Queen, in a Swarovski-crystal-encrusted white coat, literally sparkled through the gloom. She was afloat on her royal barge,
the *Spirit of Chartwell*, sailing majestically down the river Thames
as part of a thousand-boat pageant, the likes of which had not been
seen for centuries. There were Maori dugouts, Venetian gondolas,
Thames cutters, Cornish skiffs, a new royal row barge, *Gloriana*, and
even an eight-bell floating belfry. *Havengore*, the boat which bore the
wartime prime minister Winston Churchill to his funeral, was there
and so too the Dunkirk "little ships" that rescued retreating British
forces from France in 1940. There were working dredgers, colliers,
and tugs, narrow boat homes, and a flotilla of private vessels. All
bobbed along on a tide of goodwill toward Elizabeth II, the Diamond
Queen, who had been sixty years on the throne.

The date was June 3, 2012. London was at a standstill. More than a million people lined the riverbank to watch the Queen sail from Chelsea to Tower Bridge. The city hadn't seen this kind of spectacle since King Charles II introduced his new queen, Catherine of Braganza, to the British people back in 1662. Charles's pageant was described by diarist Samuel Pepys as "the most magnificent triumph that ever floated on the Thames." Two years in the planning, Elizabeth's was conceived as its modern incarnation, a contemporary image inspired by the works of Canaletto.

If only it hadn't poured.

The weather that day was more than just bad luck. It cast a shadow over the Diamond Jubilee, putting Prince Philip in the hospital.

Instead of basking in summer sunshine with the scent of the ten thousand flowers from the Queen's gardens—arranged with flowers from around her sixteen Commonwealth realms including Irish shamrocks, thistles from Scotland, Welsh daffodils, and wattles from Australia—the royal couple were chilled to the marrow by wind and rain aboard the *Spirit of Chartwell*. The Queen yielded only by drawing a small white shawl around her shoulders. The Duke, just a few days shy of his ninety-first birthday and dressed in full naval uniform, stood unbending beside her. Within twenty-four hours he would be too sick to continue and withdrew from the rest of the nation's celebrations.

The image of Elizabeth two days after the pageant on June 5, 2012, at her National Service of Thanksgiving, tiny and alone beneath the great dome of St. Paul's Cathedral, was confronting indeed. It was a stark reminder that Britain was ruled by an aging monarch whose consort was in his twilight years. She wore a youthful mint-green outfit, then another glittering ensemble reprising the diamond theme, but nothing could disguise the fact that the Queen was eighty-six years old.

So it was just as well that the Firm, her firm, was in better shape than it had been for years. It had been energized and popularized by the 2011 royal wedding of the Duke and Duchess of Cambridge, by Prince Harry's military service in Afghanistan, by the flourishing of

Camilla, and by the fact that Charles's once controversial opinions on, for example, town planning and countryside conservation were now mainstream thinking.

Britain was looking excitedly ahead to having a Cambridge baby to coo over (the palace announced Kate was pregnant before the year was out), and the prospect of a monarch with three living heirs to the throne added a sense of stability and permanence which, in the immediate aftermath of the Diana years, felt like it had gone for good. To cap it all, London was hosting the Olympics in 2012. It was exactly twenty years since the Queen had made her "annus horribilis" speech at London's Guildhall. Was 2012 her annus mirabilis? Well, it wasn't far off.

The buildup began a year earlier in 2011, when the Queen and Prince Philip pulled off one of the greatest diplomatic successes of modern times with their four-day trip to the Republic of Ireland. The first royal visit there in a hundred years, it was a pivotal moment in the reconciliation of the United Kingdom and Eire after Irish independence, partition, and in the latter part of the twentieth century, the Troubles. The Queen was so determined to show respect that after laying a wreath in Dublin's Garden of Remembrance, she bowed her head to those who died for Irish independence. It was the ultimate act, given she was honoring those who had inspired the murderers of Prince Philip's uncle Lord Mountbatten. When the Queen opened one of her speeches in Gaelic and spoke of England and Ireland being "more than just neighbors," Irish president Mary McAleese turned to the rest of the table and said quietly: "Wow."

Getty photographer Chris Jackson who covered the trip recalls: "The Queen looked genuinely happy to be there and brought an incredible energy to it. She was dressed in Irish green, a great example of her diplomacy. The Duke was by her side, a huge support, fully engaged with the people he spoke to."

Prince William, a keen student of his grandmother's statecraft, would later reflect on the personal importance of the visit, telling Robert Hardman for his book *Our Queen*: "Normally, with a lot of tours, there's a certain amount of apprehension but also 'I've done this before.' But this was like a big door opening up to her that had been locked for so long." He would also speak about the wider context, the long years of hostility between the two countries and hopes for "close relations between the state of Ireland and the UK."

Historians have described it as a turning point in Anglo-Irish relations. A decade on, both Charles and Camilla and William and Kate have made further visits to the Republic of Ireland, saying they wanted to build "a lasting relationship with the Irish people."

For the Queen and Prince Philip, the historic trip which paved the way for these later ones would be one of the last great outings for their global double act. According to Lady Elizabeth Anson, the Queen was already worried about the impact of the royal workload on her husband: "She spoke about not wanting to be overburdened at that time, more for Prince Philip's sake than hers. She was getting worried about the travel taking its toll on his health. He was never going to slow down, so the Queen made a point of scaling back so Philip didn't have to. She always said she had her substitutes to help and now was the time to call on them."

The "substitutes" was the nickname the Queen gave the senior royals who could step into her shoes for occasions that required either the gravitas or the stardust conferred by royalty. They were the Prince of Wales and the Duchess of Cornwall; the Duke and Duchess of Cambridge; and Prince Harry, now the Duke of Sussex. In fact the dynamism of that jubilee year was largely down to these substitutes, along with the Earl and Countess of Wessex (Prince Edward and his wife Sophie), and Princess Anne.

While the Queen and Prince Philip traveled extensively in the UK between March and July 2012, the rest of the family visited other Commonwealth countries in a bid to bolster support for the monarchy. According to historian Dr. Ed Owens: "These trips were important goodwill tours designed to engineer positive sentiments towards the monarchy. They are all about the monarchy trying to shore up support for the Crown around the Commonwealth."

Charles and Camilla were sent to Australia and New Zealand, while Kate and William went to Singapore, Malaysia, the Solomon

Islands, and Tuvalu. Harry managed to charm the republic-leaning Jamaica. The Earl and Countess of Wessex brought their quiet charisma to the Caribbean too, visiting St. Lucia, Barbados, St. Vincent and the Grenadines, Grenada, Trinidad and Tobago, Montserrat, St. Kitts and Nevis, Anguilla, Antigua, and Barbuda. Given that Barbados would become a republic nearly a decade later in 2021, visits to some of the Caribbean islands that were considering becoming republics was a priority for the royals.

Meanwhile Princess Anne, as president of the British Olympic Association and a former Olympic equestrian, threw herself into supporting London 2012, including bringing the Olympic torch from Athens to London.

But if the Diamond Jubilee year belonged to anyone other than the Queen, it was to Charles. In public with Camilla, he was happier and more relaxed than perhaps he had ever been. Behind palace walls, he was making some serious decisions about the sort of monarchy he would inherit.

The outcome was a shift of influence in Charles's favor, says Patrick Harrison, whose tenure at Clarence House spanned both the Golden and Diamond Jubilees. He observes: "In the previous jubilee, the Queen had gone overseas herself. This time it fell to the Prince of Wales to do most of the traveling and represent her, which was very significant. He went to Canada in May, then Papua New Guinea and Australia and New Zealand in November. I remember the crowds, everywhere, being absolutely fantastic.

"The trip to Australia was particularly important because when Charles last visited, in 2005, we were told by those helping organize the tour to manage expectations, not to expect a big turnout. In fact, Charles proved hugely popular, and I felt frustrated that we'd underplayed him. So when we went back in 2012, we didn't make the same mistake. This time we planned for success rather than for failure. We were more public-facing, more obviously populist, and less formal."

This meant the November royal tour began not in sophisticated Sydney but in the Outback with Camilla cuddling a baby kangaroo called "Ruby Blue." "There's a first time for everything," she remarked, laughing. The following days reinforced this new sense of ease and confidence about the couple. It had first emerged on the jubilee weekend itself when Charles joked at his own expense about having witnessed all three of his mother's jubilees and having the medals to prove it. The day after the river pageant, June 4, 2012, attending a jubilee rock concert on the Mall, he called the Queen "Mummy" and kissed her hand. Then he whipped up the crowd to cheer for his sick father. This wearing of his heart on his sleeve won him plaudits in both the Northern and Southern Hemispheres.

This breakthrough was critical in bolstering support for Charles and Camilla. The bladder infection suffered by the Duke as a result of the river pageant had reinforced the Queen's growing concerns about her husband's health and put the focus on the future of the monarchy. The Queen was even more determined to scale back her overseas travel to reduce the burden on them both. Confirmation of this came in May 2013 when courtiers said they would be "reviewing" her future long-haul trips, starting with her missing the Commonwealth Heads of Government (CHOGM) meeting in Sri Lanka later that year.

The Queen had attended CHOGM every two years since 1973. Sending Charles in her stead was not just a way of testing the waters for her son but an admission the Queen was getting older, while the Duke was increasingly vulnerable. Philip had been hospitalized for almost a week with a chest infection in 2008. Then in 2011 he had emergency heart surgery and was kept in the hospital for four nights over Christmas. In June 2013 he had exploratory surgery on his abdomen. Typically, he went to a garden party immediately before he was admitted for what the palace said was a prearranged procedure. The Queen knew he wouldn't slow down until she did, leaving her with little choice.

The Diamond Jubilee had been "an extraordinary show of the Queen's stoicism," said one long-serving palace aide. "She must have been desperately worried about the Duke, but it goes back to her sense of duty and commitment." Knowing she could depend on a newly popular Charles, supported by Camilla, was a game changer.

The Diamond Jubilee year also demonstrated the rising power of the Duchess of Cornwall within the monarchy. She was by the Queen's side aboard *Spirit of Chartwell* and rode with the monarch to Buckingham Palace in the 1902 state landau after the St. Paul's service. Two months earlier in April 2012, the Queen had made her daughter-in-law a Dame Grand Cross of the Royal Victorian Order, an honor bestowed for personal service to the monarchy. It was remarkable to think that just fifteen years earlier Elizabeth would not have Camilla's name uttered in her presence.

"The decision to have the Queen and Camilla ride in the carriage together was orchestrated by the Queen's private secretary Christopher Geidt and the Prince of Wales's principal private secretary William Nye," according to a senior Buckingham Palace courtier involved in planning the day. "It wouldn't have happened twenty years ago, that's for sure, but Camilla has been a flawless consort and the Queen appreciated that. It was her way of recognizing Camilla and also, very importantly, of showing that times had changed and the monarchy was moving forwards."

Four years later in 2016 the duchess would be elevated yet further to the Privy Council, the Queen's most senior advisory body. It includes the archbishop of Canterbury, the lord chancellor, and the prime minister and plays an important part in the accession ceremonies of a new sovereign.

"It was significant for Camilla to be made a member," according to Anna Whitelock, professor of the history of monarchy at City, University of London. "When the monarch ruled as well as reigned, the Privy Council was absolutely central. It was like the cabinet is today for a prime minister. But now it has a largely ceremonial function. It will be the Privy Council that the new king will meet after the Accession Council [a ceremonial body which makes the formal proclamation of the accession of the successor to the throne], so it is an important, if large, organization of about 750 members: old ministers as well as current ministers and members of the royal family."

It was another strategic move in the slow transition of power from one generation to the next. The prominence of Charles and Camilla during the Diamond Jubilee therefore subtly set out a vision of what was to come: King Charles III and Queen Camilla.

Charles also used this increased visibility to indicate his monarchy would be smaller and financially leaner than any other in history, for this is how he believed it would survive in decades to come. When the Queen stepped onto the Buckingham Palace balcony that jubilee weekend, she was flanked by just Charles, Camilla, William, Kate, and Harry. Given that the extended royal family had been cramming onto the balcony since Queen Victoria began the tradition in 1851, this was a seismic change.

According to a former courtier: "It was decided before the Duke of Edinburgh went into hospital so it was done with the Queen and Duke's blessing but, make no mistake, this was Charles's vision for the future. He wants a slimmed-down monarchy and this was a perfect opportunity to symbolize that.

"Not everyone was happy about not being up on the balcony. While Princess Anne and Prince Edward just rolled with it, it was an issue for Andrew. His view was that he had been demoted." He was right: he had been. That balcony appearance would be a turning point in Charles's relationship with his younger brother, which today remains glacial.

Tensions had already surfaced over Andrew's daughters, Princesses Beatrice and Eugenie of York, and their diminished roles within the royal family. As I wrote in the *Mail on Sunday* in 2016, Andrew had long lobbied for more significant roles for his children, along with public funding and accommodation in Kensington Palace. Even before the Diamond Jubilee, Beatrice and Eugenie had been stripped of their $0.74 million a year, permanent police protection, and told to earn their own living, but Andrew was desperate they remain in the top tier of royalty. This simply did not fit with Charles's idea of a streamlined institution—they were his nieces, but he was prepared to be ruthless.

At the time of the Diamond Jubilee there was also growing concern over Andrew's association with the convicted sex offender Jeffrey Epstein. Today Epstein is dead by suicide. Andrew faced a civil case filed by Epstein victim Virginia Roberts Giuffre but settled out of court. Their mutual friend Ghislaine Maxwell, found guilty of recruiting and grooming girls for Epstein, is in prison.

In 2011 a damning photograph had emerged of Andrew with his arm around Virginia Roberts Giuffre. Andrew claimed he had no recollection of the image being taken at the Belgravia, London, home of Ghislaine Maxwell. Giuffre, however, claimed Andrew allegedly sexually assaulted her three times, once in the Belgravia house when she was seventeen, once at Epstein's mansion in New York, and once on Epstein's private island in the US Virgin Islands.

The prince has always denied the accusations. However, he had visited Epstein's island, hosted the financier at Windsor Castle and Sandringham, and invited him to Beatrice's eighteenth birthday party. There was also a photograph of the men's now notorious stroll in New York's Central Park in December 2010, by which time Epstein had already served a prison term. Accused of paying girls under eighteen to perform sex acts, he had taken a secret plea deal and pleaded guilty to the lesser charge of soliciting a minor for prostitution.

The scandal forced the duke to stand down from his role as Britain's trade envoy. Recalls a former palace aide: "The press was outraged and rightly so and Downing Street didn't want all this negativity. They thanked Andrew but said it was time to go."

The Queen stood by Andrew but the episode highlighted the dichotomy Elizabeth faced as monarch and mother. While not everyone felt it was the right thing to do, the Queen remained loyal to her second son. This was even after Buckingham Palace announced the prince was to be stripped of his military titles and royal patronages in response to the January 2022 filing of Virginia Guiffre's civil case in New York. Andrew was a regular visitor at Windsor Castle where he often took tea with the Queen, and Elizabeth asked Andrew to escort her to her seat in full view of the world's media at Prince Philip's Service of Thanksgiving in March 2022. It was a controversial decision and one made by the Queen apparently against the advice of her courtiers and the Prince of Wales. Charles, tired of Andrew's exploits, had begun to phase his brother out many years before. In

2014 he did not invite Andrew to his sixty-sixth birthday party, even though it was being held at Buckingham Palace and Andrew was in residence at the time. Andrew ate dinner in his apartment while Charles and Camilla hosted a soirée in the grand dining room. After a slew of negative stories about Andrew's behavior and ties to unsavory foreign regimes, Charles was cutting his brother off.

I was told by a royal aide at the time: "Charles is forging a path as the elder statesman . . . and it's his way or no way at all. In some ways it's a rather Tudor court. The shutters came down on Andrew and that was it."

While it might have been upsetting for the Queen to see the once close siblings become distant, Charles had lost patience with his younger brother and could see that he was more of a liability than an asset. Hard though it is to recall, back in 2012 the Epstein affair was tawdry, murky, and humiliating but not the all-engulfing scandal it would become.

ON DECEMBER 3, 2012, came the announcement the country had been waiting for: Kate was pregnant. Unusually the palace revealed the news in the first trimester because the duchess was suffering acute morning sickness. This led to months of what was dubbed the "Great Kate Wait," with media and royal fans camping outside St. Mary's Hospital in Paddington for weeks before she was safely delivered of a son.

HRH Prince George Alexander Louis of Cambridge arrived at 4:24 P.M. on July 22, 2013. He weighed 8 lbs. 6 oz., his birth confirmed with a foolscap note pinned to a golden easel by the gates of Buckingham Palace, and celebrated with gun salutes and bell peals and landmarks lit up in blue. Just twenty-four hours later William and Kate—still showing her postpartum belly and unbelievably elegant in heels, makeup, and sporting a fresh blowout—were ready to face the cameras and the expectant public. As had become royal tradition, they introduced their baby son to the world on the steps of the hospital, with Kate paying tribute to Diana by wearing a polka-dot dress similar to the one worn by the Princess of Wales when she emerged from the same hospital cradling a newborn Prince William back in 1982.

I was among the media for the Great Kate Wait and clearly recall the excitement of the occasion. I remember seeing the royal couple emerge and thinking they looked as shell-shocked, proud, and euphoric as any other first-time parents. But of course they were not ordinary parents and this was no ordinary baby. The significance was in their son's name: George, used as the regnal name by six of the nine Hanoverian/Windsor kings. For all the talk of a "Middleton monarchy," Kate's firstborn child will be King George VII after the Queen's father and grandfather, King George VI and King George V, respectively.

In anticipation of the Cambridges starting a family, the Queen had requested a fundamental change to the law, with the 2013 Succession to the Crown Act ensuring that if they had a daughter she would retain her place in line for the throne instead of being leapfrogged by any later male siblings. "It was a real turning point," says Sally Bedell Smith. "It was a visible recognition that these kinds of discriminatory policies that have been in place for centuries needed to be changed. Primogeniture was the linchpin in the aristocracy and therefore the monarchy. This was a response to the twenty-first-century world.

"I don't know if the Queen would call herself a feminist, but this was an expression of feminism and showed her willingness to modernize."

The Cambridges seemed to embody this idea of progress being driven forward by the Queen as she headed for her ninetieth birthday in 2016. When Charles presented baby William to the world, the crown prince was formally dressed in a collar and tie, a blazer, and had a flower in his buttonhole. In contrast, William now wore chinos and a shirt with the neck open, sleeves rolled up to the elbow. He anchored his son's car seat into the family Range Rover and drove it away himself. He joked about his thinning hair and how the newborn George already had more than he did, and called his wife "poppet" in public. The Cambridges were a new and welcome kind of royal and it was clear they planned to raise their son in a modern way.

They returned to their starter home, Nottingham Cottage at Kensington Palace, so the Queen could meet her new great-grandson before she retired to Balmoral for the summer. According to Lady Elizabeth Anson, George cried throughout this first meeting. "George had a healthy set of lungs on him and screamed the entire time. It was stifling hot with just a fan to keep them cool, and although the Queen was delighted to meet the baby, she didn't stay too long," she said, laughing.

Nor did William and Kate. They packed up their belongings and headed to the country, moving into Kate's family home in Berkshire where George spent the first weeks of his life. William and Kate were tearing up tradition—royal babies usually spent their first months under the care of a maternity nurse and then a royal nanny, but it was important to the new parents that they were hands-on from the start. According to one of their aides who helped oversee the novel arrangement, the Queen was in full agreement as long as it was secure and the couple's security detail could be accommodated. According to Lady Elizabeth, the Queen found it "astonishing" that the couple did not hire a nanny. Instead Kate was supported by her mother, Carole, who prepared nourishing iron-rich smoothies, did the laundry, and made sure Kate could rest in the daytime so she had the energy for night feeds.

The couple knew the public were keen to see a first family portrait but that was notably different as well. It was not taken in a studio or by a prestigious photographer, but was snapped by Kate's father, Michael, in the back garden. The image shows Kate cradling George and William petting the family spaniel Lupo, looking like any other happy family.

The new family then returned to their home in Anglesey. Some years later Kate recalled how she had felt "isolated, so cut off" at that time, alone at home with her baby while William returned to work. But there were advantages—she had privacy and security on the remote island, meaning George could be kept out of the media spotlight, something that was crucial to the Cambridges.

The prince's christening in October 2013 at St. James's Palace was a private ceremony in the Chapel Royal followed by a reception at Clarence House. Later, however, a series of charming official pictures was released. "We had a bit of a wrestle," reveals a former royal aide. "William didn't want any cameras there, full stop. It took a team to convince him that we had to do something. It was a big step and a big give from William. Behind the scenes, Kate was quite the pacifier," adds the source. "She realized they couldn't hide George forever."

It was some time before George was seen again because both William and Kate wanted to shield him from the spotlight. Having complied with the expected tradition of seeing the newborn heir outside the hospital, a family portrait, and then the christening they felt they had earned the right to disappear from the public gaze for a while. Eventually the baby prince would emerge, taking his place on the world stage at just nine months old, when he accompanied his parents to Australia and New Zealand on their official three-week tour in April 2014. Dressed in crisp cotton rompers, cashmere cardigans, and soft shoes, he melted hearts, appearing frequently in his parents' arms and even having a couple of "official" engagements of his own. The baby prince "hosted" a playdate for children who shared his birthday in Wellington, New Zealand, then met a bilby named after him in Sydney's Taronga Zoo.

A generation earlier, at the same age William had accompanied Charles and Diana on their 1983 visit to Australia and New Zealand. Photos of Diana in a casual green dress romping on a rug in the gardens of Auckland's Government House with a barefoot William and a smiling Charles were some of the defining images of that trip. At the time the *Sydney Morning Herald* wrote: "The main fear here is that the royal couple are going to get loved to death." Thirty years later with the Cambridges, that hadn't changed. "Gorgeous George" was one nickname given to the little boy. The "Republican Slayer" was another and, constitutionally speaking, rather more important.

Australia held a referendum on becoming a republic in 1999. It voted "no," a result which still stands. But in May 2022 Anthony Albanese from the Australian Labor Party, which has long supported the republic movement, was elected as the country's new prime minister, renewing speculation that Australia will become a republic. Support for the Australian Republican Movement and its opposition, the Australian Monarchist League, fluctuates. In 2021 an Ipsos Mori poll for the *Age,* the *Sydney Morning Herald,* and TV's *Nine News* found just a third of the country supported the idea of replacing the Queen with an Australian head of state, the lowest number since the 1999 vote. Yet a year earlier a 2020 YouGov poll found 62 percent in favor of a breakaway from the monarchy. It has proved hard over the years to accurately gauge public mood on this issue because polling is often carried out just before or just after a royal visit, when affection for the royals spikes. Certainly the Cambridge family's visit did the monarchists' cause a world of good.

Once they were home, George again disappeared from public view. Soon though, Kate came up with the brilliant idea of taking pictures of her family herself, having learned photography under the tutelage of her friend Alistair Morrison. She had approached the celebrity photographer after admiring his work in the National Portrait Gallery in the years before her marriage, when she had gone so far as considering photography as a career. She was already a gifted landscape photographer. Now she turned her lens onto her family life. It was a highly successful strategy and meant the public saw intimate pictures of George and later his siblings—Princess Charlotte (born May 2015) and little brother Prince Louis (born April 2018)—without the children suffering the kind of intrusion that had blighted William's and Harry's lives.

The solution also helped sidestep some of the privacy issues that confronted the Duke and Duchess of Sussex when their son Archie arrived in 2018. When it came to his christening, the couple kept the ceremony so private that they did not even release the names of his godparents as per royal tradition, causing a storm of controversy.

"The christenings were important for both brothers of course, and how they handled the media gives you quite an insight into their characters," says a former aide. "Harry loathes the media and always has done. It's not just because of what happened to his mother but about how he feels they have treated Meghan too. William is more willing to try and make something work and that's largely down to Kate."

After George's birth the Cambridges started looking for a solution to the conflict between what they wanted as parents and what was required of them as royals; they performed their fair share of the official engagements carried out by the monarch and her family at home and abroad every year. The couple also had their work for good causes—helping to raise the profile of their chosen charities—to factor into their busy lives. As the younger, appealing face of the monarchy they were much in demand but they still had a family to raise, and as far as they were concerned, family came first.

They decided to relocate from Anglesey to their Norfolk bolthole, Anmer Hall, a ten-bedroom Georgian country home on the Sandringham estate, which had been their second wedding present from the Queen. There they would be able to give their children a chance at a normal childhood. When I revealed they were moving to Anmer Hall full time, Kensington Palace tried to damp down the story, insisting the Cambridges' London home, Apartment 1A, gifted to the couple by the Queen and renovated at taxpayer expense shortly after their wedding, remained their principal residence. But it soon became evident William and Kate did not want to spend these early family years in London.

In Norfolk they established a new kind of royal home life, and by traditional standards it was a very slimmed-down operation. There was no chef—Kate did most of the cooking—although there was a trusted housekeeper, Antonella Fresolone, who worked for them between Kensington Palace and Anmer. They entertained in their large kitchen, something else that baffled the Queen who has always believed kitchens to be staff territory. Their security detail was based in estate buildings nearby, while their private secretaries and com-munications team remained in the capital.

By then the couple had conceded they needed round-the-clock help and had hired a nanny, the Norland-trained Maria Borrallo, from one of the country's leading childcare agencies; she had joined them in 2014 ahead of their trip to Australia and New Zealand. It was just as well, for when Princess Charlotte Elizabeth Diana was born on May 2, 2015, weighing 8 lbs. 3 oz., again at St. Mary's Hospi-tal Paddington, Kate had "two under two"—a toddler and a newborn to care for.

The Middleton family, particularly Carole, was extremely hands-on, often to the frustration of Charles who privately com-plained he didn't see enough of his grandchildren. Being something of a workaholic, Charles didn't have much free time and he didn't want to impose on his son and daughter-in-law. Michael and Carole in contrast were regularly in residence at Anmer, visiting for Christ-mas, weekends, and holidays and taking care of the children when William and Kate were away on royal duties. "I couldn't do it without my mother," Kate told me on the couple's 2016 tour to the kingdom of Bhutan, when we were discussing the challenges of being working mums. William meanwhile is so close to Michael that he has affec-tionately called him "Dad" since before he married into the Middle-ton family.

Up in Norfolk George was enrolled in a Montessori school, al-beit one with newly fitted bulletproof glass in the windows, and Kate could be seen doing the school run. She shopped at the local Waitrose, and the family was often spotted walking with their dog Lupo on the local beaches of Brancaster and Holkham. Occasionally they'd surprise diners at smart gastro pubs such as the King's Head in Great Bircham where they'd blend in, dressed down in jeans and sharing dessert like any other married couple.

By that point William and Kate had never looked stronger. Their solid, sunny relationship and growing family, with all it contributed to the House of Windsor, was hugely appealing. The only cost was perhaps to Charles. So long sidelined because his mother had the top job, then coming to the fore in jubilee year, he was in danger of being outshined by his own son and daughter-in-law.

According to a former aide: "The media focused on William and Catherine. It was all about the new generation, the shiny new beautiful couple and their beautiful children. Trying to get the royal correspondents to cover Charles and Camilla wasn't easy. They were working hard and both wanted to draw attention to their charities, but the interest was always on William and Kate and then George and Charlotte. It was incredibly frustrating for Charles."

It must have been because Charles, the longest-serving Prince of Wales in history, had to make apprenticeship to the throne his life's work. He was in his late sixties when the Queen reached her landmark ninetieth birthday in 2016. When he turned sixty-five in November 2013, Camilla gave an interview to the *Daily Telegraph* and revealed: "He never, ever stops working. He's exhausting. No matter what the day, he is always working. I am hopping up and down and saying, 'Darling, do you think we could have a bit of, you know, peace and quiet, enjoy ourselves together?' But he always has to finish something. He is so in the zone . . . you are outside . . . but he is always there in the zone, working, working, working." And he had not even started the one job he was born to do.

He was however taking over more and more of his mother's workload as the most senior of her substitutes. So was William, and so too was Harry before his decision to surrender his royal role.

William left the air ambulance job he had taken after leaving military life to join the Firm full time in July 2017. He was aware the moment had finally come to fully devote himself to supporting his grandmother and his father. Harry had left the army in June 2015, turning his military service into a meaningful royal role supporting military and veterans' charities. His launch of the Invictus Games back in 2014, a sporting contest for wounded and sick service personnel, seemed as though it would define his post-military royal career. He also began traveling the world on behalf of his grandmother, clocking up visits to Australia and New Zealand, South Africa, the United States. Notably, there was a riotous 2016 trip to the Caribbean visiting Antigua and Barbuda, St. Kitts and Nevis, St. Lucia, St. Vincent and the Grenadines, Grenada, Barbados, and Guyana. Headline-grabbing highlights included meeting Rihanna, playing cricket, and helping tiny baby turtles find their way into the sea.

This "formal but fun" Harry was so cherished that even the time in 2012 when he was caught playing strip billiards in a hotel suite in Las Vegas was completely forgiven. Harry himself commented: "It was probably a classic example of me being too much army and not enough prince," and his millions of fans agreed.

In July 2016 the prince would meet American actress and activist Meghan Markle and fall headlong in love. It was at the Invictus Games in Canada the following year that the couple made their first official appearance together. Entering a wheelchair tennis match hand in hand, Meghan wore frayed jeans, flats, and a white shirt called "the Husband" by her fashion designer friend Misha Nonoo. It was clear: the relationship was serious.

The future could hardly have looked rosier. In half a decade a historic Diamond Jubilee had been celebrated, a new heir to the throne had been born, the substitutes were doing a brilliant job on behalf of the Queen, and now a new and contemporary royal love story was set to be written by Harry and Meghan.

What could possibly go wrong?

Queen Elizabeth II with Prince Charles, Princess Anne, and HRH The Prince Philip, Duke of Edinburgh, on her Coronation Day, June 2, 1953. (ULLSTEIN BILD/ULLSTEIN BILD VIA GETTY IMAGES)

Princess Elizabeth with Philip Mountbatten on their wedding day, November 20, 1947. (TOPICAL PRESS AGENCY/ HULTON ARCHIVE/GETTY IMAGES)

Prince Charles, the Prince of Wales, at his investiture at Caernarfon Castle, Wales, July 1, 1969. (RAY BELLISARIO/ POPPERFOTO VIA GETTY IMAGES/GETTY IMAGES)

The Windsors wave to photographers from the steps of Frogmore House in Home Park, Windsor, April 19, 1965. (ROLLS PRESS/POPPERFOTO VIA GETTY IMAGES/ GETTY IMAGES)

Prince Charles married Lady Diana Spencer on July 29, 1981, at St. Paul's Cathedral. Diana was the first British citizen to marry an heir to the British throne in three centuries. (TIM GRAHAM PHOTO LIBRARY VIA GETTY IMAGES)

Princess Diana with Prince William and Prince Harry at the Heads of State VE Remembrance Service in Hyde Park on May 7, 1995. (ANWAR HUSSEIN/ GETTY IMAGES)

Charles pictured with Camilla Parker Bowles in 1979. Diana famously said, "There were three of us in this marriage, so it was a bit crowded." (TIM GRAHAM/GETTY IMAGES)

At long last, Prince Charles marries Camilla Parker Bowles, now the Duchess of Cornwall, in a civil wedding at the Guildhall in Windsor on April 9, 2005. (TIM GRAHAM PHOTO LIBRARY VIA GETTY IMAGES)

Prince William met Catherine Middleton at the University of St. Andrews. Their friendship blossomed into an eight-year romance before they got engaged. (INDIGO/GETTY IMAGES)

The newly titled Duke and Duchess of Cambridge were married at Westminster Abbey, April 29, 2011. (ANTONY JONES/JULIAN PARKER/ MARK CUTHBERT/UK PRESS VIA GETTY IMAGES)

The birth of Prince George on July 22, 2013, was a moment for the nation to celebrate a new heir to the throne. This informal picture was taken by Kate's father, Michael Middleton. (MICHAEL MIDDLETON/KENSINGTON PALACE VIA GETTY IMAGES)

William gives Kate a hug after beating her at a dragon boat race in Canada on their first overseas tour in May 2011. (JOHN STILLWELL-POOL/GETTY IMAGES)

Her Majesty and two future Queen Consorts visit Fortnum and Mason, the royals' grocer of choice. (LEON NEAL/AFP VIA GETTY IMAGES)

The Prince of Wales and the Duchess of Cornwall in Adelaide during their Diamond Jubilee Tour of Australia in 2012. (MORNE DE KLERK/GETTY IMAGES)

The Diamond Jubilee was an opportunity to present a snapshot of the future of the Royal Family and back in 2012 that included Prince Harry. (PAUL CUNNINGHAM/ CORBIS VIA GETTY IMAGES)

The newly married Prince Harry and Meghan Markle, now the Duke and Duchess of Sussex, share a kiss on the steps of St. George's Chapel, May 19, 2018. (DANNY LAWSON-WPA POOL/GETTY IMAGES)

Harry and Meghan with their four-month-old son, Archie Harrison Mountbatten Windsor, on an official tour of South Africa in September 2019. (TOBY MELVILLE-POOL/ GETTY IMAGES)

The Sussexes' last engagement as working royals at the Commonwealth Day Service at Westminster Abbey on March 9, 2020. (PHIL HARRIS-WPA POOL/GETTY IMAGES)

The Duke of Edinburgh retired from public life in 2017 but he continued to support the Queen and the Royal Family until his death on April 9, 2021. (YUI MOK/ POOL/AFP VIA GETTY IMAGES)

Ever the pragmatist, Prince Philip had designed a bespoke Land Rover to carry his coffin to his funeral at St. George's Chapel. (POOL/SAMIR HUSSEIN/WIREIMAGE)

The Duchess of Cambridge is driven to Prince Philip's funeral while the Queen cuts a lonely and solitary figure, masked and dressed in black. (LEFT: CHRIS JACKSON/ POOL/AFP VIA GETTY IMAGES; RIGHT: JONATHAN BRADY-WPA POOL/GETTY IMAGES)

Having stepped down as working royals, Harry and Meghan have relaunched themselves as activists and philanthropists. (ANGELA WEISS/ AFP VIA GETTY IMAGES)

The Queen resumed public duties soon after her husband's death. She is pictured here, a new widow, at the G7 summit in Cornwall flanked by Charles and Camilla and William and Kate. (JACK HILL-WPA POOL/GETTY IMAGES)

The Queen's health took a downward turn after she suffered a back sprain and had mobility issues, but she continues to read her red box of government papers daily. (CHRIS JACKSON/ GETTY IMAGES)

The Queen used the 70th anniversary of her Accession to renew her pledge to serve her subjects and to express her "sincere wish" for Camilla to be known as Queen Consort. (JEFF OVERS/BBC NEWS & CURRENT AFFAIRS VIA GETTY IMAGES)

The Duke and Duchess of Cambridge arrive at St. George's Chapel, April 17, 2022, for the Easter Sunday church service with Prince George and Princess Charlotte. (ANDREW MATTHEWS-WPA POOL/GETTY IMAGES)

The Duke and Duchess of Cambridge being driven in the Queen's Land Rover during a controversial tour of the Caribbean in April 2022. (KARWAI TANG/ WIREIMAGE)

Prince George, Prince Louis, and Princess Charlotte make their debut carriage procession at Trooping the Colour as part of the Queen's Platinum Jubilee celebrations.

The Queen taking tea with Paddington Bear was one the highlights of the Platinum Jubilee weekend.

The Queen's state funeral took place on September 19, 2022, at Westminster Abbey. Her Majesty's final resting place is St. George's Chapel, Windsor, where thousands of people gathered on the Long Walk to bid a final farewell.

King Charles and Queen Camilla were crowned at Westminster Abbey on May 6, 2023. Accompanied by members of the royal family, it was Charles's very first balcony appearance as the sovereign.

CHAPTER 7

A Windsor Wedding

If someone slips into my life, then that's absolutely fantastic.
—Prince Harry

Harry was doing Vegas. At the Wet Republic pool party, he and a group of friends had a cabana to themselves and round after round of vodka and cranberry juice arriving from the bar. The prince wore cheerful red Bermuda shorts and a white fedora, which was more than he'd ended up wearing while playing strip billiards in his hotel room the night before.

The prince should perhaps have been subject to the rule that "what happens in Vegas stays in Vegas" but with his own "crown jewels" on show, that was always going to be unlikely. One of the twenty-five women who'd crammed into his suite at 3:30 A.M. the morning before had photographed him naked and drunk. After a night downing Jägerbombs, a potent mixture of Jägermeister liqueur and Red Bull, Harry and his friends hadn't noticed. Nor, crucially, had his security team who had for some reason allowed unvetted guests and their cell phones into the private after-party, yet kept their jobs regardless.

While the third in line to the British throne (as he was then) larked in the pool the next day, the grainy images were making their way to TMZ. "A raging party with a bunch of hot chicks," pretty much summed it up.

Harry flew home to face his father, the palace, his military bosses, and his girlfriend Cressida Bonas. He hadn't broken any army regulations, but he had let people down by putting himself in such a vulnerable position. But he was in luck: his father was protective and had already instructed lawyers in what proved to be a doomed attempt to maintain his son's privacy and any remaining shreds of dignity. After a hastily arranged summit at a secret hideaway in Buckinghamshire, Cressida forgave him too.

As for the country, it shared the opinion of Harry's former troop commander Dickon Leigh-Wood: "Vegas was an epic party. Harry was about to go back to war. He wanted to have fun. He had survived the front line, he was alive and living it up. We all thought, 'Good for him.'"

This was a fascinating and important outcome, for it demonstrated just how far public opinion of Harry had come from his party prince years, how much his military career and undisputed courage on the battlefield had changed people's perception of him. Not only was he forgiven for Vegas, but also he was quietly applauded for it. The warrior prince had earned his night off.

It had all been so different just a few years earlier. "Hooray Harry" and the "Royal Rebel" were titles given to Harry by the media. During my early career as royal correspondent for the *Mail on Sunday*, I spent many a late night partying with the prince at West London nightclubs, and watching him knock back vodka Red Bulls as he fended off the advances of well-heeled young women at charity polo matches. As one of the world's most eligible bachelors, his love life was of global interest. But those who knew him well in those days spoke of a deeply private person who longed for more anonymity and who at times struggled with his royal role. Harry once told me he sometimes wished he wasn't a prince and wanted to know what it was like to "take the tube" and "order a takeaway coffee." On the one hand he wanted to be an ordinary person, the one thing he could never be. But he also recognized that his unique position afforded him a powerful opportunity to do important work, like the Invictus Games, and raise awareness about issues that mattered to him. Harry spent most of his late twenties trying to shake off his playboy image. As he headed for his thirtieth birthday, he began a very public journey of self-discovery which would sow the seeds of his new post-royal life in California with his wife and children.

In April 2017 he sat down with *Daily Telegraph* columnist Bryony Gordon to promote the work of the mental health initiative Heads Together, launched with Kate and William, and opened up. On the podcast *Mad World* he revealed: "I can safely say that losing my mum at the age of twelve and therefore shutting down all of my emotions for the last twenty years has had a quite serious effect on not only my personal life but also my work as well. I have probably been very close to a complete breakdown on numerous occasions."

Harry recorded the podcast in Kensington Palace. Casually dressed in a blue collared shirt and a gray funnel-neck woolen sweater, he was so relaxed the journalist would describe the encounter as "like having a cup of tea with a friend who had been through a particularly difficult time and lived to tell the tale."

Harry revealed: "My way of dealing with it was sticking my head in the sand, refusing to ever think about my mum, because why would that help? It's only going to make you sad. It's not going to bring her back. I was the typical twenty-, twenty-five-, twenty-eight-year-old going around going, 'Life is great. Life is fine.'" But it led, he admitted to "total chaos."

He embarked on therapy and then took the radical decision to talk about his experience in the hope of encouraging and supporting other people struggling with their mental health. "What my mother believed in is if you are in a position of privilege or a position of responsibility and if you can put your name to something that you genuinely believe in, you can smash any stigma you want."

Hearing a senior member of the royal family speak with such searing honesty earned him both praise and criticism. There were concerns at the very top that in speaking with such candor Harry risked shattering the mystique the Queen believed vital to the survival of the monarchy. According to Lady Elizabeth Anson, the monarch feared that in revealing so much of himself, Harry was feeding an insatiable beast: "When I said to [the Queen], 'I think it's no bad thing he's opened up,' she said, 'I'm afraid I can't agree with you. [The media] will want to know more and more.'"

However, having more of the Spencers' natural openness than the Windsors' buttoned-up reserve, Harry was unwilling to observe the "Never complain, never explain" rule employed by the Queen and before her, the Queen Mother. He seized upon the twentieth anniversary of Diana's death as an opportunity for himself and William to speak publicly about the loss of their mother and the impact of her death on their lives. The result was a series of rare and deeply personal interviews for both the BBC and ITV.

The programs were a revelation, the brothers elbow to elbow poring over family photo albums, gazing at private images of one of the most photographed women in the world. Their happiness shone out, William's anger occasionally flashed, Harry held his hands together almost in prayer as he reached for precious childhood memories. It was clear that as the princes said, they thought she had been the "best mum in the world."

William said her loss was "like an earthquake's just run through the house and through your life," that her death had been "utterly devastating." He spoke too about drawing on her strength to heal himself: "I kept saying to myself that my mother would not want me to be upset, that she'd not want me to be down. She was extremely good at showing her love. She was extremely good at showing what we meant to her and what feelings meant and how important it was to feel."

Harry's words were a howl of rage and grief: "She was our mum. She is still our mum. Of course as a son I would say this: she was the best mum in the world. Even talking about it now I can feel the hugs she used to give us and I miss that feeling. I miss that part of a family, having that mother to be able to give you those hugs and give you that compassion I think everybody needs. There's not a day that William and I don't wish she was still around and we wonder what kind of mother she would be now, what kind of public role she would have and what difference she would be making."

There was more raw emotion in an interview Harry gave to *Newsweek* just weeks before the anniversary, in which he discussed his feelings about walking behind his mother's coffin. While he didn't name anyone (it was in fact Philip who encouraged William and Harry to walk behind their mother's gun carriage; he believed they would regret it for the rest of their lives if they did not), his sentiment was clear: "My mother had just died and I had to walk a long way behind her coffin, surrounded by thousands of people watching me while millions more did on television. I don't think any child should be asked to do that, under any circumstances. I don't think that would happen today."

Venturing into the wider issue of monarchy and the future, Harry, who at this stage was still a senior member of the royal family, said: "We are involved in modernizing the British monarchy. We are not doing this for ourselves but for the greater good of the people . . . Is there any one of the royal family who wants to be king or queen? I don't think so, but we will carry out our duties at the right time."

There were some who felt it was not Harry's place to speak on behalf of others, especially when it came to preaching about duty. According to Lady Elizabeth Anson: "That comment about duty I know would have upset the Queen the most. Her opinion is 'Whatever your lot is, you get on with it. You might draw the short straw, but you don't complain.'"

But just like Diana, Harry didn't fit the royal mold. Diana had always called Harry the "naughty one" and he possessed her rebellious streak. His path to freedom began with his military career. "Being in the army was the best escape I've ever had," he said in an interview with journalist Angela Levin. "I was one of the lads and could forget I was Prince Harry." In June 2015, when the scaling down of the war in Afghanistan meant he was looking at a desk job, he announced he was leaving after an illustrious decade-long career. The Queen recruited him as a full-time working royal, doubtless feeling his arrival on the palace roster could not have come at a better moment.

In September 2015 the Queen became the longest-reigning monarch ever in the UK, surpassing her great-great-grandmother Queen Victoria. Elizabeth II had reigned for 23,226 days, sixteen hours, and approximately thirty minutes. She was by then eighty-nine and Prince Philip was five years her senior, so there was a growing pressure on the next generation to step up and support them.

In 2016 the Queen celebrated her ninetieth birthday in April and then her official birthday in June. There was a national service of thanksgiving, a street party for ten thousand people along the Mall, and a tour of Windsor that seemed to have a very clear message: "One is still here." Even though she had scaled back on overseas travel the year before, the Queen had carried out 341 public engagements in the UK—more than William, Kate, and Harry combined. But despite the Queen's remarkable energy and good health, the House of Windsor was looking awfully old.

In Europe it was becoming commonplace for aging monarchs to hand over to the next generation. In 2013 the Queen's distant cousin Queen Beatrix of the Netherlands announced she was abdicating in favor of her son Willem-Alexander. Her own mother and grandmother had similarly handed on the crown in 1980 and 1948, respectively.

There have been other European abdications: in Luxembourg, Jean the Grand Duke abdicated in favor of his son Henri in 2000; and King Juan Carlos I of Spain abdicated in favor of his son Felipe VI in 2014. In Belgium King Albert II handed the throne to his son Philippe in 2013.

In the UK there was no suggestion of the Queen ever handing over or retiring. Her cousin Margaret Rhodes, interviewed by the BBC in 2016, said: "There is no possible danger of her abdicating in favor of her eldest son. She feels, I think she feels, that the vows she made on her coronation were ones she wants to fulfill to the nth degree and I think she vowed to act as Queen for as long as she lives. Her total dedication is something we should all be grateful for."

This sentiment was reinforced by my sit-down interview with Princess Anne for *Vanity Fair*. In the sunlit sitting room of her apartment at St. James's Palace, she told me: "I don't think retirement is quite the same [for my mother]. Most people would say we're very lucky not to be in that situation because you wouldn't want to just stop."

At the heart of the matter lay the holy vows the Queen—a committed Christian and supreme governor of the Church of England—made at her coronation, and the ghost of the abdication that still haunted the House of Windsor. "The word 'abdication' was still a forbidden word at the palace," says a former aide. "One did not dare utter it. When I worked for Her Majesty I felt I could talk to the Queen about *anything* except the word beginning with A. It would've been deeply offensive and got the coldest possible stare."

Retirement was, however, an option for the Duke of Edinburgh who announced he was standing down from royal duties after sixty-five years of service. Back in 2011 at the age of ninety he'd hinted it was a possibility saying: "It's better to get out before you reach your sell-by date. I reckon I have done my bit. So I want to enjoy myself now, with less responsibility, less frantic rushing about, less preparation, less trying to think of something to say. On top of that, your memory is going. I can't remember names and things."

It would be another six years before he would act on these sentiments because he believed it was his duty to be by the side of his wife, and the Queen, he knew, would never stop. The news was broken at a May 2017 meeting of 550 royal staff in the ballroom of Buckingham Palace.

Within hours of the announcement the Duke was at an engagement in St. James's Palace where he met mathematician Sir Michael Atiyah, a stripling of eighty-eight. "I am sorry to hear you are standing down," sympathized Sir Michael. "Well, I can't stand up much longer," shot back the Duke with a rueful grin. It was already his twenty-sixth public engagement of the year.

At that point his diary contained a string of engagements representing his diverse interests and responsibilities: the Royal Windsor Horse Show, the Chelsea Flower Show, a dinner marking the founding of Pakistan, a state visit by King Felipe and Queen Letizia, and of course a reception for young people who had earned a Duke of Edinburgh Award for volunteer work. He worked his way through them until the final entry: meeting a group of Royal Marines at Buckingham Palace to acknowledge their charity fund-raising. He had been captain general of the commandos for sixty-four years. Philip took the royal salute and inspected an honor guard despite the soggy, cold conditions. In return he received three cheers and a rousing rendition of "For He's a Jolly Good Fellow."

It was his 22,219th solo royal engagement, and it was no coincidence that this valedictory appearance was on the forecourt of Buckingham Palace, the building that symbolizes the monarchy around the world. The Royal Mint struck a commemorative £5 coin to mark the occasion. Under an image of the Duke's head it bore the words *Non Sibi Sed Patriae* ("Not for Self but Country")—the story of his life, well into old, old age, told in four unvarnished words.

The Duke had thrived in his nineties. He was a carriage driver, a birdwatcher, a fly fisherman, an amateur photographer, and a gifted watercolorist. A lifelong lover of new technology, he was computer literate too. He still walked and took the stairs where possible and did the daily Royal Canadian Airforce exercises he swore by. He could still fit into the uniform he'd worn on his wedding day, a fact confirmed by his personal tailor John Kent of the Piccadilly firm Kent & Haste. He enjoyed a drink occasionally, usually a pale ale, but had given up smoking overnight in 1947 to please Elizabeth. He was eighty-two before he gave up riding in Trooping the Colour (the military celebration of the Queen's birthday) and joined the Queen in her carriage. By then it was said he was in so much back pain after the ceremony, for which he always wore a full guard's uniform and a bearskin, that he had to lie on the floor to recover. His diary was still full too: in 2016 despite his age and occasional infirmity he had 110 days of public engagements, making him as busy as the younger generation of royals.

People feared the Queen would be lost without him by her side. The news turned the spotlight onto the younger royals, particularly the Cambridge family and their charming children who had been hidden from public view in Norfolk. In September 2017 William and Kate had announced they were pregnant with their third baby, Prince Louis, delighting a country that felt it had seen relatively little of George and Charlotte. For the uncomfortable truth was that while William and Kate loved their under-the-radar lives in the country, the couple were facing mounting criticism for not taking their share of the royal load. According to one senior royal source: "There was a feeling at the palace among some senior courtiers that William needed to choose between being a pilot or a prince."

It did not go unnoticed that in March 2017 he had missed the Commonwealth Day service, preferring to go on a ski trip to Verbier in the Swiss Alps with a group of male friends. Skipping such a significant service for the monarchy caused a backlash in the media. A tally of royal engagements showed that the Queen had carried out almost twice William's number of official duties so far that year, leading to unfavorable headlines such as "Throne Idol" in the *Sun*.

William was stung by the criticism, revealed a former aide: "It was the assumption that he wasn't doing anything that upset him when what he was actually doing was saving people's lives as an air ambulance pilot. It really irked him because he considered his job to be very important work, and it was just being dismissed. He felt the criticism was unfair. His view has always been that it's not just about the number of engagements you are carrying out; it's about the impact you're having and he was still very involved with the Royal Foundation and getting various initiatives off the ground."

Headstrong and determined as he always had been, William wanted time with his family and a career. His priorities were "family and flying, in that order" according to one of his senior aides. He wasn't going to be pressured into taking on full-time royal duties just yet.

In some ways, Harry leaving the army worked to William's advantage. It meant there was a young, fun, photogenic Windsor prince to do some of the heavy lifting. He had already acquitted himself brilliantly on behalf of his family, starting with a Caribbean tour in 2012, which included Jamaica, Belize, and the Bahamas followed by a trade mission to Brazil. Royal photographer Chris Jackson describes his impact on people—celebrities, politicians, children in the crowd—as "Harry Magic," and certainly he was lavished with praise when he came home.

In 2013 he was in the United States, Angola, and Australia; in 2014 Estonia, Italy, Chile, and Brazil as well as leading Remembrance Sunday commemorations at the Kandahar airbase in Afghanistan. By 2015 he was back in Australia, New Zealand, and America again, on this last trip meeting with President Barack Obama in the Oval Office and launching the 2016 Invictus Games alongside First Lady Michelle Obama and Dr. Jill Biden at Fort Belvoir. In the summer of 2015, as a sign of her growing trust in her grandson, the Queen appointed Harry Knight Commander of the Royal Victorian Order. The award recognizes people who have served the monarchy, often by representing the Queen around the world.

In conjunction with his royal duties, Harry was firmly committed to the Invictus Games. The first games opened in September 2014, and the four days that followed showcased sporting competition between more than four hundred veterans from thirteen countries. It was a roaring success. Speaking to the *Sunday Times* two years later in May 2016, Harry said: "I saw it as a chance to create a platform that [wounded service personnel] can use as part of rehabilitation for themselves. A chance for them to set goals in life, rather than sitting at home worrying about things. Sport seemed to be the linchpin. Their stories will move and inspire a whole generation." And they did.

The day after the closing concert was Harry's thirtieth birthday. William hosted a dinner at Clarence House where Prince Charles had given permission for a raid on the wine cellar. Overnight Harry became independently wealthy, inheriting the $12 million left to him in his mother's will. Most significant of all, though, launching Invictus "really helped and healed me." It had proved "a sort of cure for myself." Harry was ready to move on to the next big acutely aware of the perils which historically lie in wait for the "spare."

His first point of reference was Princess Margaret who was in her sister's shadow from the moment Elizabeth became queen. She was unable to marry her first love, Group Captain Peter Townsend, because his broken marriage and divorce flouted the then prevailing edicts of the Anglican Church. Then her marriage to Lord Snowdon ended in divorce.

"The 'spare' problem with which Princess Margaret seemed to have some difficulty," says Robert Lacey, "was that, having been brought up alongside her sister as one of the 'little princesses,' her closeness to the succession and hence her royal significance then diminished with the birth of each of her sister's children."

The parties and social power plays with which she filled her empty weeks are depicted in season four of *The Crown* where Helena Bonham Carter brings the rebel royal brilliantly to life. In a confrontation with her sister, Margaret tells the Queen: "The day stretches before me like a great yawning void," only to be told that duty and protocol mean they have to "play by the rules."

Harry was too young to remember much about his aunt Margo, but he had watched it all go badly wrong for his uncle Andrew. From a career highpoint in the Falklands War and a marriage to Sarah Ferguson, which had for a time been wildly popular, Andrew had fallen far from grace. His years as a trade envoy traveling the world supporting British business had earned him the nickname "Airmiles Andy," and he never shook off the suggestion it was of more benefit to him than to his country. There were financial scandals and, even though he was famously teetotal, stories of boorish behavior. Ultimately his disregard for the institution led to his falling out with Charles, the man who had most to gain from the long-term support of a dutiful younger brother.

As Robert Lacey says: "Spares work very well when they succeed, and we must remember that George VI was a 'spare,' as was his father, George V, the founder of the modern House of Windsor. But the problem arises for the spare when they don't get the top job and they find themselves dropping down the order of succession. They start off so strongly as virtual equals with the heir and then . . ."

Harry was acutely aware he too would slip down the line of succession and made fun of it and himself, saying in an interview with the *Sunday Times* in May 2016: "I'm in this privileged position and I will use it for as long as I can, or until I become boring, or until George ends up becoming more interesting." Following the birth of Prince Louis in April 2018 he moved to sixth in line to the throne, yet his popularity and visibility kept him to the fore of his family and on all the front pages. So too did his love life, or lack of one.

Being the most eligible prince in the world ought to have made romance easy, but he spoke of the "massive paranoia that sits inside me" over the prospect of dating. He feared for any girlfriend becoming the victim of a predatory media. "If or when I do find a girlfriend," he vowed, "I will do my utmost to ensure that me and her can get to the point where we're actually comfortable with each other before the massive invasion that is inevitably going to happen into her privacy."

It took just two meetings for Harry to realize there was something very special about the American-born actress with whom he had been set up on a blind date. Meghan and Harry's first meeting was over drinks at the fashionable Dean Street Townhouse, part of the members-only Soho House group. The couple discussed the social, economic, and environmental challenges facing emerging nations and realized that despite living on different continents and doing very different jobs, they had plenty in common. It was July 2016.

Ambitious, successful, wealthy in her own right, and three years older than the prince, Meghan was seriously impressive. As soon as he met her Harry knew he had to "up his game." There was a flurry of texts after their first meeting, a dinner date the following night, and within six weeks Harry invited Meghan to holiday with him in Botswana. It was clear to everyone in his life that Harry had met "the one."

Meghan Markle was the only child of divorced parents Thomas Markle and Doria Ragland and had grown up in middle-class comfort in Los Angeles. She became an actress and activist and wrote a stylish lifestyle blog. Winning the role of Rachel Zane in the long-running TV drama *Suits* made her globally known, but the move to Toronto where it was filmed doomed her marriage to movie industry executive Trevor Engelson. She'd had one serious relationship since then but was known to value her independence. Harry found her irresistible and the relationship swiftly became serious.

Just how serious became apparent four months after that first date when Harry's communications team confirmed their relationship and issued a powerful protective statement. It condemned "a wave of abuse and harassment" and the "outright sexism and racism of social media trolls" that was being directed at his new girlfriend. It stated: "Prince Harry is worried about Ms. Markle's safety and is deeply disappointed that he has not been able to protect her. It is not right that a few months into a relationship with him that Ms. Markle should be subjected to such a storm. He knows commentators will say this is 'the price she has to pay' and that 'this is all part of the game.' He strongly disagrees. This is not a game—it is her life and his."

After news of the relationship broke in a British tabloid, Meghan became the most googled woman on earth and the most sought after. There were paparazzi swarming around her Toronto apartment and doorstepping her mother and father. She needed extra security to get to the set of *Suits*, finding herself dealing with a level of public interest she had never experienced. Most of the coverage was positive—the contemporary idea of a royal girlfriend who was biracial, divorced, and American made a compelling story and seemed fitting for a twenty-first-century royal family.

But there was a worrying underlying racism and sexism in some of the coverage, particularly several comment pieces where Meghan was described as having "exotic DNA." One online newspaper report falsely claimed Meghan was "(almost) straight outta Compton" and noted her mother Doria's dreadlocks and nose ring. The final straw for Harry was when the *Sun* newspaper reported that some of Meghan's sex scenes in *Suits* were being streamed on a well-known porn website. It was headlined "Harry's Girl on Pornhub."

"There were some press reports that appeared to be racist," US broadcaster and journalist KJ Matthews who was covering the story in Los Angeles told me. "Tabloids talked about the texture of her mother's hair, that her lineage was exotic, that she was 'straight outta Compton' yet she has never lived in Compton."

According to veteran international broadcaster Wesley Kerr, a British journalist of Jamaican heritage who was a BBC correspondent through the nineties: "I don't think the majority of coverage in the British media was racist. I would say overall it was largely positive, but I can see how Harry and Meghan felt that a few individual stories written about Meghan in the newspapers were unkind and from their perspective racially tinged."

Harry had seen his former girlfriends Chelsy Davy and Cressida Bonas struggle with the intense media interest, and he was determined Meghan should not be subjected to the same ordeal. But the fact that she was a well-known actress with a huge Instagram following, an ex-husband, and a dysfunctional family made her an irresistible story for the tabloids. They published daily stories about Meghan and put even more strain on Harry's already tense relationship with the media.

News of the couple's engagement in November 2017 generated seemingly endless coverage in the broadsheet and tabloid media. When she made her first official appearance on a visit to Nottingham, Meghan was greeted like a Hollywood star and as though she was already royalty. Adoring fans admired her beautiful new engagement ring—set with two of Diana's diamonds and one Harry had sourced for her in Botswana—and crashed fashion websites as they hunted down her "look."

But she was to be far more than a fashion plate. Meghan wanted to show the mettle that had seen her forge a successful TV career and use her royal title as an engine for change. Charles reportedly nicknamed his future daughter-in-law "Tungsten" because of her toughness and resilience. What the Prince of Wales saw in her was made apparent to the country in February 2018, when she joined her fiancé and the Duke and Duchess of Cambridge onstage at the Royal Foundation Forum to speak. It was, according to one aide, the moment William and Kate, who was heavily pregnant, realized *they* needed to up their game.

The Cambridges had already signaled their intention to be more than "ornamental royals" and had, along with Harry, made a huge success of their mental health campaign Heads Together. But Meghan was the breakout star of the foursome. She was polished, passionate, and funny, using all her TV-honed skills to present her case. "That was a wake-up moment for William and Kate when they realized that Meghan was very impressive, very confident, and very capable," according to a source.

There were early warning signs that there could be challenges ahead and persistent rumors about fallouts between both Meghan and Kate and William and Harry. Despite Harry's hopes that Kate would show Meghan the way and the two would become close friends, there was a coolness between them. Like William, Kate could be reserved before you properly got to know her, and with two young children and one on the way, she had her hands full.

Meghan felt unsupported in the run-up to her May 2018 wedding, which was marred by members of her own family selling stories to the press and culminated with her father, Thomas Markle, having a heart attack and being forced to pull out of the ceremony. Harry meanwhile felt that while he had his grandmother's and father's backing, he didn't have the support he really craved from his brother and the "sister [he'd] always wanted."

The truth was William did have concerns and felt the relationship had moved too quickly. During one of their tête-à-têtes, which had become increasingly heated, William urged his younger brother not to rush into things. His advice fell on deaf ears. Harry resented his brother for counseling caution.

"It's probably a bit strong to say he didn't like Meghan from the start, but William had reservations," confides one of the duke's oldest friends. "He was obviously happy for Harry but he was also cautious, as he always is about people getting close very quickly to his family."

Things did not improve after the engagement when Charles, anxious for rapprochement between his sons, asked William and Kate to host Harry and Meghan at Anmer Hall over Christmas. Welcoming them into their family home was an olive branch on the Cambridges' part. Harry told the BBC Radio 4 flagship *Today* program, which he guest edited over the festive period, that it had been a wonderful first Christmas for Meghan at Sandringham. "It was fantastic, she really enjoyed it," he claimed, adding his family "loved having" Meghan with them. "I think we've got one of the biggest families I know . . . She has done an absolutely amazing job just getting in there and it's the family, I suppose, that she's never had."

In private, however, he told close friends that the Cambridges hadn't "rolled out the red carpet" for Meghan. "Harry said he felt William and Kate hadn't made much of an effort to make Meghan feel special and welcome," added the source. The Cambridges, who often have Kate's family stay at Christmas, felt they had done more than enough by inviting their brother and soon to be sister-in-law into their home at what was always an intimate and family-focused time. It was the preface to tensions that would spark more family rows up to the wedding day. Kate and Meghan disagreed over whether or not Charlotte should wear tights with her dress. Meghan wanted bare legs; Kate felt covered was more appropriate for her daughter on such a formal occasion.

In her Oprah interview Meghan revealed: "A few days before the wedding, [Kate] was upset about something pertaining—yes, the issue was correct about flower girl dresses—and it made me cry and it really hurt my feelings. And I thought in the context of everything else that was going on in those days leading to the wedding that it didn't make sense to not be just doing what everyone else was doing, which was try to be supportive, knowing what was going on with my dad and whatnot."

There was also an alleged row over which tiara Meghan was going to be permitted to borrow. "What Meghan wants, Meghan gets!" Harry is supposed to have shouted at the Queen's dresser Angela Kelly, earning him a stern telling-off from his grandmother. In a subsequent account given by Meghan herself, the Queen allowed her to choose from five tiaras, saying they all suited her and that the monarch supported Meghan's choice of the Queen Mary bandeau tiara.

According to Lady Elizabeth Anson: "The run-up to the wedding was really very difficult for the Queen. She was very upset by how Harry had behaved and some of his demands and the way he went about things his own way. For example he asked the archbishop of Canterbury to marry them before consulting the Queen and the Dean of Windsor, which wasn't the correct way to do things. I think she was dismayed by his attitude in general and I remember speaking to her and her being rather upset by how beastly Harry was being. Their relationship was quite badly damaged by it all."

While William and Kate had rewritten the royal wedding rule book so they could have the wedding they wanted, rather than a "full fat" royal wedding attended by dignitaries and people they didn't know, they were respectful of the Queen's wishes and her staff. In contrast Harry and Meghan seemed to show much less regard for anyone other than themselves as they planned their big day.

Against the odds and against this backdrop, the wedding day was a great success, even though the Queen apparently had reservations about the pure-white color of Meghan's Givenchy dress by designer Clare Waite Keller. According to a family source: "The Queen was surprised that Meghan wore pure white on her wedding day. Perhaps it's a generational thing, but she believes if you've been married before, you wear off-white on your wedding day, which is what the Duchess of Cornwall did."

The congregation, which included A-list friends such as George and Amal Clooney, Oprah, Serena Williams, and Elton John, and the tens of thousands lining Windsor's streets beyond the castle, had no such reservations. Their verdict on the medieval simplicity of her dress and its cathedral-length veil cascading over Meghan's trademark messy bun at the nape of her neck was that she looked stunning.

Curiously, the saturation coverage in the media did not seem to reflect public opinion as analyzed by YouGov on behalf of the *Times*. At the time of Harry and Meghan's engagement 52 percent of respondents declared themselves indifferent to the forthcoming wedding, with only 40 percent saying they were actively pleased. Harry remained one of the most popular members of the royal family, with Meghan racing up behind him, already ahead of both Charles and Camilla. But the excitement of their wedding did not shift the dial on British opinion over who would make the better king and queen—it was overwhelmingly the Duke and Duchess of Cambridge with 56 percent and 63 percent of the vote respectively, as opposed to Charles on 13 percent and Harry on 10 percent.

The service began traditionally enough with the hymn "Lord of All Hopefulness, Lord of All Joy" and a reading from the Song of Solomon, and then it turned into the kind of service that properly reflected the couple. American bishop Michael Curry took to the pulpit to borrow from the words of Rev. Martin Luther King Jr., speaking about the power of love to make the world new. Shortly afterward, gospel choir the Kingdom Singers gave a rendition of the Ben E. King standard "Stand by Me."

In the historic chapel of St. George's where British royals had been married and interred for centuries, these choices said Meghan's heritage mattered every bit as much as that of the man she was marrying; there was a sense of joy about the royal family as it embraced this twenty-first-century union. When Prince Charles took Meghan's mother Doria's hand as they went to sign the register, and then walked out of the chapel with her on his arm, it seemed to mark a new chapter for the monarchy.

It was a wondrous start but it swiftly soured. Meghan would learn quickly that the royal court could be a Machiavellian world that would at times make Hollywood seem tame. Within months of her fairy-tale wedding the duchess was facing accusations that she was a diva, overly demanding of her staff. It was leaked by anonymous sources that at Kensington Palace she had earned the nickname "Duchess Difficult" and "Hurricane Meghan" over her late-night and early morning emails to her team, often demanding immediate action.

"Meghan is a workhorse and that could be a problem," says one of her former aides. "She wanted everything done immediately and she could put a lot of pressure on herself and her team. Part of the problem is she comes from a world of memorizing lines, delivering them, doing a shoot, and wrapping. Her royal work was very different, as much of it was an exhaustive process that could not simply be hurried. There was a tendency for Meghan and also Harry, because they both came from a world that wasn't the real world, to not pause and process and appreciate how much time and effort goes into something."

It was in January 2019 that Meghan's first patronages were announced, all nods to causes she had previously supported. She was to become a patron of the National Theatre; the Association of Commonwealth Universities (the world's first and oldest international university network); Mayhew (an animal welfare charity); and Smart Works (which organizes coaching and smart clothing for women returning to the job market). The first two were gifted to her by the Queen who had held them herself, and the latter two were brand new.

The Queen, keen to support anyone marrying into her family, did her best to pacify the situation and get to know the new duchess. It had certainly started well, with Harry revealing in their engagement interview that Meghan had won over the Queen's notoriously snappy corgis.

The Queen was aware that Meghan's extended family had posed difficulties for the duchess, but she was less bothered about the step-siblings and distant relatives who wanted to cash in on the soap opera. The fact that Harry had not yet met Thomas Markle and that Meghan was still not speaking to her father did concern her, and while she rarely intervened she made a point of speaking to Harry and Meghan about the situation. "It was the Queen's feeling that Meghan should sort things out with her father and that Harry should have met Thomas before the wedding," reveals a close family friend. "She thought the whole thing could have been better handled."

From a practical point, the Queen did what she could for the family's newest member and given Meghan's boots-on-ground approach made sure the new duchess had the support she needed. She had dispatched her capable and loyal aide assistant private secretary Samantha Cohen over to the couple's office at Kensington Palace in 2018, believing her efficiency and unstuffy attitude would enable the Duchess of Sussex to learn her new role. Cohen would help Meghan choose her causes and identify what she could do to support them. She had such a lot to offer the arts, women in the workplace, and the Commonwealth.

She was also a potentially uniting figure for Britain's diverse communities, as evidenced by her work with survivors of the 2018 Grenfell Tower fire in which seventy-two residents of one tower block died. Mehgan began visiting the Hubb Community Kitchen based in a West London mosque that supported the traumatized community in the aftermath of the tragedy, eventually helping publish a charity cookbook, which raised over $600,000 for the organization.

Along with Harry's youthful appeal, his mental health outreach, and his serious work on the Invictus Games, the Sussex brand was captivating. A trip to Chester in June 2018 was specifically organized for the Queen and Meghan to appear together on an official royal visit: opening a major new bridge and visiting a theater. The new duchess was invited to travel in the royal train with the monarch, an honor that had not then been afforded to William, Harry, or Kate. The Queen would have made Meghan feel at home, making sure her preferred food and drinks were available, and showing the animal-loving duchess the stepladder she'd had specially made to help her beloved corgis get onto the train. By the following month the Sussexes were being entrusted with a mini-tour of their own to Ireland. Meghan handled the pressure well, meeting the Irish taoiseach (prime minister) and the Irish president. The tour was deemed a success, but once again her wardrobe courted controversy and she was criticized for the extravagance: more Givenchy, Roland Mouret, and Emilia Wickstead.

The trip was intended to maintain the improving relations between the two countries since the Queen's historic 2011 visit and came against the backdrop of Brexit. Irish taoiseach Leo Varadkar admitted as much saying, "I think with the United Kingdom leaving Europe, we are really going to need to focus a lot more on bilateral relationships, and visits of the president to the UK or members of the royal family to Ireland help cement that very close relationship between Britain and Ireland. So we will be rolling out the red carpet [for the Duke and Duchess of Sussex]."

The attention on Meghan's designer wardrobe was a distraction. Back at the palace she had been advised to take a leaf out of Kate's book and mix High Street with designer labels, and recycle her wardrobe like the Queen. I was told there was a fraught exchange between Meghan and palace staff when she was firmly told she could no longer accept freebies and generous discounts on clothes because it was contrary to royal guidelines and too close to advertising or endorsing. It was just one of many frictions as Meghan navigated her new life.

Despite these issues, she was making a great success of her new role. She was living up to her engagement interview promise: "I think you realize once you have access or a voice that people are willing to listen to, with that comes a lot of responsibility, which I take seriously. And now being boots on the ground in the UK, I'm excited to just really get to know more about the different communities here, [and learn about the] smaller organizations who are working on the same causes that I've always been passionate about under this umbrella."

Following Philip's retirement that energy could not have been needed more. In October 2018 the Sussexes headed to the other side of the world and completed seventy-six engagements over sixteen days in Australia, New Zealand, Fiji, and Tonga. They received a rock-star reception at events such as a morning on Bondi Beach raising awareness for youth mental health. During an iconic visit to

drought-ridden Dubbo in New South Wales for which Meghan baked
banana bread for a local farming family, rain famously fell during the
couple's address. The couple had announced they were expecting
their first baby within hours of touching down in Australia, which
only added to the success of the tour with the *Sydney Morning Herald*
describing it as "an important brand-building exercise for the British
monarchy within a key Commonwealth realm."

It ought to have embedded them in the royal family, but by the
end of the year there had been an announcement they were quitting
London. With a baby on the way they had outgrown Nottingham
Cottage. The Queen offered them Frogmore Cottage in Windsor
Great Park as their new home, not a suite of apartments at Windsor
Castle as they had hoped. "The cottage was a big give," recalls Lady
Elizabeth Anson. "The Queen's entrance into the gardens is right
next to their cottage. It is essentially her backyard, her solitude, and
her privacy. She was giving that up in gifting Harry and Meghan
Frogmore Cottage. We all thought it was very big of her. She said, 'I
hope they'll respect it.'"

Perhaps it was just as well that the Sussexes were moving, for relations between the new Fab Four were far from fabulous.

In leaving Kensington Palace the Sussexes were setting up their
own Household and paving the way for a split from the Royal Foundation, a break designed to allow the Sussexes to pursue their own
philanthropic ventures. The Royal Foundation had been founded in
2009 by William and Harry and joined by Kate in 2011 and Meghan
in 2018. Yet now it was to be the Royal Foundation of the Duke and
Duchess of Cambridge while the Sussexes worked on their own philanthropic organization. This led to great speculation that the couple
wanted to strike out on their own and not be constrained by the
constitutional protocols that tied William and Kate. But just how far
Harry and Meghan were willing to go in pursuit of their dreams and
ideals no one could then have guessed.

CHAPTER 8

Another Annus Horribilis

The path, of course, is not always smooth, and may at times
this year have felt quite bumpy.
　　　　　　　—HER MAJESTY THE QUEEN

T he Queen must have hoped to only endure one annus horribilis
　　during her reign. In fact she would weather two—the second
in 2019 more than a quarter of a century after 1992, the year which
made the Latin phrase famous.

It began with a car crash and ended with car-crash-TV. The first
involved her beloved husband the Duke of Edinburgh, the second
her son Prince Andrew the Duke of York, mired ever deeper in the
global sex scandal surrounding Jeffrey Epstein.

Despite the generation between the two men and the fact that
one was a private incident and the second a global furor, they both
had the same result: a retirement of sorts for two of the Queen's loyal
lieutenants, which would force an entire rethink about the future
of the monarchy. In between came the series of small fractures that
would ultimately lead to Megxit, perhaps the most seismic event of
the Queen's reign since the death of Diana.

First there was the March 2019 announcement that the Fab Four of William and Kate and Harry and Meghan were splitting their joint Household into two. Two months later the joyous arrival of baby Archie Harrison Mountbatten-Windsor was marred by a bitter privacy row. In October Meghan delivered her devastating "surviving not thriving" line in her interview with Tom Bradby in South Africa. And in the same program Harry confirmed the rumored rift with his elder brother, saying: "We're certainly on different paths at the moment . . . as brothers you have good days, you have bad days."

It was a period of public turmoil and personal sadness for the Queen, so it was perhaps no surprise the monarch acknowledged it had been a "bumpy" year in her Christmas broadcast. She used the national address to reflect on the ancient carol "It Came upon the Midnight Clear" and its hopes in a divided world. "It's a timely reminder of what positive things can be achieved when people set aside past differences and come together in the spirit of friendship and reconciliation," she said. "And as we all look forward to the start of a new decade, it's worth remembering that it is often the small steps, not the giant leaps, that bring about lasting change."

She reached back into history referring to the challenges of reconciliation after World War II, but with the modern world in turmoil—democracy protests in Hong Kong; the first impeachment of President Donald Trump; tensions rising in the Persian Gulf; the US-China trade war; and of course the toxic aftermath of the Brexit vote in Britain itself—her words had global contemporary currency. For Elizabeth the reminder that even her life could change in an instant came just after three o'clock on a crisp January afternoon: she was informed via an urgent phone call that Prince Philip had been involved in a car crash.

The then ninety-seven-year-old was turning onto a main road at the edge of the Sandringham estate when, blinded by sunlight, he pulled into oncoming traffic and hit another car. His Freelander flipped across the road leaving the Duke to crawl from the wreckage "very, very shocked and shaken," according to an eyewitness.

Mercifully the three passengers in the other vehicle, two women and a young baby, were not seriously hurt.

However, the crash turned into a PR disaster after courtiers initially tried to downplay it, issuing a discordant press statement: "The Duke of Edinburgh was involved in a road traffic accident with another vehicle this afternoon. The Duke was not injured. The accident took place close to the Sandringham Estate. Local police attended the scene." The palace also defended Philip's right to drive, confirming he had an up-to-date license, renewed every three years as required from anyone his age.

There was no heartfelt apology, no wringing of royal hands. Yet the crash had been Philip's fault. He looked graceless.

It didn't help that twenty-four hours later a brand new replacement Freelander was delivered to the prince and he was photographed behind the wheel on the Sandringham estate without wearing a seatbelt. While not mandatory on private land, the optics were awful.

It took a week and a half before he wrote to the woman injured in the crash, apologizing and saying on Sandringham House–headed notepaper: "I would like you to know how very sorry I am for my part in the accident. The sun was shining low over the main road. In normal conditions I would have no difficulty in seeing traffic coming . . . but I can only imagine that I failed to see the car coming, and I am very contrite about the consequences."

The following month in February 2019 he let it be known that he had surrendered his driving license voluntarily, prompting speculation about how that might impact the fiercely independent duke who was living alone at Wood Farm and loved to drive around the royal estate. According to Lady Elizabeth Anson, it was the Queen who suggested it was time for him to give up driving. No one else had dared.

The imminent birth of baby Sussex should have given the entire royal family a boost but the media and public narrative—in the UK at least—was already shifting. Harry and Meghan were rarely out of the papers, and for all the wrong reasons.

The costly refurbishment of Frogmore Cottage was one. There was controversy over the $2.9 million of taxpayers' money spent on the conversion of five separate sets of living quarters into one home, complete with a rumored *Gone with the Wind*–style double staircase, grand fireplaces, and vegan paint for the nursery.

William and Kate had faced a similar backlash when they embarked on a costly refurbishment of Apartment 1A at Kensington Palace, especially when I reported they did not plan to use it as their permanent residence when Prince George was born.

There was comment too on Meghan's lavish February 2019 baby shower in the penthouse of New York's Mark Hotel with familiar A-list guests including tennis ace Serena Williams and human rights lawyer Amal Clooney. Baby showers are not a tradition widely enjoyed in Britain and the extravagance was a protocol-buster for the royals. Although the party itself was privately funded, Meghan was accompanied by taxpayer-funded royal security, and there was a sense that for this environmentally conscious couple hopping across the Atlantic on a friend's private jet was incongruous and somewhat hypocritical. There were also raised eyebrows when Harry and Meghan declined an invite from the Queen to spend a long weekend at Balmoral in the summer of 2019—when she traditionally hosts a weekend for her grandchildren and a special sleepover for her great-grandchildren—preferring instead to take Archie to Ibiza and the South of France. "Playing happy families at Balmoral didn't really fit their narrative," I was told by a source close to the Sussexes.

On social media an ugly war broke out between loyal Cambridge admirers and Sussex fans, and there were real and frightening consequences to the tide of negative publicity. Shortly before their wedding in February 2018, a letter containing a suspicious white powder had been intercepted by staff at St. James's Palace, triggering an anthrax terror scare. It was harmless, but proved the threat was real.

According to a palace insider the couple were left shaken by the experience and increasingly concerned by the online trolling of Meghan, which grew exponentially as she transformed from royal girlfriend to new duchess. Her work ethic, style, and self-belief led to a steady stream of negative stories. At first they related to her attitude toward palace staff. Soon and more alarmingly, they would concern her relationship with her sister-in-law the Duchess of Cambridge. It should be pointed out that Catherine also had to tolerate unpleasant and derogatory press coverage during her tenure as a royal girlfriend and fiancée, specifically about her middle-class upbringing and her mother's former job as a flight attendant.

"Not everything written about Meghan was positive, but I think the overwhelming point about the coverage of Meghan in the media is that it focused less on her race and more on her behaving like a Hollywood actress. The baby shower is a good example," observes broadcaster, author, and cultural commentator Trevor Phillips. "First it didn't include any British friends, and by going back to New York and having such an ostentatious and expensive party, felt as though she hadn't really become part of a national institution.

"The stories about Harry and Meghan became more critical when the couple made missteps. It seems to me that Meghan never understood the nature of the institution that she was marrying into and perhaps Harry didn't properly explain it to her. This was not an ordinary marriage. It is not an ordinary institution. You go into the enchanted castle and you're accepting a deal and to a degree that includes a deal with the media.

"The fact is the treatment of royal women is pretty gruesome. The Duchess of Cambridge had years and years of being reported on as 'Waity Katie' and being seen as desperately trying to climb the social ladder. There were the jokes about her mother being an air hostess, which were humiliating. Princess Anne back in the day was constantly in the media for being rude and high-handed. Fergie had a tough time in the media and still does, and as we know, so did Camilla before the media finally warmed to her."

The Queen, in tune with Meghan's capabilities and perhaps mindful of some of what Meghan was having to navigate, had put her new grand daughter-in-law on the royal fast track, granting her the patronages of the National Theatre and the Association of Commonwealth Universities, which the monarch herself had held for forty-five years and thirty-three years respectively. It was now Meghan's turn to bring the public gaze to these high-profile causes, promoting their work and fund-raising for them. It amounted to a very public endorsement of the monarch's newest recruit. In March 2019 she elevated the duchess to vice president of the Queen's Commonwealth Trust to work alongside Harry, who was already serving as its president. The start of her new position was timed to coincide with International Women's Day.

These were plum roles for the Sussexes, who'd been vocal about wanting to work in the Commonwealth, the Queen's pride and joy, since their engagement. The countries of the Commonwealth worked together across multiple issues: trade, education, and training; protecting democracy and human rights; gender equality; the environment; building peace. So there were real opportunities to effect change, particularly with Meghan being both mixed race and a feminist determined to help close the gender gap, an issue she believed was worldwide and where she could make an impact. The appointments were so significant they made William "slightly jealous," according to one source close to the brothers. "It was a role William had rather fancied for himself," added the insider.

The troubled relationship between the Cambridges and the Sussexes was becoming obvious in other areas too. First there was Harry and Meghan's move from Kensington Palace to Windsor, announced in November 2018 and completed in April 2019. In a 2018 article I wrote for VF.com I disclosed for the first time the rift between the brothers that was behind the change. "Tension Between Harry and William May Have Inspired Harry and Meghan's Move to the Suburbs," read the headline.

In March 2019, as the Sussexes finalized their geographical split, Buckingham Palace announced an even more significant departure: Harry and Meghan were moving their Royal Household—that is their office and administrative support base—from Kensington Palace to Buckingham Palace. The brothers' royal double act was officially over.

For the Queen it was all deeply disappointing. She had expected, as a grandmother and as the head of the family business, that the Fab Four would work closely together and that their teamwork would bring popularity, modernity, and stability. Instead she found herself issuing the following statement: "The Queen has agreed to the creation of a new Household for The Duke and Duchess of Sussex, following their marriage in May last year. The Household, which will be created with the support of The Queen and The Prince of Wales, will be established in the spring. This long-planned move will ensure that permanent support arrangements for The Duke and Duchess's work are in place as they start their family and move to their official residence at Frogmore Cottage."

A "Royal Household" is the name given to the collection of departments that support the entire life—the diary for domestic and overseas official visits, transport, security, finances, HR, IT, telecoms and press, hospitality and housekeeping, ceremonial activities—of the royals in its care. It's symbolic as well as practical, so this was a statement about differing directions and beliefs, not just logistics.

As William prepared for kingship with statesmanlike engagements, tours, and speeches, Harry was setting his own agenda with Meghan by his side. The Sussexes had created a new, rival court.

Royal aides were keen to play down suggestions that the restructuring was the result of fallings-out between the two couples, but this did little to quash talk in royal circles that Kate and Meghan were not close. According to one insider: "Kate did everything she could to make the peace for Harry" but the sisters-in-law had little in common. "A personality clash," was how it was put to me by someone close to the Duchess of Cambridge.

There were other clashes too, between Meghan and her staff. When her personal assistant Melissa Toubati sensationally quit after just six months in late 2018, it reminded everyone that the Queen had personally spoken to Meghan about her attitude to staff in the run-up to her wedding. There was a high turnover on the Sussexes' payroll. Other members on what was called the "quit list" included deputy communications secretary Katrina McKeever, a female royal protection officer; Meghan's assistant private secretary Amy Pickerill; and Archie's first nanny.

The Queen may have felt the creation of a new Royal Household would give both the Sussexes and their staff a fresh start, though she did put her foot down over its location. Harry and Meghan had wanted it at Windsor near their new home, but the monarch decreed it should be at Buckingham Palace where it would work closely with her own communications team headed by Donal McCabe. Her Majesty, it appeared, did not want the couple freestyling.

Their biggest hire would be Sara Latham, a PR hotshot from corporate firm Freuds; she had formerly worked for Bill Clinton, Hillary Clinton, and Barack Obama and on London's Olympic bid. At Freuds she worked on "executive thought leadership and purpose-led campaigns." Trusted aide Samantha Cohen came across from the Queen's Household to act as Harry and Meghan's private secretary, with one deputy and two assistant private secretaries—one for the duke and one for the duchess—beneath her. The couple also hired a projects manager and a digital communications lead to keep the heat under their social media channels.

Jason Knauf was the well-regarded communications secretary to both the Duke and Duchess of Cambridge and the Duke and Duchess of Sussex until the March 2019 division of the households. At that point he jumped ship to become a senior advisor to William and Kate. So too did Christian Jones, formerly deputy communications secretary to both royal couples, who left to work exclusively for the Cambridges just a month after his boss.

In June 2019 came the bombshell news that Harry and Meghan were splitting from the Royal Foundation, the decade-old charity in which they were, alongside the Duke and Duchess of Cambridge, the headline act. "The Duke and Duchess of Sussex will establish their own new charitable foundation with transitional operating support from The Royal Foundation," the charity said in a statement every bit as banal as the one issued by Buckingham Palace about the Sussexes' new Royal Household.

In July the world learned that their new venture was to be called "Sussex Royal, the Foundation of the Duke and Duchess of Sussex." It was registered as a charitable company but it was far more than that: Sussex Royal was Harry and Meghan's public face, their brand, their savvy new website, and the heartbeat of their social.

Harry and Meghan were powering ahead with their passion projects and philanthropy, overturning stolid royal tradition just as they had done with the birth of their son two months earlier.

Archie had arrived on May 6, 2019. There was no happy photo opportunity on the hospital steps as there had been for Prince George, Princess Charlotte, and Prince Louis, or for William and Harry themselves a generation earlier. Meghan was not comfortable showcasing her newborn baby just hours after the birth, and even though there was an expectation that she would follow tradition, the couple made it clear they planned to do things differently. They had hoped to have a home birth, but given Meghan's age and her being a first-time mother, it was decided a hospital delivery would be safest. Harry had always enjoyed outfoxing the media; he and Meghan were thrilled to be safely delivered of their son in London's private Portland Hospital even before the palace press office had confirmed the duchess was in labor.

The Sussexes served an ace in their quest for privacy and tore another page out of the royal rulebook by choosing a hospital better known for celebrity births over royal. But the reality was that it was deeply damaging to the Crown's relations with the press, the broadcasters, and by extension the public, who felt duped by the experience—whether that was a fair expectation or not. Having been so behind the couple's royal wedding and invested in their future (not to mention paying the bill for the renovation of their home), there was a feeling the public had been cheated of what it had come to expect: that first sighting of a new prince on the hospital steps.

The royal family is unelected, but it is not unaccountable. It sits atop Britain's social structure and is funded by the public purse. It lives in castles and palaces, cosseted and protected. What is asked in return is that people get to see the royals as they go about their business, which is to embody Great Britain. People get to share a little in the royal family because fundamentally every British citizen holds a life share in them. The media is the conduit for this even if, as journalist and radio presenter Stig Abell once observed, the relationship is "a hug that was always threatening to become an assault."

One source described Harry as being "almost morbidly obsessed" with keeping Archie's birth as secret as possible, breaching the unwritten contract between the royals and the public. "Behind the scenes," wrote Rebecca English, royal editor of the *Daily Mail*, "matters were so fraught that more than one official—as I know from personal experience—was reduced to tears of frustration and despair."

Harry and Meghan had wanted some time as a new family before they presented their son Archie to the world. A brief photo opportunity with a single reporter to ask questions took place two days after the birth in the grandeur of St. George's Hall at Windsor Castle. A historic photograph of the Queen and Prince Philip and Meghan's mother, Doria, with the baby (not yet named) and Harry and Meghan was an unexpected bonus.

But it all felt stage managed, with preapproved questions, one journalist, and one photographer. It demonstrated the growing gulf between public expectations of Harry and what he felt obliged to give.

Meghan had looked exhausted and occasionally uncomfortable at the photo opportunity and it's worth recalling that although the Duchess of Cambridge viewed such appearances with her new babies as mandatory, she has admitted she found them a challenge too. She acquiesced because she will one day be queen and the mother of a king, so there was a legitimate public interest. Meghan however was married to the spare. Little wonder she wanted, like any other ordinary new mother, to be safe among family and friends.

Afterward the Sussexes retreated to Frogmore Cottage to begin their new life as a family of three, with Meghan's mother, Doria, on hand to help out. There were visits from luminaries such as Ellen DeGeneres and her wife, Portia, and Hillary Clinton. When William and Kate visited just over a week later it was hardly a family affair—they left Archie's cousins at home with the nanny. Later that summer in July the two families were finally seen together at a polo match. According to one onlooker the atmosphere was icy. "There was a private drinks reception for the sponsor and you could sense there was a tension," according to one of the organizers. "Kate was on one side of the pitch and Meghan on the other."

As for the public, the next they would officially see of baby Archie was at his christening on July 6, captured in part by fashion photographer Chris Allerton. The Queen could not attend; she had a prior engagement and had not been given enough advance warning to make the shift. According to Lady Elizabeth Anson, she was very sorry not to be at the service. Her absence raised eyebrows, but what proved far more controversial was the couple's decision not to publicly name Archie's godparents. This is far more than a royal convention. The "sponsors" of royal children, as their godparents are known, are significant. Harry has six, all tasked with helping raise a boy who was third in line to the throne when he was born. Prince George has seven, ranging from old and trusted friends of William's and Kate's, to one of Diana's best friends, to William's cousin Zara Tindall, and finally Jamie Lowther-Pinkerton, the former private secretary to William and Harry. They are stewarding him toward kingship.

A royal godparent helps raise a child who will play some part in British public life; that's why there has always been an expectation their names will be known. What Harry and Meghan were legitimately asking was, why does this hold true for Archie if he's going to be a member of the royal family but not so much the institution of the monarchy? The Sussexes were asking if it was not time for change and if that change should not start with their son. It was a valid question but given the existing tensions in their relationship with the media, not one that was explored in a calm or conciliatory way.

Harry did not want to uphold this media contract, or a "game," as he would later come to refer to it. What he wanted was far more privacy and a direct line of communication with the public via social media. This was a more modern approach, more in keeping with celebrities who liked to engage directly with their fans, and it was a great success. Harry and Meghan were heavily invested in their Instagram account which had launched so successfully that it had acquired 2.1 million followers in a day.

In time the Cambridges as well as Charles and Camilla would follow their lead in embracing social media over more traditional media.

The couple were doing all they could to reclaim the Sussex narrative by posting exclusive pictures and video footage on their Instagram account and pointedly ignoring the British press pack on official occasions.

"The gentleman's agreement between the royals and the British media was always based on the fact that they needed each other," said Stig Abell, quoted in the *New York Times* in January 2020. "But we are seeing the fragmentation of the media, combined with the fact that [Harry and Meghan] are a brand in and of themselves. They are a global phenomenon. If they don't need the media, the question is, why would they have a relationship with the media?"

It was a confronting question. Elizabeth and Philip had encouraged the media at the dawning of the age of mass television. Sometimes it had felt like the War of the Waleses between Charles and Diana had been played out in the tabloids at the height of their power in the eighties and early nineties. But here was the first generation whose communications landscape was social media and whose appeal was morphing into something beyond royal.

It didn't help that although Harry and Meghan were supported by a razor-sharp comms team, they sometimes chose not to take the expensive media advice they'd paid for. When a group of Meghan's friends spoke anonymously to *People* magazine for a positive cover story—"The Truth about Meghan, Her Best Friends Break Their Silence"—in February 2019, it had serious ramifications. The piece blindsided Kensington Palace and ultimately triggered a complex and costly legal battle over privacy and copyright with the *Mail on Sunday* in Britain, after it encouraged the duchess's father, Thomas

Markle, to respond by releasing excerpts of a private letter sent to him by Meghan.

When in September and October the couple embarked with Archie on an overseas tour of southern Africa on behalf of the Queen, the media and PR stakes were high. I was covering the trip for *Vanity Fair* and right from the start it was apparent the imprimatur of the trip was all their own. Rather than the usual official welcome on the tarmac, the couple began their visit in the Nyanga township, which had one of the highest murder rates in Cape Town. Meghan delivered a rousing speech to women and girls supported by the charity the Justice Desk. She applauded them for "standing up for what's right in the face of adversity" and told them: "While I am here with my husband as a member of the royal family, I want you to know that for me I am here with you as a mother, as a wife, as a woman, as a woman of color, and as your sister."

It was a powerful and impressive start and showed that the couple planned to incorporate their hands-on approach within an official royal-tour program. They met representatives of Waves for Change, an organization in which surfers support youth mental health in Cape Town; and the Lunchbox Fund, which ensures daily meals for schoolchildren. They visited the Commonwealth Litter Program, which takes action on plastics in the ocean; and Harry went out on the water with Cape Town's maritime police and British Royal Marines to see how they tackled poaching. The couple had taken their four-month-old son to meet Archbishop Desmond Tutu, and then while Harry went to Botswana, Angola, and Malawi, Meghan stayed in South Africa visiting female entrepreneurs and supporting the Association of Commonwealth Universities.

While in Angola Harry went to the HALO Trust anti-landmine charity, whose work had led to one of the most famous images of Diana ever taken—footage of her walking through a minefield. He would retrace his mother's footsteps, seeing the area was now safe enough to house schools, businesses, shops, and homes. He would also echo her walk with one of his own, wearing similar blue body armor and a face shield, in a partially cleared minefield nearby.

Reunited, Harry and Meghan visited a township near Johannesburg to hear about youth unemployment and met Nelson Mandela's widow, Graça Machel. They educated themselves further on apartheid, honored the business relationships between the UK and South Africa, and finally had an audience with South Africa's president Cyril Ramaphosa.

It was an unalloyed triumph.

What no one saw coming after a blaze of brilliant coverage at home and internationally was that they about to declare all-out war on the British press.

While still in South Africa, Meghan had revealed her court action against the *Mail on Sunday*, backed in an explosive statement by Harry who condemned what he called a "ruthless campaign" by the media against his wife. After they returned, details of legal action taken by the duke against the publishers of the *Sun* and the *Daily Mirror* for allegedly hacking his phone were confirmed by Buckingham Palace.

Then later in October came the behind-the-scenes documentary that set fire to whatever hopes anyone may have had about the couple's anger fading. They spoke to Harry's friend of twenty years, the TV anchor Tom Bradby, for *Harry and Meghan: An African Journey* and made it clear they were unhappy and had been for some time. While the most jaw-dropping of their interviews was yet to come, their confessional with Bradby packed a punch and signaled the Sussexes were attempting to seize control of the narrative.

Historically, sit-down interviews in which members of the royal family bare their souls have not fared well. Diana regretted some of the things she said in her *Panorama* interview with Martin Bashir, and the Queen has always stuck to the mantra "Never complain, never explain." According to journalist and broadcaster Wesley Kerr: "There is a great deal to learn from Her Majesty's example of really thorough presentation and sticking to an agreed, relatively brief and uncontroversial script that promotes the good work of the institution or place being visited or highlighted. In a free country with a lively media any big public figure will be criticized from time to time, not simply swathed in praise. As a senior royal you have to play the long game and let your good works speak for themselves."

But Harry deliberately—and controversially—used the global spotlight focused on this important official tour to confirm the reported rift with William and reveal the pressure he was under.

"Every single time I see a camera, every single time I hear a click, every single time I see a flash, it takes me straight back," Harry said in the TV documentary *Harry and Meghan: An African Journey*, revealing how the relentless press attention dragged him back to the summer he lost his mother.

As for Meghan, she described herself as feeling vulnerable in pregnancy and then with her newborn son. She went on: "You add this [media scrutiny] on top of trying to be a new mom, trying to be a newlywed and . . . Also, thank you for asking, because not many people have asked if I am okay."

She had looked so utterly accomplished on the tour, dressed down in casual cottons, laughing and dancing in public, and giving that powerful opening speech which went viral. Harry's pride in his wife and Archie when they met Archbishop Desmond Tutu—Archie's first official event—had been infectious. So to hear Harry and Meghan's reality was devastating, especially for Prince Charles and the Cambridges watching at home.

"It was a wake-up call, the moment when the family reached out," reveals one palace insider. "To see Harry and Meghan so raw, it was like, 'Oh my goodness, they are in so much pain.' William was the first one to pick up the phone to his brother."

The call was too little, too late. Harry and Meghan were already considering a life in which they were not full-time working royals, a break which would be swiftly nicknamed "Megxit" in a nod to Brexit, Britain's departure from the European Union (EU).

The celebratory narrative in the press during the lead-up to the wedding had soon soured, and Harry and Meghan had increasingly felt the British newspapers were out to destroy them. Harry would later speak freely about how unhappy he was, telling Oprah the British press was one of the key reasons they chose to leave

England: "I was trapped but I didn't know I was trapped. Like the rest of my family are, my father and my brother, they are trapped. They don't get to leave and I have huge compassion for that. For the family, they very much have this mentality of 'This is just how it is. This is how it is meant to be. You can't change it. We've all been through it.'"

But in his mind he could and should change the kind of life his royal birth had mapped out for him. Instead of Meghan coming into his world, why could he not be free to cross into hers?

Soon the Sussexes were off again, this time to Canada for a much needed break. According to their spokesman they were taking a "sabbatical," but it was a vacation with a very specific agenda—planning their resignation from the Firm. Holed up in a mansion on Vancouver Island, they were free from the media spotlight, which conveniently had turned to Harry's uncle, Prince Andrew.

.———.——.

ON NOVEMBER 16, 2019, Prince Andrew's interview with Emily Maitlis from the BBC current affairs program *Newsnight* was broadcast. It had taken her team a year to woo the prince, whose relationship with Jeffrey Epstein had come under intense and lasting scrutiny.

Arrested again in July 2019, accused of sex trafficking girls as young as fourteen, Epstein died in his New York prison cell on August 10, 2019. His death did not sever the link to Andrew in London, and tough questions about the prince's judgment and morality remained unanswered. Additionally Andrew had been a friend of Epstein's long-term companion and alleged procurer of girls, Ghislaine Maxwell.

The Duke of York had consistently denied allegations by one of Epstein's victims, Virginia Roberts Giuffre, that she was made to have sex with him three times. He had always done so through palace statements. Now he wanted to speak for himself.

In an essay published in the *Guardian* on December 19, 2019, Emily Maitlis wrote: "We began to record. I thought about how reasonable he sounded. He was explaining why Jeffrey Epstein was never really his friend, more 'a friend of a friend.' For one moment, I imagined I had got everything wrong, misunderstood the story entirely. But I stuck to the line of questioning. And it paid off. Does he regret the visit to stay with Epstein? 'Yes.' Does he regret the whole friendship? It was around sixteen minutes into the interview, and it was the answer that, for me, changed everything.

"'Still not,' he said. And told me of the opportunities he was given by Epstein that were 'actually very useful . . .'

"It was such a candid admission, such a bald refusal to play the game with any wider apology or regret and it would become the pivotal moment of the entire hour. This is a man—a prince—who did not come to repent. He came to earn back his right to tell the story his way."

It detonated a scandal that saw the duke banished from court. He was airbrushed from public life and stripped of his royal roles. Plans for a glittering sixtieth birthday party in February 2020 were scrapped in favor of a muted gathering for just a dozen people, which included his daughters, Princesses Beatrice and Eugenie, and his ex-wife, Sarah. He was not promoted to the rank of admiral. Town halls across the country did not fly the Union flag in his honor on his birthday. The humiliating announcement was made by a Department for Digital, Culture, Media, & Sport spokesman: "Following the decision by the Duke of York to step back from public duties for the foreseeable future, there is no longer a requirement for UK Government buildings to fly the Union flag on Wednesday, February 19."

It was all the result of arrogance—for which Andrew was well known at the palace, particularly among the staff, whom he was often rude to and dismissive of—and served to widen the gulf between him and Charles. It also meant there could be no way back when his brother assumed the throne.

Earlier Andrew had hoped to make a comeback and volunteered to support the Queen on public engagements after the retirement of the Duke of Edinburgh in 2017, but his overture was rebuffed. "There was some concern that Andrew would see an opportunity following Prince Philip's retirement and try to insert himself in place of his father and that wouldn't be a good look, so [the rebuff] was quite carefully choreographed," says a former palace source. "It was made clear that while it was good for the Queen to have someone from the family occasionally to assist her on engagements, it was always going to be more appropriate for it to be the Prince of Wales or the Duke of Cambridge. It was primarily a seniority issue, although of course the other dimension was ever present."

The necessity of confronting this was something Charles and William agreed on. In the past, father and son hadn't always seen eye to eye. There was a well-documented clash of opinions in 2013 over the palace's priceless collection of ivory, for one. And Charles was sometimes irritated that Kate's frocks got more media attention than his good works. He also had been hurt by not seeing as much of his Cambridge grandchildren as he might have liked.

But on the Andrew issue father and son were united. According to a family friend, William very much supported his father's decision over Andrew and it was essentially the two princes taking charge of the situation. It was really the start of them forming an allegiance with each other for the sake of the good of the monarchy. They might have different points of view over certain things, but the one thing they are united on is the importance of the Crown and preserving its reputation. For them it's not about celebrity or popularity; it's about royalty and sovereignty. That is the thing that bonds them and links Charles with his mother and with his son.

"Like every father and son relationship, there have been clashes," says the aforementioned family friend. "William can have a hot head and Charles can be quick to lose his temper, but over the years the relationship has become more relaxed and organic. There was a time when there was a sense of competition over each other's popularity but that has fizzled. You get the sense that there is more of a relationship between them these days, and of collaboration."

The urgency of the Epstein scandal, especially after the disastrous *Newsnight* interview, cemented that collaboration, not least because the Queen seemed unable to distance herself from her second son; in January 2020 she appeared publicly alongside him at church in Sandringham, Norfolk, toward the end of her Christmas and New Year break.

Andrew still lives at Royal Lodge in Windsor Great Park and had the Queen's ear during their long walks and regular horseback rides together. According to a close family friend, he gave his mother his word on more than one occasion that he was innocent. But those close to the Queen wondered whether she should have been tougher, more ruthless. According to one insider who worked closely with the monarch: "There was a question being asked: Had some of her sharpness softened?"

The BBC's long-serving royal correspondent Nicholas Witchell summed up the thoughts of many in late November 2019, when he said bluntly of the Queen's decision to stand by Andrew and also Harry's rant at the tabloids while in South Africa: "The Queen . . . is ninety-three years old now, and she is not exercising the strong control she had." It was a rare and brave questioning of the Queen's judgment that would surface again when she allowed Prince Andrew to escort her to the Service of Thanksgiving for the Duke of Edinburgh.

It was unusual for the Queen to be at the center of a controversy, but in September 2019 the monarch was unwittingly dragged into Britain's Brexit saga when the prime minister asked her to suspend Parliament for five weeks. This can be a routine event, but in this case the suspension or proroguing was irregular. It came at a time when an embattled Conservative government was struggling to progress its Brexit plans in a parliamentary chamber divided between Brexiteers and Remainers: those who wanted Britain to leave the European Union and those who wanted the country to stay. A parliamentary suspension effectively broke the deadlock, but Commons Speaker John Bercow (the chief officer and highest authority in Parliament) spoke for many when he declared the proroguing a "constitutional outrage." Crucially it required the permission of the Queen as head of state.

Writing for the BBC news website Nicholas Witchell explained: "Throughout her reign she has been punctilious about the principles of a constitutional monarchy. One of those principles is that she does not involve herself in politics. She has played her part with what even most of her critics would accept has been a high sense of duty. In return, she and her advisors would always hope and expect that her governments would accord her the respect of not involving her in controversial decisions. I say decisions, though the reality is that once it became clear that the prime minister was seeking the prorogation of Parliament, the Queen and her closest advisors will have known that she had no choice other than to accede to the request."

Elizabeth agreed, as she was constitutionally bound to, only to find that a fortnight later on September 24, 2019, Britain's Supreme Court would declare the suspension illegal. It was nullified and Parliament returned. Prime Minister Boris Johnson telephoned the Queen personally to apologize. It was a rare moment of political controversy for an avowedly apolitical monarch.

Two years earlier in September 2017 she had parted company from her trusted aide Sir Christopher Geidt. Although it was never officially acknowledged, Geidt was toppled in a palace coup. He had made an enemy of Prince Andrew—Geidt had been instrumental in the decision to make Andrew stand down as British trade ambassador in 2011 over his Epstein links—and then of Prince Charles. Geidt's rallying call to palace staff on behalf of the Queen after the retirement of the Duke of Edinburgh enraged Charles, who had ambitions to fill the gap left in public life himself. According to newspaper reports there were differences of opinion between Geidt and Charles's senior aides over how to manage the handover of power between the monarch and the heir. Geidt's ousting was a shock, for he had been one of the powers behind Elizabeth's throne for a decade. He had masterminded her Diamond Jubilee, her ninetieth birthday, and the gradual handover of her duties to Charles, albeit not as fast as the Prince of Wales might have wanted.

So his departure sent aftershocks reverberating through Buckingham Palace. According to one former palace aide: "An air of authority had gone. He walked the corridors with such presence because he had the authority of the Queen. Everything was about the service of the monarch. It's the old cliché, but if you cut him open he'd have the good of the monarchy running through him. He was very good at keeping the focus on the Crown and the institution while never forgetting it is a family.

"He's quite an imposing figure; people knew who was in charge and he knew everybody by name, from the housemaids through to the butlers through to people working at the private office. He was very visible and had the Queen's blessing on what he did, which probably set some hares running. I think maybe people were jealous of his influence and power, but Christopher wore power very lightly. I think people in government would probably say the same thing."

The Queen appeared to acknowledge that Geidt's going was an error and in early 2019 she asked him to return as her permanent lord-in-waiting. According to Robert Lacey, Geidt's job was to be the Queen's "eyes and ears."

In his book *Battle of the Brothers* Lacey ponders what might have been. "Had Christopher Geidt been private secretary when the question of Harry and Meghan's new role in the family had landed on the royal desk at the end of 2017, he would have applied his customary vision and analysis to a task that was actually weightier than the technicalities of how Charles should succeed his mother.

"Here was the great step forward, to integrate a mixed-race recruit—the first-ever—into the all-white royal family, which needed to maintain its position in a society that was becoming more racially diverse by the day. It was a profound challenge, with massive implications for the long-term identity and relevance—and even perhaps the survival—of the crown in a changing world.

"But it was also an immense opportunity, since the interracial union of these two popular headliners, Harry and Meghan, 'the royal rock stars,' represented a unique chance to knit the monarchy closer to the people—people of all races and classes."

Geidt, in his new role as the Queen's permanent lord-in-waiting, came up with a characteristically imaginative and progressive solution: that the couple should go to live and work for a time elsewhere in a Commonwealth country, with South Africa the most likely candidate. There, in a place they loved, away from the goldfish bowl of London and its predatory media they could use their individual talents and the emblem of their mixed-race marriage to work in support of all fifty-four nations. It would have been a period akin to the Queen and Prince Philip's blissful years in Malta and would have raised the royal status of the spare. It's also undeniable that it would have put six thousand miles between what was being labeled the "Sussex problem" and other Royal Households.

In the end of course there was no move to South Africa and it was the Sussexes who pressed the eject button in spectacular fashion. On January 8, 2020, Harry and Meghan announced they were standing down as senior royals. "We intend to step back as 'senior' members of the Royal Family and work to become financially independent, while continuing to fully support Her Majesty The Queen," they revealed in a dramatic statement issued by their communications officer at Buckingham Palace and posted on their newly launched Sussex Royal website. They explained that they planned to balance their time between the UK and North America while "continuing to honor our duty to the Queen, the Commonwealth, and our patronages. This geographic balance will enable us to raise our son with an appreciation for the royal tradition into which he was born, while also providing our family with the space to focus on the next chapter, including the launch of our new charitable entity."

Harry and Meghan felt their stardust was being kept corked in a bottle. They would be able to reach more people and do more good outside of the monarchy than in it, and they had mapped their futures out. In their eyes they were a millennial couple up against a historic institution, two emotionally open people who'd been struggling in an arcane environment. Not anymore. The only option was to leave.

But in their haste to create new roles for themselves, they had jumped the gun. The Queen hadn't signed off on their ambitious plans, which I was told by a senior courtier were at an "embryonic stage," and the couple did not seek permission from Her Majesty or her courtiers before issuing the statement. At Buckingham Palace courtiers had just ten minutes' notice. The palace switchboard was overwhelmed as news programs around the world tried to get a comment. I was called to *Entertainment Tonight*'s satellite studio in London to discuss the extraordinary announcement, but it was almost impossible to truly convey the magnitude of what had just happened and what it meant for the future of the Firm. This was Harry and Meghan quitting their roles as senior royals less than two years after their magical Windsor wedding, and announcing they would also be leaving Britain to start a new life in America.

At this stage there were still many unanswered questions. What did this "progressive new role" they envisaged look like? Would they retain their honorary titles? Where were they going to live? How were they going to be financially independent while also representing the monarchy and, crucially, did this have the green light from Her Majesty?

It was clear from Buckingham Palace's short and hasty response that the Queen had been taken by surprise: "We understand their desire to take a different approach, but these are complicated issues that will take time to work through," the statement read.

Britain's right-leaning *Spectator* magazine would go on to compare Harry to Diana in a piece published in January 2021: "Like Diana, Harry's decision to leave the royal family was based on a sense that she could do her thing—relating to people and helping them—just as well outside the family as within it. But what was never really thought through was how to manage to play royal without being anchored in the royal family. She, like Harry, could not have become the phenomenon she was without that status. She wanted to keep that mystical element, the royal touch, without the constraints of royal life, without a relationship with the Queen. Well, that's now her son's—or his wife's—project."

Diana divorced herself from the royal family. Now Harry was doing the same, and a generation on, it promised to have even more devastating consequences.

CHAPTER 9

A Sea Change

Recollections may vary.
—HER MAJESTY THE QUEEN

For a monarch in the twilight years of her reign, 2019 onward forced a lightning revision of the future. This turbulent time was a reminder that an institution built on a thousand years of history could not afford to become complacent. With Prince Andrew banished from public life and the loss of Harry and Meghan as working royals, the Firm was down by three key players.

It was a dizzying time globally, the world in the grip of a pandemic that would claim 6 million lives by early 2022. The new coronavirus ravaging China's Wuhan province by the close of 2019 crossed continents to arrive in Britain at the end of January 2020.

Lockdowns and social distancing tested Elizabeth's ability to remain at the helm of her country, to lead the British people and be seen doing so, her raison d'être.

"We will meet again," she promised them, echoing Dame Vera Lynn's wartime song in a spine-stiffening speech made on April 5, 2020. Within twenty-four hours Britain's prime minister Boris

Johnson would be so sick with Covid that he would be in intensive care in a London hospital. The country's National Health Service was teetering on the brink of collapse, its economy was in the deep freeze, and people were attempting to work from home while schooling their children in their kitchens. Britain would face another dark year of lockdowns, both national and regional, until the accelerating vaccination rollout offered real hope.

Yet this was not the only crisis facing Elizabeth. In March 2021 came the news that the Sussexes, by then living as private citizens in Montecito, California, had sat down with Oprah to tell the story of Megxit. Their bombshell interview, broadcast in the United States on March 7, made incendiary claims of racism against the royal family.

"It was damaging to the royal family not just because of what Harry and Meghan revealed, but because the mystique was suddenly gone. Meghan has pulled the curtain back and let us see what was going on behind closed doors," says KJ Matthews. "Americans have always been Team Monarchy but after Oprah there was a startling shift in attitudes towards the royal family."

At the same time the Duke of Edinburgh was in hospital following heart surgery. He would be allowed to go home, weak and much diminished, to Windsor Castle where he would die peacefully on April 9, just weeks before his hundredth birthday. He and the Queen had been married seventy-three years and he'd been her "liege man of life and limb" as long as she'd been wearing the crown.

A pandemic. Megxit. Widowhood. It was the worst of times for the monarch.

And yet, and yet . . .

For a nonagenarian leader her pandemic performance was stellar. Elizabeth could have retreated to Windsor, the castle that is literally her fortress. Instead she stepped up, putting country before self as she had since 1952. Working from home: check. Zoom glitches: check. Outdoor exercise: check. Vaccine: check. Elizabeth deftly refashioned her monarchy to stay in lockstep with its people.

Remarkably she achieved this while facing a cataclysm of her own. While Harry and Meghan's departure wasn't an abdication, or technically a constitutional crisis because Harry was not a direct heir to the throne, it felt like one.

The Sussexes had left Great Britain for the sake of their own mental health and happiness. The notion of self before duty was anathema to the Queen. This was a battle between the old ways and the new, between the British stiff upper lip and an American unpacking of feelings. It pitted the constraints of the Crown against the right to personal freedom and asked one crucial question: Was the House of Windsor still relevant in this changed and changing world?

——— · ———

It was March 2020 when the UK entered its first lockdown, which saw schools and shops shuttered until June and pubs and restaurants closed until July. The Duke of Edinburgh, who had retired to the solitude of Wood Farm on the Sandringham estate, was helicoptered to Windsor Castle so he and the Queen could isolate together.

Courtiers called the couple HMS *Bubble*, a wry reference to "bubbling up," the national strategy in which people formed a single household to limit contagion. HMS *Bubble*'s mission was to support Britain and the Commonwealth as it came to terms with this new way of living. The Queen, having never forgotten the separations and privations of World War II, unexpectedly proved to be a dab hand.

During the pandemic she mastered Zoom—still in her trademark double- or triple-strand of pearls—and made electronic royal visits to her subjects at home and armed forces personnel serving around the world. She conducted her weekly audience with the prime minister by telephone and her social media teams posted homeschooling resources on Twitter. Although her garden parties were canceled, the palace kitchen's recipes for those royal staples, the Victoria sponge cake and fruit scones, were shared on YouTube.

Amid the panic, which saw many elderly people too scared to emerge into the outside world even as it became safer to do so in the summer months, the monarch demonstrated that age should be no barrier to getting fresh air and exercise after the long weeks of lockdown. She mounted up on her fell pony Balmoral Fern and was pictured riding in jodhpurs, a tweed jacket, white gloves, and a silk headscarf in Windsor. That was June 2020. By October she was undertaking some face-to-face duties, visiting the UK's Defense Science and Technology Laboratory to support scientists leading Britain's Covid response.

While there was some consternation that she was not always wearing a mask on engagements (palace officials insist she always followed government regulations), her no-nonsense approach to the pandemic was apparent when in January 2021 she allowed courtiers to publicly confirm she'd had the vaccine. In doing so she set aside her right to medical privacy as the government desperately tried to convince everyone to get jabbed. On a Zoom call to officials leading the vaccine rollout in the UK, the Queen did something rare and told the British people what to do, encouraging the populace to "think about other people rather than themselves" and get jabbed when their turn came. It was a powerful message no politician could have communicated so successfully.

Like her subjects the monarch marked birthdays and family celebrations in lockdown. She released a sunny photo of herself and Prince Philip—impeccable in a navy blazer, burgundy striped tie, and white handkerchief—to mark his ninety-ninth birthday in June 2020. Then in November she shared a touching image of herself and Philip opening a card from their Cambridge great-grandchildren to celebrate their seventy-third wedding anniversary. "You can be assured that my family and I stand ready to play our part," she had pledged at the start of the pandemic.

Back then no one had known what that would look like or, more significantly, if it would help. But to a beleaguered people the royal family represented constancy and unity in the face of an unprecedented threat to life, security, and prosperity. The Queen's leadership proved constitutional expert Robert Hazell's point that "monarchies can speak to and for their nations in ways no partisan politician can."

The pandemic also made a Zoom star of Charles, sitting with his iPad propped up on a copy of his own book *Harmony*, and also of Camilla, whose cheerful appearances from her mint-walled drawing room at Clarence House added to her national-treasure status. The princess royal was her usual blunt self. "You don't need [to see] me; you know what I look like," she guffawed to her mother, giving her a speedy Zoom tutorial during a live video call. Edward and Sophie, the Earl and Countess of Wessex, were ever-present online: Sophie baking cheese and bacon scones from the kitchen of their Surrey home, Bagshot Park, or looking sharp in a navy-print Victoria Beckham dress to award a fashion design prize, or joining her husband on virtual royal engagements. In Norfolk, William, Kate, and their children were pictured and filmed for their newly updated Instagram account on the doorstep of Anmer Hall during the regular Thursday night Clap for Carers, which saw Britons on their doorsteps applauding the country's health workers.

This novel opening of royal homes created an air of authenticity and intimacy and engendered a real affection for their inhabitants. It drove forward Charles's modernizing agenda and achieved an outcome that prior to the pandemic would have appeared contradictory. Charles had never looked and sounded more like a king in waiting, yet at the same time he connected with his future subjects in a familiar and informal way that saw his popularity soar and traffic to his Clarence House Instagram account peak.

The only glitch in the royal machine was that the family was without the two senior members with a proven ability to reach a younger, more diverse demographic: Harry and Meghan. Over in Los Angeles the Sussexes were photographed delivering food parcels to vulnerable communities, dressed down in sneakers and baseball caps. In contrast to William and Kate who were more willing for their children to be seen in public—perhaps to be seen as ordinary and more accessible—Harry and Meghan made a point of keeping Archie behind closed doors. At Tyler Perry's house where they were staying, they had their own security detail and lawyers on standby to take action against anyone who photographed their son. Given they had moved to California partly to escape the media, the irony was that the Sussexes found themselves more sought after by the paparazzi in America than they ever had been in England.

"I don't think the Queen ever truly understood Harry's decision to leave," reflected the late Lady Elizabeth Anson who spoke with the monarch via frequent telephone calls during this period. "Turning one's back on duty is completely alien to the Queen and she has been very hurt by it all. William was angry and Charles was distraught, but Harry wasn't prepared to back down over Meghan." When Harry and Meghan made their announcement that they were standing down as senior royals, the Queen was faced with a crisis. She didn't want them to leave, and she could foresee the damage Megxit posed to the institution and needed a solution. Back in January 2020 she had demanded a royal quartet—herself, Charles, William, and Harry—meet at Sandringham to find a way forward. She asked her son and grandsons to join her for lunch beforehand. William refused, leading to speculation he was so incensed with his brother that he could barely be in the same room. Prince Philip left Sandringham before it began.

The meeting would become known as the Sandringham Summit and its outcome was not at all what the Sussexes had hoped. It required the couple to step back from royal duties completely, and since they would not be representing the Queen they would not be permitted to use their HRH titles publicly. The military appointments and titles such as Harry being Commonwealth Youth Ambassador, which were theirs by dint of their royal roles, would ultimately have to be forfeited too. This was not a hostile act—they went with the jobs from which the couple had just resigned. The Queen did not strip Harry and Meghan of their HRHs. She simply forbade them from leveraging their royal status in their commercial lives. The brand "Sussex Royal" would be ruled out for the same reason.

"They have every right as individuals to be domiciled where they like and to make a living how they like. But living in America and earning large amounts of money from media deals means you can't be an active member of the royal family. That wasn't going to work," says Wesley Kerr. "The royal family are there to serve the British state. They are essentially very grand civil servants." To a furious Britain, Megxit looked like betrayal. To a sympathetic America, the outcome of the Sandringham Summit looked like punishment. Either way, it created turmoil between father and son and brother and brother, and it destabilized the whole House of Windsor. Harry and Meghan's departure was a painful and public repudiation of an institution that was meant to harness and represent the very best of Great Britain.

According to Robert Lacey: "The indignation of Prince Charles, Prince William, and the palace with Meghan and Harry was over two things; firstly the way that they revealed their entire 'Sussex Royal' plan as a done deal on their new website when it wasn't a done deal at all, and secondly the fact that the Sussexes were daring to pronounce on royal matters that were far above their pay grade. There was a very strong feeling that went right to the top that the only person who can talk about the royal family doing things in a different style is the Queen herself or possibly Prince Charles. On top of that the Sussex Royal website was the work of Meghan's American team of staff but had been paid for by Charles's subsidies to Harry. That was a big source of grievance."

Nonetheless on January 13, 2020, the Queen issued a statement saying: "My family and I are entirely supportive of Harry and Meghan's desire to create a new life as a young family. Although we would have preferred them to remain full-time working Members of the Royal Family, we respect and understand their wish to live a more independent life . . . while remaining a valued part of my family."

The statement was loving and conciliatory, a master class in diplomacy. But it would not be enough to stop Harry and Meghan seizing control of the narrative in the weeks and months to come—and speedily moving to Los Angeles.

According to Charles Anson: "The Queen has high standards but she is also tolerant by nature. It's partly her role, partly her temperament, and also her faith that guide her. She is also a realist in good times and bad, and even when there are setbacks she keeps going through thick and thin. It is a bit of that wartime spirit she possesses. The Queen has a strong sense of family and values her family, but she can be firm when necessary."

A year later, on February 19, 2021, after the twelve-month transition period agreed to at the Sandringham Summit came the inevitable announcement: "The Duke and Duchess of Sussex have confirmed to Her Majesty The Queen that they will not be returning as working members of the Royal Family. While all are saddened by their decision, The Duke and Duchess remain much loved members of the family."

Historian Hugo Vickers explains: "It was Harry and Meghan's decision to leave and it was deeply disappointing for the Queen but I think she handled the situation well. As always she took the long view. She couldn't have been fairer. In the UK the general feeling was that the Sussexes had behaved very badly but the Queen came out of the whole thing very well."

Former courtier Patrick Jephson adds: "To progressives Meghan can be celebrated as a survivor of toxic British snob culture. To conservatives she has exercised a red-blooded American's right to give the finger to the Queen. At home in Britain they look like they're turning their back on a country that offered them everything." This was utterly at odds with Harry and Meghan's view that life in the UK had been unbearable. Exhausted by the press scrutiny, a racism they felt was both overt and covert, and the primal need as parents to protect their baby son, they opted to break out of their gilded prison.

Privately the Queen confided to a close friend that she was exhausted by the turmoil of it all. "She was very hurt and told me, 'I don't know, I don't care, and I don't want to think about it anymore,'" I was told.

Behind closed doors family members including Camilla and Sophie reached out on a number of occasions to Harry and Meghan, while Kate attempted to ease relations between Harry and William who were barely speaking. All three women were outsiders who had married into the royal family and like Meghan had had their own challenges. They hoped they might be able to help or at least empathize.

"It was upsetting for all the family and we mustn't forget that they are a family. I know that Camilla did her best and was a tremendous sounding [board] and support for Charles, who was deeply troubled. I think Camilla could foresee cultural differences and problems from the start," says a close friend of the Duchess of Cornwall. "Don't forget that for years Camilla was vilified in the press, she was ostracized by the [royal] family. She has felt that pain of being at the center of a family drama and so she did play a key role behind the scenes. She threw a hand of friendship out to Harry and Meghan at various points. Before their wedding, when Meghan was going through a difficult time with her own father, she helped navigate things. It was Camilla who told Charles that walking Meghan up the aisle was the right thing to do. She's a very family-oriented woman and she really wanted to help."

Camilla could also see that unless relations between the Sussexes and the wider royal family were soothed, Megxit would not just cast a shadow over the end of the Queen's reign but it would also blight Charles's. A rival Sussex court operating in America also had the potential to undermine William's accession, given that many of the causes the Sussexes championed, from the environment to mental health awareness, overlapped with William and Kate's work. The very presence of the Duke and Duchess of Sussex—two of the most famous people on the planet—flexing their substantial muscle as global philanthropists inevitably raised fundamental questions about the influence and possibly the relevance of royalty in the twenty-first century.

William and Kate will always be in a unique position: royalty will forever stand as a symbol of its country and give a nation a focal point in times of happiness and tragedy. They are also public servants. Harry and Meghan are not, which is the most important distinction. Even though Harry and Meghan have claimed that "service is universal," as an institution the royal family dedicates itself entirely to public service. Harry and Meghan have the freedom to pursue lucrative commercial deals now that they are no longer working royals. But in terms of campaigning and good causes, the gap between royalty and the heavyweight celebrity of the Duke and Duchess of Sussex has never looked so slim.

Professor Anna Whitelock explains: "Megxit wasn't a constitutional crisis, but it raised a lot of issues and asked a lot of questions about the future of the royal family. What was it going to look like? Was it going to be vastly scaled down? Was there a sense that people could opt out of it? What did it all say about the expectations of the spare?"

Megxit also triggered an immediate restructuring of the royal family that left Charles reassessing his plans for a scaled-down monarchy. "It was always the Prince of Wales's intention that Harry and Meghan would be part of the official lineup. That has now changed," according to one of Charles's former aides. So it seems the Buckingham Palace balcony scene Charles long imagined—that of a lean, modern monarchy headed by a father supported by his two sons—is now set to be a very different spectacle with the Wessexes and Princess Anne possibly set to have bigger roles than Charles intended, in order to support the work of the monarchy.

It was William who felt Harry's departure most acutely because of the immediate repercussions on his own life. Friends of his say one of the reasons he won't forgive Harry is due to the consequences of Megxit for Kate and their children. The Cambridges now have a significantly increased royal workload while trying to raise their young family.

"We've seen the Cambridge children performing in front of the cameras in a way that cannot have been part of the original plan," observes Robert Lacey. "We know that William and Kate want to bring their children up in relative seclusion and privacy, but the children have had to become a prominent part of the show. A combination of Covid and Megxit has forced them all into the spotlight."

The appearance of all three children on the doorstep of Anmer Hall clapping for Britain's carers alongside their parents at the height of the first lockdown was a prime example of this.

William was so concerned that he is understood to have convened his own crisis summit with his most trusted advisors shortly after the Sandringham Summit. Held at Anmer Hall it was swiftly dubbed the "Anmer Summit." It was intended to help the Cambridge team work out strategies for life post-Megxit without Harry, William's trusted deputy, to support him. For so long they had been a double act and then a formidable trio with Kate. William had leaned on his brother for support, and Harry had shouldered a great deal, relieving some of the pressure on William and always acting as an honest and loyal sounding board.

The Sussexes' final engagement, the Commonwealth Day Service at Westminster Abbey on March 9, 2020, showed just how fraught relations between the two couples had become. Meghan clearly wanted to go out in style, choosing an Emilia Wickstead emerald-green dress with a dramatic half cape and matching veiled hat. She looked lovely, and it was a vivid visual reminder of what Britain was about to lose.

I was seated just a few rows behind them and the tension was palpable. Not once did William and Kate turn to acknowledge Harry and Meghan; instead they kept their backs to the other couple, gazes fixed ahead. Kate, usually so warm in her demeanor, seemed stern and distant. The Cambridges were seated in the front row alongside the Prince of Wales, Camilla, and the Queen, while the Sussexes were in the row behind, next to Edward and Sophie. This is hierarchically correct, but being in the bottom of the royal league bothered Harry and Meghan who were upset to have been demoted from the procession into the abbey. It depicted life as they felt it—overlooked—and was another reason why they wanted to break free.

The Sussexes couldn't wait to get on a plane back to Canada. But as Covid spread and international borders started to close, they made a last-minute decision to fly to Los Angeles instead. Movie producer Tyler Perry sent his private jet, a $147 million Embraer E190, to collect the family from Vancouver Island and fly them to his $18 million hilltop mansion in Beverly Hills.

This flit to California prompted speculation that a new life in Los Angeles had been their plan from the outset. "Canada was never going to be their forever home. The big plan, for Meghan at least, was always LA," says one of the Sussexes' former aides. Reflecting on the couple's decision to leave the UK, the aide added: "What happened is tragic and very disappointing. Personally I don't think it [Harry and Meghan having traditional royal roles] was doomed from the start, but it was very apparent that some sort of drastic change needed to happen because it just wasn't working."

For the Sussexes, the ensuing lockdown had a silver lining. While it meant postponing their "launch" in California, it gave them time out of the spotlight to work through their next moves. What emerged was their new Archewell foundation, the beginnings of their own global brand. Just before Covid stopped travel, the couple flew to Miami to speak at a JP Morgan event for a fee reported to be more than $1 million. Deals with Netflix, Spotify, and Apple TV were in the pipeline.

Their vision, to couple philanthropy with making a personal fortune, was working. It was as they had wished, a new way of being royal five thousand miles away from the Crown.

Harry could not have felt farther from home when on March 24, 2020, he received a phone call to say the Prince of Wales had been diagnosed with Covid and was isolating at Birkhall. Charles was well enough to speak with his son and it was an opportunity for William and Harry to be in touch, having barely been on speaking terms. The news would be made public by Clarence House two days later. What would not be reported until the end of the year was that William had also contracted the virus around the same time as his father. His diagnosis was kept private to avoid alarming a nation which knew the heir to the throne had been sick during a time when its prime minister had almost died.

The Queen remained well, emerging in July 2020 with Prince Philip to attend Princess Beatrice's small, secret, socially distanced wedding to property developer Edoardo Mapelli Mozzi in the Royal Chapel of All Saints at Royal Lodge, Windsor. The bride wore a vintage Norman Hartnell dress loaned by the Queen, who'd worn it for the premiere of *Lawrence of Arabia* back in 1962. Beatrice also borrowed the Queen Mary diamond fringe tiara that the Queen had worn for her own marriage ceremony. (It was perhaps a nod to her family name since before her husband's accession, Queen Mary had been Duchess of York.)

It was a trailblazer of a royal wedding, not announced in advance and with few official images made available afterward. Tellingly, none of them featured the bride's parents, for Prince Andrew was mired in the Jeffrey Epstein scandal and it would have been awkward for Sarah Ferguson to be pictured on her own, so instead the newlyweds were flanked by the Duke of Edinburgh and the Queen. The wedding was a notable departure from the October 2018 nuptials of Beatrice's younger sister, Eugenie. She had married her longterm partner Jack Brooksbank in St. George's Chapel, Windsor, with Grenadier Guards, the state trumpeters of the Household Cavalry, and a carriage ride around Windsor in celebration. Intimate by contrast, with its borrowed dress and a handful of guests, Beatrice's wedding, postponed when the original date in May fell within a lockdown, resonated with the public.

Something similar was happening with Charles and Camilla, for whom digital connection with the public was enabling them to show their humanity and their industry rather than their royalty and social polish. On their fifteenth wedding anniversary the couple released a picture on Instagram of themselves and their dogs on the porch at Birkhall. It spoke of a couple deeply content with each other and willing to embrace social media in their seventies.

In Charles's study an abundance of framed photos showed his fondness for family. The backdrop to his Zoom calls was analyzed in great detail; there were pictures of his wedding, his mother, his children and grandchildren, and even one of himself and Princess Anne as children, both dressed in peach outfits and holding hands in Malta. There were lilies spilling out of a vase, a pair of ceramic hens, and books ranging from an encyclopedia of tropical plants to thrillers written by jockey-turned-author Dick Francis. Camilla's study, meanwhile, revealed a ball tosser for her rescue Jack Russells, Beth and Bluebell, propped up against a wall, crime novels, and pictures of her horses and dogs. It all felt familiar to millions of ordinary Britons. Unsurprisingly traffic to the couple's social channels peaked and they accrued thousands more online followers.

In an April 1, 2020, address to the country Charles sounded more kingly than ever before, his authority leavened with emotion and warmth. "None of us can say when this will end, but end it will. Until it does that, let us all try and live with hope and with faith in ourselves and each other," he encouraged. It was a perceptible shift toward King Charles III.

"In many ways the pandemic helped the royals, their visibility, and their sense of purpose," says Anna Whitelock. "The Queen managed to get to grips with modern technology so that she could be seen and interact with her subjects. Charles and Camilla and William and Kate were all very high profile and came across as doing a lot. It was very much a case of focusing the attention on the principal players, but we also saw Princess Anne, Edward, and Sophie coming more to the fore to help share the workload."

Royal diaries were reconfigured: royal visits became online events with the royals dropping in via Zoom from home, with a particular focus on acknowledging the efforts of frontline workers, medical staff, and armed forces personnel. The Countess of Wessex also joined a telephone support group reaching out to elderly people isolated in lockdown.

"What the pandemic showed in many ways was that the royal family was a solid working unit and they represented a national symbol [of] unity," continues Anna Whitelock. "They showed how work could be divided up, that they could speak to different ages and do something useful. This was the royal family at its best—in action and being visible."

The pandemic also proved that the Queen was still the boss and that her seven decades on the throne had given her matchless experience in steadying Britain's nerves and raising its spirits. Personal addresses from the monarch were rare—prior to the pandemic she had only addressed the nation four times in her reign outside of her traditional annual broadcasts. These were during the first Gulf War in 1991, when Diana died in 1997, on the death of the Queen Mother in 2002, and for her Diamond Jubilee in 2012. During the pandemic she took to the airwaves with unprecedented frequency.

In her first broadcast she wore a vibrant green dress with a rarely seen brooch of turquoise—a stone associated with protection and healing—and called for her people to remain united and resolute in the fight against the disease. She ended with a personal promise: "We will succeed and that success will belong to every one of us . . . we will be with our friends again, we will be with our families again, we will meet again."

Then she recorded an audio address for Easter Saturday 2020, reaching out to Christians across the world marking the holy days in isolation at home. "Coronavirus will not overcome us," she vowed. "As dark as death can be, particularly for those suffering with grief, light and life are greater. May the living flame of the Easter hope be a steady guide as we face the future."

And on May 8, 2020, the seventy-fifth anniversary of the end of World War II in Europe, she gave another speech, reminding her country she'd been there during those brutal years. In the silence of lockdown she told Great Britain: "Our streets are not empty; they are filled with the love and the care that we have for each other and when I look at our country today, and see what we are willing to do to protect and support one another, I say with pride that we are still a nation those brave soldiers, sailors, and airmen would recognize and admire."

Historian Peter Hennessy believes that "these speeches captured the British mood of decency and solidarity and taking care of each other with calmness; they spoke of the way Britons can come through if they work together carefully and thoughtfully. They're beautifully phrased. The Queen has a high input into her speeches and these bear reading every word of, because it's the inner her. It really is. They were very beautifully delivered at a time of high anxiety."

Charles Anson agrees: "In her Easter message and her Christmas address in 2020 it was clear that people were very responsive to that calm and increasingly authoritative voice with seventy years' experience on the throne. It's not just what the Queen says but also her tone that people find wise and comforting."

The monarch used the break from royal business as usual to offer the Cambridges a plum job which ought perhaps to have gone to Charles and Camilla. She dispatched the younger couple on the royal train (a rare privilege) for a 1,250-mile whistle-stop journey across Scotland, Wales, and England to thank key workers and then welcomed them back in person at Windsor Castle. It was a significant moment for the Cambridges, a deliberate choice by the Queen to send William instead of his father. At the end as the Queen turned to go back up the steps into Windsor Castle, the Duke of Cambridge said, "Bye, Gran," a reminder that the Firm really is a family business.

"What that showed is that William and Kate represent the future," reflects Charles Anson. "The Queen is well aware of the comparative weight and popularity of the Cambridges." It was a positive end to a challenging year and, although the couple were saddened by the deterioration of their relationship with Harry, they were, according to one person who knows them well, "both relieved that there was no more drama" now that Harry and Meghan had left Britain.

But there was more drama to come over the most unlikely—and inappropriate—of dates in the royal calendar: Remembrance Sunday. Held on the second Sunday in November, this is the day the Queen leads the nation in remembering British and Commonwealth soldiers, sailors, and airmen and -women who died in world wars and other conflicts. The royal family leads the national act of mourning at the Cenotaph, where there is a two-minute silence at 11:00 A.M. and the solemn laying of wreaths.

From across the Atlantic, the Duke of Sussex asked for a wreath to be laid in his name. The Queen declined on the grounds that he was not a working royal and that it was in this capacity that he had attended the Cenotaph in years gone by. Harry was dismayed. Charles, William, Prince Edward, and Princess Anne all laid wreaths. The only exception was Andrew.

As a mark of their respect, Harry and Meghan laid a wreath in the Los Angeles National Cemetery and left flowers on the graves of two Commonwealth soldiers instead. Again they demonstrated a new way to be royal. "Service is universal" is their mantra, and this they felt was a valuable tribute to the military and veterans' community.

However, their gesture drew criticism, not for the action itself so much as the fact that the couple took a photographer along to capture the moment. It could be viewed as shameless self-promotion. To the Sussexes however it was not an act of vanity, just the legitimate chronicling of their work for a global audience.

There was happy personal news for them too. On Valentine's Day 2021 Harry and Meghan announced they were expecting their second child, having revealed in November 2020 that Meghan had miscarried in July of that year. The notice came on Instagram with an artistic black-and-white shot of the couple barefoot in their California garden. It was beguiling and contemporary and connected directly with their followers.

Despite having moved to LA for a more private life, the Sussexes seemed to be on a major publicity drive now that they were established in their new home and the world was learning to live with Covid. Harry appeared on *The Late Late Show* with British comedian James Corden, traveling around LA on an open-top double decker while enjoying English high tea and performing a running gag about *The Fresh Prince of Bel-Air*. Rumors were swirling that the couple were to sit down with the queen of the TV interview, Oprah Winfrey. When they did, it was incendiary.

Meghan revealed a mental health crisis severe enough to make her consider suicide when she was pregnant, while also accusing courtiers of not taking it seriously; she alleged a member of the royal family had raised concerns about the likely color of Archie's skin; said the Duchess of Cambridge had made her cry before her wedding; and that she was silenced as soon as she became a royal girlfriend. Harry would go on to say he'd been cut off financially by his father, who had stopped taking his calls.

The special aired in the United States on March 7 and in the UK on March 8. The Queen did not watch the interview, but she was fully briefed on the content. It was another day before she responded with the briefest of statements: "The whole family is saddened to learn the full extent of how challenging the last few years have been for Harry and Meghan. The issues raised, particularly that of race, are concerning. Whilst some recollections may vary, they are taken very seriously and will be addressed by the family privately. Harry, Meghan, and Archie will always be much loved family members."

The pointed phrase "recollections may vary" was the sharpest of barbs. The fallout from the interview caused not just a global sensation but something of a cultural divide between the US and the UK. In the UK an Ipsos Mori poll showed no shift in the Sussexes' favor, and the general consensus in Britain was that Harry and Meghan had behaved shoddily toward the Queen and turned their backs on Harry's homeland. In the United States the Sussexes found compassion and encouragement for speaking their truth.

"Many people here were rooting for Meghan to be the progressive link in the royal family but after a while, seeing it wasn't working, it wasn't worth it. There is a lot of sympathy for her here," KJ Matthews told me.

Many Americans felt that stripping Harry of his military titles had been petty and unfair given that he had served two tours of duty, and when reports surfaced in the *Times* alleging that Meghan had bullied members of staff at the palace (allegations she strenuously denied) just before the Oprah interview aired, for some it was proof enough of a smear campaign designed to discredit her. Amid the fallout from the Oprah interview the royal family were also preparing for the loss of their patriarch, the Duke of Edinburgh, whose final instructions to Charles were "Look after the Queen" and "Keep the family together." A royal epoch as well as a royal marriage was coming to a close.

According to a family friend: "Philip slept a lot but [Elizabeth] made sure he was comfortable. She read to him, played him music, and they reminisced, going through family albums together. Charles got time with his father as well and Philip told him, 'Whatever you do, promise me you will take care of your mother.' Charles was very emotional."

Philip's death brought Britain to a standstill. Just short of his hundredth birthday, the Duke had been in public life since the 1940s; few could remember the United Kingdom without its handsome, clever, irascible consort. He had taken the notion of military service—dedication to a country and a cause—and repurposed it for royal life. His legacy was in the modernization of the monarchy and the stability of his wife's reign. As the Queen had said on their golden wedding anniversary: "He is someone who doesn't take easily to compliments but he has quite simply been my strength and stay all these years."

Covid restrictions meant a vastly different funeral from the one that had been planned. Scaled back and socially distanced, it was a royal funeral unlike any other. The Queen sat alone and masked, unable to be consoled by her children and grandchildren. As her eldest grandson Peter Phillips, son of Princess Anne, said in an interview with the BBC: "Our thoughts immediately went to my grandmother. We've been trying to support her as much as we can. Everybody saw the image of Her Majesty sitting alone. It would have been the same for any other family; the hardest part is not being able to hug those closest to the person who's been lost."

In some ways it was the funeral the Duke would have wanted. It reflected the private man he had been before he had made himself, for love of the then princess Elizabeth, public property. Far from a gathering of the eight hundred guests who would have filled St. George's Chapel, there were just thirty members of his family there for his farewell.

I was commentating for the BBC and noted as the Queen was driven past, masked and dwarfed in her black mourning dress, that she looked vulnerable and suddenly very old. On a day which was focused on the past—the Duke's life and achievements—this image also asked, what of the future?

The answer lay in several iconic moments captured throughout the day. There was the sight of a masked Kate, regal and reassuring, in the back of a funeral car. Above a four-strand pearl and diamond necklace loaned to her by the Queen, she gazed straight into the lens, drawing instant comparisons to the Queen Mother, another Windsor wife whose grace hid an inner iron.

"In that single image you see Kate as absolutely fundamental to the future. She inherently understands what the job requires and embodies that sense of duty," comments Robert Lacey.

The funeral brought Prince Harry back to the UK and offered an opportunity for the feuding brothers to come together. The image of William and Harry walking up Castle Hill after the ceremony, jollied along by Kate, was something the world wanted to see—the brothers finally together and talking. But it was a short-lived reunion with the Cambridges seen leaving Windsor Castle after around thirty minutes or so and not joining Harry and their royal cousins, Princesses Beatrice, Eugenie, Zara and Mike Tindall, and Peter Phillips for an impromptu wake at Frogmore. "All the cousins got together for a drink up at Frogmore after the funeral. There was quite a lot of alcohol and quite a few tears too," according to a family friend. "Harry was so happy to see his cousins but William and Kate did not stick around."

Charles was stoic at his father's funeral but made clear the depth of his loss in a tribute given in front of his Highgrove bolthole. Referring to the Duke as his "dear Papa," he said his father was a "much loved and appreciated figure" who had given "remarkable, devoted" service to his country and his family. Charles added that he was a "very special person who . . . above all else would have been amazed by the reaction and the touching things that have been said about him."

The world's final glimpse of Philip was a somber one, with his coffin being lowered into the royal vault and then the mournful sound of a lone piper's lament. There he lay until the death of the Queen when they were interred together the George VI Memorial Chapel, which is also the resting place of her parents and her sister, Princess Margaret.

According to Alastair Bruce, historian, royal commentator, and currently governor of Edinburgh Castle, it was the Queen's request for Philip to be held in the royal vault until they could be buried to-gether: "When the Queen dies they will be interred together along-side her family, and so I think it was a practical decision that seems to speak of 'I shan't be long after.'" Or perhaps it was more about romance than pragmatism. Perhaps she wanted her last journey to be made alongside the love of her life.

Ultimately the enduring image of Philip's funeral was the Queen alone in her time of greatest grief. Less than a year later the coun-try would be stunned to learn that the night before, staffers from 10 Downing Street had partied into the early hours at the seat of government, in direct contravention to social distancing rules. One set of partygoers created a sound system with a laptop placed on a photocopier in the basement. Another group went shopping for wine with a suitcase. Later the two groups combined as the revelry spilled out into No. 10's back garden.

It was also reported that No. 10 offered the Queen a relaxation of Covid rules for the day of the Duke's funeral. Elizabeth declined. Almost seventy years on the throne and deep in mourning, she led as she always had—by example and not by decree.

CHAPTER 10

One Final Hurrah

She's so dedicated and really determined to finish everything she started . . . she'll want to hand over knowing . . . that she's done everything she can for the country and that she's not let anyone down.

—PRINCE WILLIAM

The Duke of Edinburgh's death was a turning point for the royal family. As one courtier observed, "Prince Philip's death sharpened the sense that things will change, and that day is getting closer."

While she hid it well, Elizabeth's health started to decline after she lost Philip. During the early months of widowhood, the monarch had surprised her family, royal courtiers, and her subjects by returning to duties just weeks after Philip's funeral. She traveled to Cornwall to meet world leaders at the G7 summit. In a surprise move Buckingham Palace announced that Charles, Camilla, and the Cambridges would be joining her. It was a calculated projection to the country and the wider world of the "new royals."

Surrounded by the world's most influential leaders, all eyes were on Elizabeth as she headed a royal delegation with two future kings and two queens of tomorrow.

The Queen wore a dress which looked like an English country garden, a pale cream patterned with pink and orange wildflowers and green sprigs. Her brooch was in the shape of a spray of sorghum, a flowering grass. Her Majesty was literally wearing her team's colors. She did not linger, for she had to be back in Windsor to receive President Biden and the First Lady. President Biden is only the fifth president to be invited to the castle the Queen considers home, and there was no question the royal red carpet was being rolled out for this particular American visit.

During her reign there were presidents Elizabeth got along with particularly well, notably President Ronald Reagan, with whom she went horseback riding in Windsor Great Park. President George W. Bush once winked at her by way of apology for making her sound more than two hundred years old in a speech. President Barack Obama and First Lady Michelle Obama were famously collected in person from their helicopter by the Queen and Prince Philip, the Duke driving the First Couple back to Windsor Castle himself.

There was also one American leader who despite the Queen's shrewdness seemed to elude her understanding: President Donald Trump, who rudely kept the Queen waiting ahead of their meeting and then walked in front of her during an inspection of the Guard of Honor at Windsor Castle. Privately the Queen is said to have described Trump as "an enigma." Perhaps it explains why, when she posed for an official photograph with President Trump and his wife, First Lady Melania Trump, her staff failed to move a dog bowl that was on a plastic mat right by his foot.

President Biden was the thirteenth US president she'd welcomed to the country in her seventy-year reign. It was all about keeping the so-called "special relationship" special.

Despite the loss of Philip, the Queen was determined for the royal show to carry on, and later in June 2021 she headed to Scotland for Holyrood Week as she had always done throughout her reign. Now that she no longer had Philip to support her, the Queen was often accompanied by family members when she carried out engagements. The Duke of Cambridge joined his grandmother for the traditional welcome ceremony known as the Ceremony of the Keys at Holyroodhouse, and he was by his grandmother's side for a visit to the AG Barr factory, where the Queen opened a new process facility and William sipped on the famous Scottish soft drink Irn-Bru.

Their shared trip had a double significance. The first was from the same playbook as anointing Camilla a future queen consort; this was the monarch showing off the intergenerational stability at the heart of the House of Windsor. And second, it was a display of royal soft power. In the face of an energetic Scottish independence campaign, this was an apolitical bid to keep the United Kingdom united. "When Prince William went with his grandmother to the Irn Bru factory and drank a bottle, you could have captioned that picture 'The things one does for one's Union,'" joked Peter Hennessy.

Interestingly, a poll for the *Sunday Times* at the time showed that 47 percent of Scottish people would vote to keep a royal head of state even if Scotland broke away from the Union, compared to 35 percent who would prefer an elected head. The same poll asked the Scots how they felt about the royals intervening in the issue of Scottish independence. Almost half, 49 percent, thought it was "unacceptable." Around a third, 32 percent, said they would accept it. The conclusion seemed to be that while the monarch and her family remained personally popular in Scotland, any attempt by them to influence the course of the independence struggle in the country would not go down well. (And worryingly for William, support for keeping the monarchy was stronger in the over-fifty-fives than it was with younger voters.)

The Queen was keen to keep the traditions that had come to define her reign, and after completing her official engagements in late July she left Windsor Castle to begin her annual summer break in the Scottish Highlands. It was her first time at the castle without Philip, but she was visited by various family members, including her children, grandchildren, and great-grandchildren. While the visits delighted the Queen, her health was ailing. She had lost a noticeable amount of weight in the months since Philip's death, which was to be expected, but alarm bells were sounded when she was suddenly admitted to the hospital in October 2021. The news broke in a tabloid paper, panicking the palace and forcing them to issue a statement about the Queen's health. A spokesman said the Queen had undergone "preliminary investigations" and was under doctors' orders to rest. It meant having to cancel a planned visit to Northern Ireland at the last minute. The Queen was back at Windsor Castle by lunchtime the next day, but despite the palace's assurance that the monarch was in "good spirits," there was widespread concern about her health. There was speculation in the media about what was wrong with the monarch and fears over her forthcoming Platinum Jubilee celebrations in June 2022. The year did not start well for the Queen, who contracted Covid early in the new year.

Thankfully, she recovered and was well enough to attend Prince Philip's memorial service at Westminster Abbey on March 29. She managed the occasion, under the full glare of the press cameras, by entering through a side door to avoid a lengthy walk down the aisle.

The palace had consistently refused to go into detail about her health, insisting it would not be drawn into a running commentary about private matters. This was understandable but did little to stem the rumors that she was suffering from a serious illness. *Cancer* was the whisper going around newsrooms of the national press. The official line from Buckingham Palace was that the Queen was suffering "episodic mobility issues." She had long suffered from knee and back problems, and during one face-to-face audience, the Queen let slip that there were some days when she was in so much pain she could not walk.

Reluctant to be seen in a wheelchair like her sister, the late Princess Margaret, she occasionally attended engagements in an electric buggy, which made its debut in May 2022 in suitably regal style at the Chelsea Flower Show, one of the Queen's favorite events. She was in good spirits, though increasingly dependent on a walking stick, and chose to use her late husband's.

While she continued with light desk work, her regular engagements and audiences were usually carried out via videoconference calls rather than in person.

Charles and Camilla carried out the lion's share of royal engagements, supported by William and Kate. At times "the new fab four," as they were now known in the press, carried out visits together. Kate joined Charles and Camilla for their first joint engagement to a Prince's Foundation arts and culture training site in February 2022; a few months later Kate teamed up with Princess Anne to visit the London headquarters of the Royal College of Midwives for their first-ever engagement together. There was a sense of pooling resources to support the Queen while filling the void left by Harry and Meghan, who were pressing ahead with their own lives in California. With a fracture at the heart of the family ever since the Sussexes' departure, the Windsors needed to put on a show of unity.

Having relocated to Windsor during the pandemic, the Queen was still not back at Buckingham Palace, which was undergoing a ten-year-long refurbishment. (The £425.5 million bill was being picked up by the British taxpayer.)

Up until the pandemic Elizabeth had happily divided her week between London and Windsor, but Windsor was more private and the wing occupied by the Queen was easier to navigate as opposed to the long corridors and spiraling staircases of Buckingham Palace. However, the fact that there was no monarch living day-to-day in Buckingham Palace, the globally recognized HQ of the Firm, felt significant.

The palace has been the official London residence of British sovereigns since 1837, yet Charles, in residence at Clarence House next door, was now closer geographically to the heart of the monarchy than the monarch herself. Was he running the royal show? Not yet, although behind palace walls the Regency Act (which makes provision for a regency in the event of the monarch being incapacitated through illness) was being brushed off and revised.

Charles was assisting his mother more than at any other time in her reign, and in November 2021 he had traveled to Barbados to represent the Queen to witness the country become a republic. The prince was clearly moved to see the Queen's standard lowered and new president, Dame Sandra Mason, sworn in. While the Queen had never publicly spoken about Britain's colonial past, Charles addressed the country's history in a powerful speech: "From the darkest days of our past and the appalling atrocity of slavery which forever stains our history, the people of this island forged their path with extraordinary fortitude," he said.

Then, in May 2022, Charles stood in for the Queen at the State Opening of Parliament, his highest-profile substitution ever. The lengthy service involves walking and standing for several hours and was deemed too much for the Queen. She had missed the important occasion, in which she outlines the government's legislation, only twice in her reign—when she was pregnant with Andrew and then with Edward. The image of Charles on the throne with the imperial crown next to him was a poignant one. It was a reminder of how close Charles was to the throne and the responsibility being granted to him by his aging mother.

"In the army it's called *succession planning*, and the Queen has been very responsible about doing just this," notes Alastair Bruce. "It would be a gross dereliction of her reign not to expose the heir apparent to the work that will one day be his responsibility. The Queen is well aware that her life will end and that the institution she serves needs to be well tuned in order to take the next step. She knows that her troops are rehearsing, but she needs to be certain they are ready to go at any moment."

It was why in the later years of her life, the Queen was closer to Charles than ever, seeing him more regularly to discuss matters of state and the future of the institution. According to Charles Anson: "It's the nature of our monarchy. Each monarch coaches and brings on the next generation. It's that continuity that appeals to so many people, because it's not just an elected person who suddenly arrives in public life. It's this sense of generations, one after another, being trained and committing themselves to public service, to the nation, and to the Commonwealth in a constitutional monarchy above the fray of daily politics."

Against the backdrop of the Queen's declining health, it had been a turbulent period for the royals. Prince Andrew was headline news once again after announcing a reported $14.7 million out-of-court settlement with Virginia Roberts Giuffre. There was no admission of guilt but full acknowledgment that she was a victim of abuse and, finally, an expression of regret for his association with Jeffrey Epstein. Meanwhile, Scotland Yard detectives were looking into allegations that Prince Charles's senior aide Michael Fawcett had offered Saudi tycoon Mahfouz Marei Mubarak bin Mahfouz a knighthood and help securing British citizenship in return for donations to the Prince of Wales's charity. (Clarence House has said the prince had no knowledge of possible wrongdoing, while the Prince's Foundation has said it is investigating.)

Across the pond, the Sussexes were laying the foundation for an alternative royal court in California. In September 2020 they signed a $100 million deal with Netflix. The first project, it was rumored, would be a fly-on-the-wall series about their lives. Harry had already made a series about mental health with Oprah Winfrey for Apple TV, signed on as chief impact officer for mental health start-up BetterUp, and the couple signed a deal with Spotify worth an estimated $20 million, which included a podcast hosted by Meghan called *Archetypes*, which featured the duchess in conversation with celebrities, historians, and experts about women and the stereotypes that get leveled against them. As well as redefining themselves as global philanthropists using their Archewell Foundation, they were mental health advisors, content creators, and ethical investors. In short, they were reinventing themselves as a billion-dollar brand.

While their business plans were taking off, family relations had stalled. Harry was not speaking to his father or brother and had not flown home for his grandfather's memorial service. He had cited security issues and was engaged in a legal wrangle with the UK government, claiming his private security arrangements didn't give him the protection he needed while on UK soil and that he was prevented from paying the government to beef them up. But his absence was taken as a snub. It was only the reckless, self-serving behavior of the Duke of York—who emerged from the shadows to walk the Queen to her seat in full view of the TV cameras—which prevented Harry's no-show from dominating the service.

In No. 10 Downing Street, Prime Minister Boris Johnson's administration faced a lengthy police probe into multiple alleged breaches of Britain's lockdown rules and a leadership challenge after Johnson was forced to stand down following a series of Tory scandals. Abroad, Russia's invasion of Ukraine on February 24, 2022, posed the gravest threat to peace in Europe since the Second World War.

Peter Hennessy summed up the national mood: "Heaven forbid we should lose the Queen in the middle of all these crises. Of course one day she will go, and when she does it's going to be the most tremendous shock, because everybody has an idea of the Queen in their head. It's an individual thing as well as a collective thing. We have been formidably lucky all these years to have her. Through the ups and downs any country endures, you have continuity embodied in a woman who has not put a foot wrong since 1952.

"We've been absolutely blessed by having a gold-standard constitutional monarch. When she dedicated her life to the service of the Commonwealth and its people aged twenty-one, she meant it."

Indeed Elizabeth had used her accession anniversary statement on February 5, 2022, to renew her vow of lifelong service, declaring, "It gives me great pleasure to renew to you the pledge I gave in 1947 that my life will always be devoted to your service. . . . I look forward to continuing to serve you with all of my heart." She signed it, "Your servant, Elizabeth R."

She had also used the important anniversary to pave the way for Camilla to become Queen Consort, thus addressing a conundrum that had carried on for decades. "When, in the fullness of time, my son Charles becomes King, I know you will give him and his wife

Camilla the same support you have given me; and it is my sincere wish that, when the time comes, Camilla will be known as Queen Consort as she continues her own loyal service." Elizabeth effectively willed "Queen Camilla" into being in her own lifetime. There was a sense that she was tying up loose ends.

As well as the dusting off of the Regency Act, Charles was quietly revising his own coronation plans, code-named Operation Golden Orb, and had sketched out both his first address to the nation as King and an outline of the first five years of his reign. His vision was for a streamlined monarchy with the focus on him and Camilla and their support act—William and Kate—the next generation upon whom the future of the monarchy depended.

Charles did not plan to be a caretaker monarch, simply minding the family firm until William and Kate take control. As Prince of Wales, he had a clear idea of how he would reign and what he wanted to achieve. The issues he had championed for so long, such as his global campaigning in the critical area of climate change and his work around youth employment and inner-city housing, to name just a few, would be issues he would continue to promote as King.

First and foremost, Charles planned to be Britain's first eco-king, a monarch with green fingers and green ideals who has lived an environmentally aware life since he was a teenager. He's the prince with solar panels on his homes and an Aston Martin DB6 that runs on surplus English white wine and whey from the cheesemaking process. Addressing the 2020 World Economic Forum in Davos, Switzerland, the prince pointed out that he had "dedicated much of my life to the restoration of harmony between humanity, nature, and the environment" before issuing a call to arms on sustainability, saying, "We simply cannot waste any more time—the only limit is our willingness to act, and the time to act is now." It was a mission statement for his monarchy and one he would repeat at the United Nations Climate Change Conference, COP26, held in the UK the following year. Climate change and biodiversity loss pose an even greater existential threat than the Covid pandemic, he told world leaders. "We have to put ourselves on what might be called a warlike footing."

He acknowledged to filmmaker John Bridcut in the documentary *Prince, Son and Heir: Charles at 70* back in 2018 that he understood his role would change as King, saying, "Clearly I won't be able to do the same things I have done as heir. Of course you operate within the constitutional parameters."

And Charles understood that when his time came, it would be a very different climate from when his mother acceded. He had already decided that while his coronation ceremony would honor the traditions and religious elements of previous coronations (the coronation of a British monarch is the only remaining religious coronation in Europe), it would be smaller in size and shorter in length. While the service would be Anglican, it would be culturally diverse with people of many faiths and guests representing Britain's religious cultural and ethnic diversity.

But for now the palace was planning for a jubilee and Elizabeth was determined that despite her health problems, she would set yet another record by becoming the first British monarch to celebrate a Platinum Jubilee. Four days of pomp and pageantry had been planned, including the monarch's 260-year-old birthday parade known as Trooping the Colour, a Service of Thanksgiving, a pop concert at Buckingham Palace, and a street pageant.

Ahead of the celebration, the Queen issued a statement: "[I] hope that the coming days will provide an opportunity to reflect on all that has been achieved during the last seventy years, as we look to the future with confidence and enthusiasm."

Perhaps it was because this was the first time since the Covid pandemic that the nation had come together. Perhaps it was the realization that this could be a final farewell to the platinum queen. But from the start to the end of the celebrations there was a swell of emotion and patriotism that swept across Britain in a colorful tide of bunting, street parties, Union Jack–themed bowler hats, and a hefty dose of British eccentricity.

It took every inch of the Queen's stoic strength to be there in person, facing her subjects from the balcony of Buckingham Palace not once but twice. Having reigned by the mantra "I have to be seen to be believed," the Queen ensured she was visible at the start and close of the national holiday, engraving those important balcony moments into the hearts of the nation.

The ninety-six-year-old monarch had promised, during her rousing speech during the first lockdown of 2020, "We will meet again." She honored that promise, greeting her subjects—who had gathered in their hundreds of thousands—with her first balcony appearance since 2019. At Trooping the Colour, she took the salute from the palace and watched the flyover, a tradition her father, King George VI, had begun. This was the balcony where she had first appeared when she was just one year and two months old.

Leaning on her now-essential walking stick, the monarch looked frail and at times uncharacteristically emotional, but undeniably happy to be present. I was in the BBC's commentary box with news anchor Huw Edwards and Prince William and Prince Harry's former private secretary Jamie Lowther-Pinkerton. We all agreed it was one of those moments that made your hairs stand on end, and there was a lump in my throat as I reflected on the significance of the moment. Prince Charles paid a moving tribute to his mother at the party at the palace, saying, "What really gets my mother up in the morning is all of you." He captured the spirit of the nation when he exclaimed, "You laugh and cry with us and, most importantly, you have been there for us!"

The crowds lined the Mall, stretching from the Queen Victoria Memorial outside Buckingham Palace half a mile back to Trafalgar Square, and were a testament to Elizabeth's enduring popularity and the affection of her nation.

Young, middle-aged, elderly, from all ethnicities and walks of life, people simply wanted to witness this moment. For most, the Queen was the only monarch they had known, and with her century in sight, it was a reminder that she would not be here forever.

The crowds, at points twenty-five people deep, and the sea of giant Union Jack flags all waving for her must have been quite a spectacle to witness. "Incredible," she murmured.

When she next appeared just moments later for the crescendo, a flyover of seventy aircraft, she was followed by her family. There were the Prince of Wales, the Duchess of Cornwall, and the Duke and Duchess of Cambridge and their children (Prince Louis, who was making his very first balcony appearance, wore a sweet sailor's outfit identical to one William had worn in 1985).

The Prince of Wales's role as her chief substitute, with the Duke of Cambridge by his side, was evident throughout the jubilee, as it had been in the months since the death of the Duke of Edinburgh. Also present were the princess royal and her husband, Vice Admiral Sir Timothy Laurence, and the Queen's cousins the Duke of Kent, the Duke and Duchess of Gloucester, and Princess Alexandra. But they were the support act. The star of the show was the Queen, and the fifteen Typhoon fighter planes that formed a spectacular 70 in the bright blue sky made that clear.

Later that day the Queen lit the principal beacon at Windsor Castle, starting a fiery chain of three thousand beacons around the Commonwealth—from Tonga to Belize, New Zealand, and Australia. Even as republicanism loomed Down Under, there was affection and nostalgia for the Queen.

There was one particularly poignant moment during the Service of Thanksgiving (which the Queen was unable to attend): Hubert Parry's "I Was Glad" rang out, just as it had in Westminster Abbey in June 1953 when the twenty-seven-year-old Elizabeth was crowned.

"Your long reign reflects the distance of Aintree rather than the sprints of Epsom," the archbishop of York observed in his sermon, prompting smiles from the royals. "We are so glad you are still in the saddle. And we are all glad that there is still more to come. So, thank you for staying the course. Thank you for continuing to be faithful to the pledges you made seventy years ago."

It all felt deeply personal. The Queen agreed to open the family's private photo albums for a BBC documentary called *Elizabeth: The Unseen Queen*, which she narrated. Her mobility issues had slowed her down, but her voice was still strong, warm, and engaging. Never before had we heard the Queen telling the story of her life and, in doing so, giving the public a rare glimpse of the woman who wore the crown.

The Queen also had a starring role in a charming sketch of her taking afternoon tea at the palace with Paddington Bear. Proving she had lost none of her humor or comic timing, there were gasps of delight and cheers of approval from the audience and those in the royal box when the monarch was seen pulling a marmalade sandwich from her trademark Launer handbag.

When Prince Charles took the stage to pay tribute to his mother later that evening and asked the audience to cheer for "Mummy," as he had done at her previous jubilees, they clapped and stamped and cheered three deafening, "Hip, hip, hoorays!" that might almost have reached her at Windsor Castle, where she watched the concert on television.

The Platinum Jubilee Pageant was the highlight of the weekend with thousands of performers and dancers, carnival-style floats, and life-size corgi puppets, which made front pages across the United States and Europe. Even in China, nearly four million people watched the festivities on live stream.

Such support had not been a given. As with her previous jubilees, there had been concerns that the platinum might be met with a muted reception; given Britain was on the verge of a recession, not everyone felt the then chancellor, Rishi Sunak, should put aside over $34 million to fund the celebrations. Russia was at war with Ukraine, and in the UK the spiraling cost of living—as household bills soared and interest rates rose—was being felt by millions.

The polls at the time also made for worrying reading for the royals, indicating the younger generation was not interested in the monarchy. According to a YouGov poll, just 9 percent of Gen Z was in favor of keeping the royals. Meanwhile, the percentage of people who thought the monarchy was the best thing about Britain had dropped by 8 percent since the 2012 Diamond Jubilee. Undoubtedly, the family scandals of recent years involving Prince Andrew and the

Sussexes had impacted the royal family's popularity, and while support for the Queen remained consistent, for others in the family it wasn't a case of smooth sailing.

———————

THE DUKE AND Duchess of Sussex arrived in the UK from Los Angeles with their young children, Archie and Lilibet, to join the celebrations. It had been the Queen's wish for them to attend, but to avoid any awkwardness over how they would be represented, the palace announced only working family members would be invited to join the Queen on the balcony. This also allowed the Queen to neatly deal with Prince Andrew, whose high-profile attendance at the Service of Thanksgiving for the Duke of Edinburgh had been so controversial. In the end, the Duke of York, whose attendance could well have cast a cloud over the occasion, was forced to bow out of the jubilee entirely after testing positive for Covid, thus saving palace aides a further headache.

There were fears too that the Sussexes might dominate the news headlines, and they were warned that under no circumstances would they be allowed to film any of the official celebrations or their participation for their Netflix series. Lilibet's first birthday fell in the middle of the long weekend, and Harry and Meghan hosted a small tea party at Frogmore Cottage for select family members and close friends. Charles, William, and Kate were busy on official engagements, but the Queen was reported to have briefly attended; however, there was no official photograph of the monarch meeting her namesake. It was all part of the palace's strategy for keeping Harry and Meghan low profile during the Queen's celebrations.

Apart from their attendance at Trooping the Colour (they arrived by car, not in a state landau like the senior royals), the Sussexes were peripheral; at the Service of Thanksgiving at St. Paul's Cathedral, they were seated in second-row pews, behind the working royals and at an obvious distance from the Cambridges. The hierarchy was quite deliberate, with Harry and Meghan taking their seats next to Harry's cousins Princesses Beatrice and Eugenie and their husbands.

Elegant in a white Dior dress suit and broad-brimmed hat, Meghan looked the part and smiled for the cameras, but Harry, bedecked in his jubilee medals, seemed at times lost in thought.

Harry had last seen his father, stepmother, and grandmother in April 2022 when he and Meghan stopped off in Britain on their way to The Hague for the Invictus Games. The meeting with Charles and Camilla was awkward compared to their cordial tea with the Queen. The Sussexes were late, and Charles had just fifteen minutes with his son and daughter-in-law before he had to leave for the Royal Maundy Service at Windsor Castle, where he was standing in for the Queen for the very first time. While father and son are said to have greeted each other warmly, there were moments of tension. "Harry went in with hugs and the best of intentions and said he wanted to clear the air," according to a family friend. "He actually suggested that they use a mediator to try and sort things out, which had Charles somewhat bemused and Camilla spluttering into her tea. She told Harry it was ridiculous and that they were a family and would sort it out between themselves."

William and Kate were skiing with the children, and William pointedly did not change his holiday plans. He was not really speaking to his brother and hadn't seen him since the summer when they briefly put aside their differences to unveil the long-awaited memorial statue of Diana in Kensington Gardens on July 1, 2021. They had put on a decent show for the cameras, but there was no reconciliation. William simply couldn't forgive Harry for the things that had been said in the Oprah interview, and he was deeply concerned about his and Meghan's documentary and Harry's forthcoming autobiography, both of which were being kept closely guarded secrets. There were real concerns about what the couple might say and expose about a tumultuous and difficult period for the family. Given they had been so open and critical of the institution in the numerous interviews they had given since moving to America, there was a lack of trust and concerns within the family that private conversations could be relayed to the media.

There were raised eyebrows at the palace when, days after the meeting with the Queen, Harry spoke about their reunion on NBC's *Today* program. He revealed his grandmother was "in great form" and added he wanted to make sure she was being "protected" and had the right people around her. It wasn't clear whether Harry was referring to his father and William or the aides who were closest to the Queen—chiefly her private secretary, Sir Edward Young, her dresser, Angela Kelly, and favorite courtier, Paul Whybrew.

It seemed Harry's drive to win back some of the trust that had been shattered was dashed.

Many had hoped the jubilee weekend would be an opportunity for Harry and William to finally reunite, but it was not to be the case. There was no private meeting between the estranged brothers and no meeting of minds. I was reporting for CBC in Canada on the day of the Service of Thanksgiving and had seen Harry and Meghan leaving Clarence House, Prince Charles's official London residence, where the prince had organized a rendezvous before the church service. But the Cambridges were not in attendance and the chasm between the brothers was painfully evident.

While the Sussexes stuck to their background roles, the Cambridges were in full view. Having all three children ride in carriages to Trooping the Colour had been a brave decision by William and Kate given Louis was so young, but with George and Charlotte to help keep him in check, the little prince behaved impeccably, waving enthusiastically to the crowds.

After deliberately keeping their young children out of the spotlight for many years, William and Kate were more willing for their two eldest children to join them on certain occasions in public. George and Charlotte had been seen just months earlier at Prince Philip's memorial service and then the following month at the Easter Day service at St. George's Chapel, where each had demonstrated an innate understanding of their roles and a maturity beyond their years with their perfect behavior and easy tolerance of the assembled press pack. However, it was the first time Louis had appeared in public, and while riding in the carriage, he dipped his head as they passed the color—flag—during the trooping ceremony.

During the jubilee celebrations Prince George and Princess Charlotte accompanied their parents on a trip to Cardiff, where, during a rare walkabout, their confidence and interest in meeting people stood out as they shook hands with members of the public and watched rehearsals for a concert in the city that night. By the evening they were back in London at Buckingham Palace for the Platinum Party at the Palace, where the siblings were seen singing and waving their flags in the royal box. The following day they were back in the royal box for the Platinum Jubilee street pageant with Louis, who like most preschoolers had a limited attention span and the occasional tantrum. Their parents, however, were keen for them to witness this historic moment and to understand the duty that would one day fall to them. That the Sussexes were already en route home to California by the time the others were watching the ten-thousand-person pageant spoke volumes. While they were, as the Queen had said, "much loved" family members, they were no longer frontline royals.

When the Queen made her final appearance, she used it to signal the future she had referenced at the start of the celebrations. While her appearance was laden with symbolism and called back to the past (her walking stick belonged to Prince Philip and the black hatpin at the center of her emerald-green hat was a sign of mourning), this moment was about what would come next.

In a statement the Queen said she had been "humbled and deeply touched that so many people have taken to the streets to celebrate my Platinum Jubilee. While I may not have attended every event in person, my heart has been with you all, and I remain committed to serving you to the best of my ability, supported by my family."

It reaffirmed the vow she had made as a twenty-one-year-old princess in her first public address: to serve her whole life.

CHAPTER 11

Operation London Bridge

Thank you for your love and devotion to our family and to
the family of nations you have served so diligently all these
years.

—His Majesty the King

It was just before 4:00 p.m. on Thursday, September 8, 2022. "She's
gone," my source whispered tearfully down the phone. After a
morning of high alarm, it would be a further two and a half hours
before Buckingham Palace officially confirmed the rumors circulat-
ing around the world, on social media, and within Whitehall that
Queen Elizabeth II had died. According to the official death cer-
tificate published by the registrar general for Scotland, the Queen
passed away at Balmoral at 3:10 p.m. She was ninety-six years old,
and the cause of death was old age. For the doctors who had been
taking care of the Queen in the final weeks of her life, it was not
unexpected. According to Dr. Douglas James Allan Glass, who had
been keeping an eye on the Queen over the summer and who lives
less than twenty miles from Balmoral, "We had been concerned
about the Queen's health for several months." But when the moment

came it was still a shock. Charles and Anne received urgent calls from the royal doctors, who were informing the immediate family that the Queen's health had taken a sudden and serious downturn, and they were the first to reach Balmoral.

Just that morning I had met with the Queen's head of communications at a café around the corner from Buckingham Palace, and when I asked him about the Queen's health, he was very concerned. His phone had been ringing all morning, and he said a statement would be released shortly and urged me to be ready.

There had been further concerns just two days previously when the Queen was photographed meeting the new prime minister, Liz Truss. She was to be the Queen's fifteenth and final prime minister, following one of the most tumultuous periods in recent political history. Boris Johnson had stepped down as leader after a series of scandals involving himself and members of the cabinet, and Truss was appointed his replacement. She was required to travel to Scotland to ask the Queen's permission to form a new cabinet. Press Association photographer Jane Barlow was there to capture the moment and take what was to be the final picture of the monarch. She recalls: "Obviously she was very frail but she was very smiley." Barlow was allowed to photograph the Queen by herself after the brief meeting. Wearing spectacles and dressed in a beige cardigan and tartan skirt and leaning on her walking stick, the Queen was smiling, but her hands were black and blue with bruises—presumably from a cannula through which she had been receiving medication, or possibly blood transfusions.

Despite her frail health the Queen had insisted on carrying out one final duty, but the exertion took its toll on the monarch, and the following evening a virtual meeting with the Privy Council was canceled. The alarm was sounded, and over the course of the next twenty-four hours the Queen's health took a turn for the worse. Following my meeting with the Queen's press secretary, I headed straight back to my office, and at 12:32 p.m., the palace issued an unusually detailed statement that the royal doctors were concerned about the

Queen's health and stating that she was under medical supervision. It was clearly gravely serious.

The immediate family had been alerted earlier that morning that the Queen was unlikely to survive the day and that they were to come to Balmoral as quickly as possible. Anne, who was in Scotland at the time, was the first one by her mother's bedside. Fortunately, Charles and Camilla were at Dumfries House and able to take a helicopter to Balmoral, where they were seen arriving at 10:30 a.m. The rest of the family did not arrive until later that afternoon.

At 3:10 p.m., the Queen passed away peacefully in her bed. Charles is understood to have been by his mother's side the very moment he became King. Accession is immediate. It requires no ceremony or signature but is an immutable fact which flows from hereditary monarchy, making its code name, Operation Springtide, most apt. The new prime minister was telephoned at 4:30 p.m., once all family members had been informed, and told, "London Bridge is down," so that the wheels for the well-rehearsed D Day plans could be put into action.

Prince William, who had only the day before been seen with Kate taking their three children to their new school in Windsor, where the family had relocated over the summer, hurried to Scotland via a private flight that morning together with his uncles Andrew and Edward and Edward's wife, Sophie. They arrived just after 5:00 p.m.

By a stroke of luck, Harry was in the UK for a charity event with Meghan, but after an argument with his father over whether Meghan should be allowed to join him, he was forced to travel alone on a charter flight from London to Scotland and didn't arrive at Balmoral until later in the day, some hours after the Queen had passed. There was no time to say goodbye.

By lunchtime, rumors were spreading around Whitehall and beyond that the Queen was dying, possibly even dead. BBC News switched to rolling coverage on the Queen's decline as presenters in black ties filled airtime until the announcement came from the palace. At 6:30 p.m. Huw Edwards broke the news on the BBC to a stunned nation that the Queen had "died peacefully at Balmoral this afternoon." It was one of those moments the nation would never forget.

In keeping with tradition, a black-bordered notice of death was pinned to the gates of Buckingham Palace, where thousands of mourners, many in tears, had gathered to pay their respects and leave flowers as eleven days of official mourning commenced. There were so many bouquets that there was no space on the pavement outside the palace and people were asked to leave flowers in neighboring Green Park and St. James's Park. At Windsor, William, Kate, Harry, and Meghan put on a show of unity when they went to meet mourners at the castle gates to accept flowers and words of condolence from the grieving public. It was the first time the brothers and sisters-in-law had seen each other since the jubilee celebrations in the spring, and there had been little contact between them. William had asked Harry to join him and Kate on the impromptu walkabout to appease Charles, who felt the family needed to put on a show of unity at such a time.

Around the country flags were flown at half-mast on royal and government buildings, bells tolled at Westminster Abbey and St. Paul's Cathedral, and gun salutes were fired in Hyde Park and at royal palaces. In Paris, the lights were dimmed on the Eiffel Tower. In New York, the Empire State Building lit up in purple and silver to honor the Queen's life and legacy while the flag flew at half-mast at the US Capitol Building as a sign of respect. In Sydney, flags were also flown at half-mast on the Harbour Bridge. When the Queen's father, King George VI, died, the then prime minister Winston Churchill observed how his passing "stilled the clatter and traffic of 20th-century life in many lands."

Queen Elizabeth II's death brought the world to a stop. Tributes flooded in from around the world. US president Joe Biden, the last world leader to see the Queen during his 2021 visit to the UK, was one of the first to pay his respects, saying Her Majesty was "more than a monarch. She defined an era."

Because the Queen had died in Scotland, Operation London Bridge was executed in tandem with Operation Unicorn—the contingency plan should the monarch die in Scotland. Shielded from the public gaze by rolling hills and dense forests, the turreted castle had been the Queen's sanctuary. Now, finally she was at peace and the first monarch to die in Scotland since James V in 1542. According to Operation Unicorn, her body would be escorted to Edinburgh to lie in rest at Holyroodhouse before being moved to lie in state at St. Giles's Cathedral. Afterward, she would make her final journey back to England for a full state funeral before her final resting place at St. George's Chapel in Windsor.

The last monarch to have a funeral at Westminster Abbey was George II in 1760. Since then, the funerals of kings and queens have taken place at St. George's Chapel in Windsor. But in a break with tradition, the Queen decided she wanted her funeral at Westminster Abbey, where she had been crowned, so that more members of the public could attend and pay their respects. The plans were complex, extensive, well rehearsed, and overseen by the Duke of Norfolk, the Earl Marshal.

As members of the public flocked to royal palaces around the country to lay flowers, a double rainbow appeared over Buckingham Palace and another at Windsor Castle.

According to the D Day—"Death Day"—plans, which had been leaked over the years and were, therefore, widely known, the new King would be proclaimed by the Accession Council at St. James's Palace within twenty-four hours. It was confirmed by the palace that the Queen's body would lie in state in Westminster Hall for five nights and four days ahead of the state funeral, which would take place on September 19 at 11:00 a.m. There was to be a public holiday in the form of a day of national mourning. After the funeral service, the Queen's body would be taken by car to St. George's Chapel for a smaller family funeral and the interment at the memorial chapel, where she would finally be reunited with her beloved parents, sister, and Philip.

While the nation tried to come to terms with the loss of its Queen, there was no time for the royals to grieve. Charles and Camilla headed to England so that the new King could convene the Accession Council, which is made up of privy councilors, including the prime minister, the leader of the opposition, and members of the royal family. The ceremonial body only convenes on the death of the monarch and was last active in 1952 when George VI died. Members meet as soon as possible after the monarch dies, usually within twenty-four hours, at St. James's Palace in London, where Charles would be proclaimed King before traveling around the country on a nationwide tour as the new monarch.

When the Queen returned to Britain from Kenya following the sudden death of her father, she was a twenty-five-year-old mother and a glamorous young Queen who promised to breathe new life into the House of Windsor. When Charles III took the throne, it was the start of the Carolean age, the reign of Charles III, which looked very different from the Elizabethan age. At seventy-three, he was an aging monarch destined to rule in a very different socioeconomic and political climate. Elizabeth was loved and revered, but the age of deference was well and truly over, and there was no predicting how Charles would be received as King. Would this moment of transition give way to a new wave of republicanism? Would the crowds boo or cheer? And would they accept Queen Consort Camilla?

I was reporting live for NBC's *Today Show* when Charles and Camilla arrived at Buckingham Palace for the very first time as King and Queen Consort. Crowds of thousands had gathered, just as they had for the Queen's Platinum Jubilee. There was a sense of people wanting to witness the moment, pay their respects to the late Queen, and meet the new King and queen. Some were crying, but most were respectfully silent, simply trying to come to terms with the enormity of what had happened. As Charles and then Camilla stepped out of the car, the silence was punctuated with clapping and cheers and chants of "Long live the King." It was an incredibly moving moment, and while Camilla stood back, allowing Charles to take the lead, people clamored to shake his hand and offer words of support. There was even a peck on the cheek from one enthusiastic supporter.

This walkabout had not been planned. Charles was due to meet the prime minister at the palace, but upon seeing the crowds, the King asked his driver to stop. He seemed to draw comfort from the words of support and encouragement that he received, words which would buoy him over the coming days. As he walked through the palace gates with the Queen Consort by his side, it seemed as though all was not doomed. Britain had lost one monarch but gained another, and one it seemed who had already laid out a blueprint to be the people's King.

When he delivered his address to the nation and Commonwealth that night, Charles showed leadership and heart. Sitting at his late father's desk in the blue drawing room at Buckingham Palace with a photograph of the Queen by his side, he paid tribute to his "darling mama," saying, "As you begin your last great journey to join my dear late papa, I want to simply say this: thank you. Thank you for your love and devotion to our family and to the family of nations you have served so diligently all these years. May flights of angels sing thee to thy rest."

This was the most important address of his life, and it ticked every box. Quoting Shakespeare, one of his favorite playwrights, Charles pledged to renew the Queen's promise of lifelong service, thus stamping out speculation that he would allow the Crown to leapfrog a generation and move to William. He announced that his eldest son would succeed him as both Duke of Cornwall and Prince of Wales (the twenty-second in history), making Kate the Princess of Wales, the first woman to hold the title since Diana. "With Catherine beside him, our new Prince and Princess of Wales will, I know, continue to inspire and lead our national conversations helping to bring the marginal to the centre ground where vital help can be given."

The titles, laden with history, signaled a seismic shift for the former Duke and Duchess of Cambridge. William was now the heir to the throne, ever closer to the Crown, and Kate was inheriting a title not used since Diana. Kate "appreciates the history" associated with the title, sources close to her revealed, but insisted that she was keen to create "her own path."

When Charles was given the title of Prince of Wales at the age of nine, there were fears of nationalist violence at his investiture ceremony in 1969; however, William had no plans for such a ceremony, and his aides made it known early on that there would be no ornate antiquated investiture. Father and son agreed that such a ceremony would feel out of touch. Instead William and Kate had already forged a deep connection with Wales and its people, having lived on the island of Anglesey as a couple and newlyweds and taking George and Charlotte on their first official engagement to Cardiff during the Queen's jubilee celebrations. William and Kate were also planning an imminent visit to Wales after the new King had visited the country and after the official period of royal mourning. A seamless transition and boots-on-ground approach was far more in keeping with William's vision of the beginning of his tenure as Prince of Wales. This was the start of a new era, and it felt unusually intimate.

During his important address to the nation, Charles spoke of his "darling wife, Camilla" promising she would "bring to the demands of her new role the steadfast devotion to duty on which I have come to rely so much." And in a gesture of reconciliation to his younger son he said, "I want to also express my love for Harry and Meghan as they continue to build their lives overseas."

It wasn't just personal—there was politics too—and Charles addressed his critics head-on by making it clear he would be a convening King, but not a meddling one. He said he would respect "our system of parliamentary government" and vowed to "uphold the constitutional principles at the heart of our nation." He also promised to serve the Commonwealth realms—a reminder that the countries overseas were very much in his thoughts, as were his many patronages and charities, although he acknowledged that he would no longer be able to dedicate so much of his time to them.

For the first time in history, the formal proclamation of the death of the monarch and the accession of the new sovereign was televised from St. James's Palace.

The Accession Council is made up of 250 dignitaries, including privy councilors and high commissioners of the fourteen Commonwealth countries where the monarch is head of state. The ceremony is divided into two parts—a meeting of the King's Privy Council, and a litany of official proclamations for the King to sign. William, a privy councilor, watched his father, knowing that he would be the next person to take the oath and be sworn in as King. As a member of the Privy Council, Camilla was also by Charles's side, which was just as well, for when the King's fountain pen started to leak at the crucial moment of signing, it was Camilla who saved the day by calming him. The episode trended on social media with GIFs of the King losing his patience.

Yet it was a reminder that while he was King, he was also under great pressure and still Charles, a man known for being quick to lose his temper, which goes as quickly as it comes.

For all that was modern about this reign change, there was plenty of tradition; the public reading of the proclamation was delivered by the most senior herald in the realm from the balcony of the palace, followed by a forty-one-gun salute in Hyde Park. In keeping with centuries-old protocol, Charles was then proclaimed King Charles III at the Royal Exchange in the City of London while heralds on horseback rode from the palace and began passing the proclamation across the country. No wonder this spectacle, this piece of ancient theater, was being watched with interest around the globe. Most people had never witnessed anything like it in their lifetime.

When the Queen's coffin left Balmoral for Edinburgh, it was the moment, for most, when the reality that she had really gone set in. For Scotland, it was a chance to pay tribute to a monarch who had in fact been more Scottish in ancestry than English. The Queen Mother, who'd died aged 101 in 2002, was of Scottish ancestry, as she was a member of the Bowes Lyon family descended from the Royal House of Scotland. According to National Records of Scotland, the Queen's parents shared Robert II, King of Scots, as a common ancestor. But the Queen's connection with Scotland extended beyond heritage. She had always held Scotland dear to her heart. It was the country where she had given her first public speech as a teenager in Aberdeen in 1944 and a country she had visited for her Silver, Gold, and Diamond Jubilees. Each year she spent long summers at Balmoral riding her horses, picnicking in the hills, fishing, and deer stalking. She was as fond of the people as she was of the countryside, and they in turn of her. Many locals, who were used to seeing the Queen around the Royal Deeside area, had come to the gates of Balmoral to lay flowers and see the Queen's children and some of her grandchildren, including Princesses Beatrice and Eugenie and Zara Tindall, as they carried out a walkabout to thank people who had stood outside for hours waiting for a glimpse of the family. There were grandparents and families, toddlers and babes in arms, and teenagers videoing the moment. Each had wanted to come and pay their respects.

When the Queen's coffin was transported from Balmoral to Edinburgh via Royal Deeside, thousands more locals took to the streets and countryside lanes. Accompanied by Princess Anne and her husband, Tim Laurence, the hearse made its way through Aberdeenshire past Forfar and Dundee and skirted Perth before embarking on the final lap south to Edinburgh. It took six hours and twenty minutes and gave the people of Scotland a chance to say a final farewell.

In Ballater, the Aberdeenshire village where the Queen had often been seen in the streets and the shops, it was as though the tight-knit community of residents had lost a cherished neighbor. After passing Crathie Kirk, the small granite church in the shadow of the Cairngorm mountains where the Queen attended Sunday service when she was in residence at Balmoral, the hearse slowed to a walking pace. The Queen had not been seen in public since July 21, when she'd arrived in Aberdeen. Unlike previous years, there was no welcoming ceremony at the gates of Balmoral, and the Queen did not go to church. Nor was she well enough to attend the Braemar highland games. But that wasn't to say she hadn't been missed. It took more than six hours for the hearse to reach Edinburgh because it slowed continually to allow the many mourners a moment of reflection. When it arrived in Edinburgh, the coffin remained at Holyroodhouse Palace for a night before being taken to St. Giles's Cathedral in a royal procession up the Royal Mile, the main street of Edinburgh's old town.

The King, stoic, led his siblings in procession behind the coffin from the palace down the Royal Mile to the cathedral. The hearse was flanked by a bearer party formed by the Royal Regiment of Scotland and the King's Body Guard for Scotland.

The crowds of around sixty thousand crammed every inch of the famous Royal Mile. Some waved Union Jacks, others carried homemade posters paying homage to the Queen. There were shouts of "God save the King" and a brief disruption when a lone man heckled the Duke of York before being arrested by police for breaching the peace. The strain on Charles's face as he walked uphill was evident, but once again he drew support from the people.

The first minister of Scotland, Nicola Sturgeon, said that the passing of the Queen in Scotland and her lying in rest "will for evermore form a very special part of the history of Scotland." Two and a half months before, Sturgeon had announced plans to hold a referendum on independence on October 19, 2023. It was no secret that the late Queen had not wanted Scotland to become independent, and the breakup of the union is one of Charles's greatest concerns as King. Yet here were the Scots in their thousands, not just turning out to grieve their Queen, but to welcome the new King. There were cheers of support for Charles when after the ceremony, he performed his first engagement as head of state, receiving condolences at the Scottish parliament and meeting with First Minister Sturgeon.

Hundreds of thousands of mourners queued through the night to see the coffin, which was draped in the Scottish Royal Standard. This is different from the usual royal standard in that it has the lion rampant—the arms of the kings of Scots—whereas the standard has the three lions of England. The Crown of Scotland, which was made in 1540 for King James V, rested on top of the coffin alongside a wreath of white flowers. After sunset, there was a Vigil of the Princes in which Charles, Andrew, Edward, and Anne each stood by one of the four corners of the coffin for ten minutes as members of the public filed past. The King, who was wearing the Prince Charles Edward Stuart tartan and white heather in his lapel from Balmoral, looked toward the floor as he stood alongside four suited members of the Royal Company of Archers, who were standing guard dressed in long-feathered hats and armed with arrows and quivers.

The royals were grieving very publicly, and seeing them by their mother's coffin was an extraordinary sight. Charles had entrusted the responsibility of flying the Queen's body home to England to his sister. According to the original plans for Operation Unicorn, the Queen was to be taken from Scotland to London by the royal train, but these plans were altered while the Queen was still alive so that she would be flown back to England instead to avoid any risks of overcrowding at stations and along the route. On the evening of September 13, Princess Anne boarded an aircraft for RAF Northolt. "It has been an honour and a privilege to accompany her on her final journeys," Anne said in a statement. "Witnessing the love and respect shown by so many on these journeys has been both humbling and uplifting."

The journey from RAF Northolt to Buckingham Palace was extraordinary. Traffic came to a halt in the driving rain as the cortege drove through the streets of London, bringing the capital to a standstill. Charles, Camilla, and the immediate family were waiting at the palace, their heads bowed.

It was a grueling time for the King, who was not only coming to terms with the death of his mother, but also carrying out a carefully choreographed tour of the UK. Keen to meet his new subjects, Charles and Camilla traveled to Northern Ireland and Wales as well as Scotland ahead of the state funeral. His mother had not carried out such a tour upon her accession, but Charles had wanted to and thousands of well-wishes greeted him on the streets outside Hillsborough Castle (the monarch's official residence in Northern Ireland). Just as she had in life, Elizabeth transcended politics in death, and at a ceremony the acting speaker of the Northern Ireland Assembly, Alex Maskey, a member of Sinn Féin, which seeks the reunification of Ireland, paid tribute to the Queen, who, he said, "personally demonstrated how individual acts of positive leadership can help break down barriers and encourage reconciliation." Crucially for Charles, he also said that the new King had understood the importance of reconciliation and was committed to it.

There had been fears that the death of the Queen would give way to a growing trend for republicanism across the UK, but a poll taken at the time showed Charles had enjoyed a surge of support since becoming King. According to the YouGov poll, 63 percent thought he would be a good king, a rise of 24 percentage points since March, while 15 percent believed he would do a bad job, compared with 31 percent six months earlier.

Even in Wales, where there had been campaigns to abolish the role of the Prince of Wales, the new King and Queen Consort received a warm welcome at Llandaff Cathedral in Cardiff, where they attended a remembrance service. Among the thousands of supporters there was just a handful that held banners protesting against the monarchy. Charles charmed members of the Welsh Senedd when he addressed it in Welsh.

Whether that support would continue remained to be seen, but for now Charles had the public on his side, and they looked to him to shepherd the nation through this time of transition.

The Queen's journey from Buckingham Palace to the medieval Westminster Hall for the lying-in-state service was particularly poignant. I was reporting for the BBC when the ceremonial procession left the palace, and there wasn't a sound from the crowd as the horses pulled the gun carriage bearing the coffin, which was adorned with the Imperial State Crown, down the Mall. Just months earlier, the Queen had greeted her subjects lining this very route on the occasion of her Platinum Jubilee. As the coffin passed me by, I felt a lump in my throat. Elizabeth had known that balcony appearance at the close of her jubilee celebrations would be her last. And secretly, so had we.

Perhaps the most moving sight was William and Harry walking behind the coffin, in lockstep, just as they had at Diana's funeral, and more recently at their grandfather's. William stared straight ahead as he processed directly behind his father, in keeping with his place as the new heir to the throne. To the sound of funeral marches played by the Scots Guards and Grenadier Guards, the procession stepped off at a slow pace of seventy-five steps per minute. The Queen Consort,

Princess of Wales, Countess of Wessex, and Duchess of Sussex followed the cortege by car.

At the ancient hall, the coffin was set on a catafalque with the Queen's crown, orb, and scepter placed on top of the coffin. After the service, which was attended by all extended members of the Queen's family, her four children kept a vigil just as they had in Edinburgh. On this occasion, however, Charles allowed Andrew to wear his military uniform as a mark of respect, even though the duke had been stripped of his military titles. Harry was given the same privilege at a separate vigil of the grandchildren on the Saturday night before the funeral. Prince William, Prince Harry, Zara and Peter Phillips, Princesses Beatrice and Eugenie, and Lady Louise Windsor and Viscount James Severn took their places by the catafalque as members of the public filed past. It was a reminder that Elizabeth hadn't just been a queen, she had been a much-loved grandmother too.

William paid a moving tribute, saying, "She was by my side at my happiest moments. And she was by my side during the saddest days of my life," while Harry described his grandmother as a "guiding compass" and said how grateful he was for the "special moments" they had shared. Perhaps the most emotional tribute was from Eugenie, who said, "We, like many, thought you'd be here forever. And we all miss you terribly."

The last royal to lie in state had been the Queen Mother in 2002. Then some 200,000 filed past her coffin. Back in 1952, there were four-mile queues as 300,000 mourners paid their respects to King George VI. Over the coming four days and five nights, more than 250,000 people queued up to four miles to see the Queen's coffin, waiting up to thirteen hours or longer in the cold in a line that snaked along the Thames from Westminster to Tower Bridge. Millions logged on to the queue tracker for a live view of members of the public filing past the catafalque.

I was reporting for *Vanity Fair* and spoke to some of those who had queued through the night. One mother with three young children said she had packed a bag full of sugary treats to keep them going, and that despite having to queue through the night, this was something they "simply had to do." "The queue," as it was quickly known, became a phenomenon, with celebrities like David Beckham joining members of the public and other household names coming under fire in the media for using their VIP status to jump the queue. The everyday Britons who queued did so without complaint. After the Queen's lifetime of service, standing in line, which was a peculiarly British concept after all, was a small sacrifice for Britons to make.

Charles and William arrived unannounced one morning to speak to those who had queued overnight, lifting the spirits of everyone who saw them. There was a sense of community and camaraderie as strangers struck up conversations with one another and shared blankets and picnics.

The morning of the funeral was unseasonably cold and crisp. The capital was on lockdown, streets were closed to traffic, and there was a no-fly zone over the abbey. The two-thousand-strong congregation assembled from 8:00 a.m., when the abbey's vast doors were opened. The guest list embodied every aspect of British and Commonwealth life, with overseas government representatives, heads of state, and members of foreign royal families arriving by coach in what was one of the biggest security operations ever staged in Britain.

In keeping with protocol, kings and queens from Europe and afar were the last to arrive. Queen Margrethe II and Crown Prince Frederik of Denmark were seated nearest to the catafalque, with King Carl XVI Gustaf and Queen Silvia of Sweden, King Willem-Alexander, Queen Máxima, and Princess Beatrix of the Netherlands alongside them. The former Spanish King Juan Carlos and Queen Sofia were surprise attendees along with reigning King Felipe VI and Queen Letizia. King Harald V and Queen Sonja of Norway, King Philippe and Queen Mathilde of the Belgians, and Prince Albert and Princess Charlene of Monaco were seated alongside grand dukes and duchesses and other crowned heads of Europe and beyond, including Emperor Naruhito and Empress Masako of Japan, the sultans of Brunei and Oman, and King Tupou VI of Tonga, and the queen of Bhutan. The vast and eclectic guest list reflected the loyalty to Queen Elizabeth II around the globe.

More than four billion people around the world tuned in to watch the state funeral on television while hundreds of thousands of mourners took to the streets of the capital to witness the historic day unfold.

At 10:30 a.m., the coffin was transported in yet another ceremonial procession from Westminster Hall to Westminster Abbey, but this was on a scale not seen in England for many years. The State Gun Carriage was drawn by 148 sailors, the Royal Navy personnel marching arm in arm and pulling it forward by ropes in a solemn tradition dating back more than a century. The two-and-a-half-ton carriage was first used at Queen Victoria's funeral on February 2, 1901, and then for the funerals of King Edward VII, King George V, King George VI, Sir Winston Churchill, Lord Mountbatten, Princess Diana, and the Queen Mother.

I was broadcasting with the BBC from a rooftop position overlooking the abbey, and it was quite a moment to see the hearse and procession arrive. On the stroke of eleven o'clock, the country fell silent. The one-hour service conducted by the Dean of Westminster with the archbishop of Canterbury was televised and beamed across giant screens around the capital's royal parks. Baroness Patricia Scotland, secretary-general of the Commonwealth, read the first lesson; Prime Minister Liz Truss read the second. The Queen had chosen her favorite hymns, including "The Lord Is My Shepherd," which was sung at her and Philip's wedding.

In the front row, her family looked on solemnly. The cameras panned in on the two youngest members, George and Charlotte, who with their parents had walked the length of Westminster Abbey behind the coffin, looking so small compared to the vastness of the great abbey where their parents had been married. George was dressed in a dark blue suit and black tie. Charlotte was in a black dress and wide-brimmed hat, and as they entered the abbey they looked around at the sea of faces staring back at them. Kate placed her reassuring hands on their small shoulders.

The decision for them to attend couldn't have been an easy one, and it was a break with tradition. At previous state funerals, children have not had prominent roles, but George and Charlotte were part of the procession into the abbey, with George walking alongside his father. William understandably had reservations, having walked behind his mother's coffin as a boy, and he didn't want to subject his children to anything traumatic, particularly with such a huge media presence. But the image of the next generation of royals sitting in the front pew sent out a powerful message to the UK and the Commonwealth. It symbolized the future of this great family and that the succession of the House of Windsor was secure. Here was the next heir and spare. The Queen's great-grandson is now second in line to the throne. Charlotte is the new spare, and her presence was a reminder of how her birth had ended years of male primogeniture. Charlotte is third in line to the throne while Louis, who was not present at the funeral, is fourth. Both Charlotte and George know their place in the line of succession. Princess Anne was leapfrogged by her younger brothers, but the Queen ensured this would not be the case with Charlotte.

This was the first funeral the children had attended, and it was for their beloved "Gan Gan," as George and Charlotte called her. They adored her and wanted to say goodbye.

———·———·———

WHILE WILLIAM AND Kate did their best to keep things normal at home following the Queen's death, the Wales family, as they are now known, had gone through a period of great change. Just weeks before they had enjoyed a short holiday at Balmoral with the Queen. It was a relaxing end to a busy summer during which the family had relocated from their twenty-one-room apartment at Kensington Palace, where they had lived since 2017, to the much smaller four-bedroom Adelaide Cottage in the grounds of Windsor Great Park. It was downsizing—there was not enough space for the nanny to move in—but William and Kate sometimes felt like they were living in a goldfish bowl at the palace, and they wanted their three children to have a more ordinary—and rural—upbringing. They could enjoy more privacy, freedom, and open space in Windsor, and they had also wanted to be closer to the Queen as she neared the end of her life.

The nineteenth-century Grade II–listed retreat, nestled in the heart of the Crown Estate's Home Park, is just a short walk from Windsor Castle, required no major renovations, and was deemed perfect for the family. George, Charlotte, and Louis (five at the time of writing) had been photographed arriving at the nearby Lambrook School for their first day. The next day, the Queen died.

Louis was deemed too young to attend the state funeral, but George and Charlotte, who by now had some experience in the public eye, coped admirably. While her legs didn't reach the floor as she sat straight-backed on the pew, Charlotte looked older than her seven years. George seemed nervous, biting his lip and often turning to his sister for support, and at one point she urged him to bow his head when the coffin passed them.

Two generations removed, Charles sought that same sibling support and reassurance from Anne, whose stoicism he leaned on heavily throughout. At points, the King looked close to tears, gripping the handle of his ceremonial sword, his face somber and strained, but he was always under the watchful eye of Camilla and his sister. It was evident from Anne's high-profile role throughout the period of mourning, and the responsibility she had been given in escorting her mother's body from Balmoral to Edinburgh and from Edinburgh to London, just how much Charles valued and depended on her.

After the commendation, the Dean of Westminster pronounced the blessing. Last Post was sounded by the State Trumpeters of the Household Cavalry from the steps of the Lady Chapel. Two minutes of silence was then observed around the country, broken by Reveille, and then the congregation singing the national anthem with the words "God save the King" sung for the first time in seventy years. As "Sleep, Dearie, Sleep," performed by Pipe Major Paul Burns, echoed around the abbey, the Queen's coffin was carried outside and placed back on the State Gun Carriage and the royal funeral procession moved through Parliament Square, Whitehall, Constitution Hill, and the Mall, arriving at Wellington Arch at 1:00 p.m. to make the very final journey by car to Windsor.

In total, nearly 6,000 soldiers were deployed on Operation London Bridge, along with around 175 troops from Commonwealth countries. Mounties of the Royal Canadian Mounted Police were followed by representatives of the George Cross Foundations from Malta, the Royal Ulster Constabulary, and National Health Services of the United Kingdom, along with detachments from Commonwealth armed forces, including troops from Australia and New Zealand. At the forefront of the procession alongside the King, the Prince of Wales and other family members, including the Queen's children and grandchildren and former equerries to the Queen, marched alongside her hearse. Her faithful page Paul Whybrew walked alongside the royal family. Paul had stayed with the Queen throughout the pandemic, supported her after Philip's death, and been by her side during the final weeks of her life. Like many of the Queen's staff, his future was uncertain. The palace had announced there would be redundancies during the transition, and a letter warning of job cuts had been sent out to staff at Clarence House. The Queen had wanted her most trusted and loyal staff to have the honor of walking alongside her family behind her coffin, and her sergeant at arms, Barry Mitford, also walked at the top of the procession.

The crowds that lined the route were quiet, the only sound hooves on tarmac and minute guns fired in Hyde Park while Big Ben tolled throughout. A sea of smartphones suspended in midair captured the historic moment. Some mourners threw flowers into the road, others shed tears, but most just watched in awe. People had traveled the length and breadth of the country to witness this moment. One sixty-eight-year-old woman from Canada had camped on the south side of the Mall for five nights to secure a ringside seat.

The procession down the Long Walk at Windsor was a moment most would never forget. Thousands had gathered along the one-thousand-year-old, three-mile-long, oak- and chestnut-lined route, which had been transformed into a carpet of flowers. As the hearse approached the chapel, there was loud applause. This was the Queen's ultimate homecoming, and there to greet her was her faithful Fell pony Emma and her loyal groom Terry Pendry, who had touchingly placed the Queen's headscarf on top of the saddle. It was a moving sight, as were the Queen's corgis Sandy and Muick, who were waiting for her with two members of the Royal Household. The Queen's last dorgi, Candy, had died just a few weeks before, at the ripe age of eighteen. It had already been agreed that Prince Andrew and Lady Sarah Ferguson would take care of her two remaining dogs, which he had given the Queen as puppies following the death of the Duke of Edinburgh.

The arrival of the Queen's Company First Battalion Grenadier Guards, who protected her in life and death, at the chapel marked the beginning of the committal service. Many of the Queen's staff past and present had been invited, including her close friend and senior dresser and personal assistant Angela Kelly, the Master of the Horse, the lord chamberlain, the Keeper of the Privy Purse, the Earl Marshal, and the archbishops of York and Canterbury.

In the chapel, the King sat where his mother had during Prince Philip's funeral, alone and masked because of the Covid restrictions, while the Dean of Westminster conducted the service. The Queen had chosen the music, including John Donne's "Motet," which was composed by Sir William Henry Harris, who taught Elizabeth piano when she was a young girl. At the end of the short ceremony, the "instruments of state"—the scepter and the orb—were removed from the coffin by the Crown Jeweller and conveyed by the Queen's bargemaster and a sergeant of arms to the Dean of Windsor, who placed them on the High Altar. Princess Charlotte, who was sitting next to her mother with her uncle Harry to her other side, watched curiously, pointing. Back in 1953, a young Charles had watched in similar amazement as his mother was crowned, marveling at the occasion and trying to understand it all.

It was the King who placed the Queen's regimental crimson silk flag known as the Company Camp Colour on his mother's coffin, having received it from the regimental lieutenant colonel of the Grenadier Guards, an act of such emotion and solemnity that

Charles was moved to tears. The flag, the oldest in the armed forces, was finally being retired after seven decades. But perhaps the most moving moment was when the lord chamberlain Lord Parker broke his wand of office to mark the end of his service to the sovereign. It truly marked the end of Queen Elizabeth's reign.

As the Dean of Windsor read Psalm 103, which ends with the words "Go forth upon thy journey from this world, O Christian soul," the coffin was lowered into the vault while in the north quire the Queen's piper, who played outside the Queen's bedroom each morning, piped a final lament which echoed around the church before the choir and congregation sang "God Save the King."

The King appeared exhausted, emotionally and physically. While cameras had been permitted into the service, the actual burial was a strictly private moment and a final chance for the family to say their goodbyes. Alongside the ledger stone bearing the names of the Queen's parents was a new black marble one bearing the names "Philip and Elizabeth II." Finally, Elizabeth was united with her beloved parents, the ashes of her sister, and her late husband. It was the end, but it was also the beginning.

CHAPTER 12

The New Royals

If you become the sovereign, then you play the role in the way that it is expected.

—His Majesty the King

In an interview to mark his seventieth birthday in 2018, the Prince of Wales, as he was then, was asked if he planned to change his ways when he became King. He retorted, "The idea that somehow, I am going to go on in exactly the same way . . . is complete nonsense because the two are completely different. If you become the sovereign, then you play the role in the way that it is expected."

Now we are seeing that in action. The man who was the longest-serving Prince of Wales in history has taken the throne for what will be a short but highly significant reign, charting a new course for the entire royal family in the twenty-first century.

Out has gone the loud lobbying for his passion projects and favored causes, replaced with a quiet advocacy for what he believes is best for his people and country. His warmth and ease in public remain, but there is also a new gravitas befitting a head of state. His beloved Camilla has become—officially—his Queen and, unofficially, his greatest asset.

So what can we expect from King Charles III and this new Carolean age?

Those who know him best say the monarch is a passionate man with a strong moral compass and an enduring belief that we can all be better humans. They highlight his enormous capacity for empathy (he often tears up listening to opera) and his dogged pursuit of social issues such as youth employment and inner-city housing. They flag his support for neglected communities, including rural sheep-farming villages, and his global campaigning in the critical area of climate change.

Nothing that he has done in the months since his mother died in September 2022 suggests he is going to sacrifice that side of himself to become an austere, unopinionated ruler.

In fact, says royal documentary director John Bridcut, the Charles he knows will not reign remotely but by reaching out to his subjects to serve them better: "He looks for a connection with people, however brief—their shared experience. Charles is natural, warm, and funny."

Undoubtedly, Charles is Britain's first eco-king, a monarch with green fingers and green ideals, who has lived an environmentally aware life since he was a teenager.

That's not going to change either. In fact, one of his first notable acts upon taking the throne was to ask for profits from a £1-billion-a-year Crown Estate wind farm deal to be used for "the wider public good" rather than as extra funding for the monarchy.

In taking such a radical step he highlighted his ongoing support for alternative energy sources and acknowledged the crippling cost-of-living crisis confronting Europe as a result of the Covid pandemic and the war in Ukraine. His first Christmas speech in December 2022 showed similar thoughtfulness when he spoke of those struggling with "conflict, famine or natural disaster" and also "those at home finding ways to pay their bills and keep their families fed and warm." Compassion has been the hallmark of his leadership from the start.

Much of what Charles believes is shared in his 2010 book, *Harmony: A New Way of Looking at Our World*. It's an unusual piece of work which asks if the challenges of the built environment, engineering, medicine, and farming could be met by creating a more balanced and sustainable world. It calls for people to reconnect with nature, philosophy, and spirituality to rebalance modern life.

Anyone wanting a blueprint for the next decade of his reign would do well to read it.

"Charles has always been ahead of his time," points out former royal aide Patrick Harrison. "He really believes in what he does and I think that now he is finally getting some credit."

That said, as his seventieth-birthday interview made clear, he knows that his days of hard campaigning on controversial issues are over. "If Charles did speak out of turn," says constitutional expert Robert Hazell, "if he continued to support causes that were seen as political, I think the prime minister of the day would move quite swiftly to say, 'Sir, that's unacceptable. Now that you're King, I'm sorry, but you can't go on speaking in public about those things.'"

It's definitely a new way of working for Charles and as well as having to master it, the new King has come to the throne with what you might call multiple in-box issues.

At the very beginning of his reign there seemed to be a revolving door at No. 10 Downing Street and in the nation's treasury. The existential threat posed to the United Kingdom by the rise of Scottish independence has not gone away, and the sands beneath the Commonwealth are shifting too. Then, of course, there's Megxit, a constitutional headache and a family disaster, plus the unresolved issue of Prince Andrew, whose name and reputation has been tarnished by his association with convicted pedophile financier Jeffrey Epstein.

Even Charles's first international trip of his reign in March 2023 was dogged by problems. President Emmanuel Macron of France canceled the royal visit to Paris, ostensibly fearing for Charles and Camilla's safety amid civil unrest over French pension reform. However, there was some suggestion the real reason was that the French leader didn't want the damaging optics of a splendid state dinner in the Palace of Versailles while he was supposed to be dealing with a domestic crisis.

Would he have dared cancel on Queen Elizabeth? Charles does not seem to have his mother's international clout yet.

Thankfully the second leg of the royal pair's trip, to Germany, went ahead as scheduled and was a riotous success. Charles addressed a state dinner in flawless German. Camilla was resplendent in royal jewels, notably the City of London fringe necklace (a wedding gift to her later mother-in-law back in 1947) and the Greville tiara, a decadent favorite of the Queen Mother. The visit was designed to shore up relations with the UK's closest neighbors post-Brexit, and it's fair to say the royal couple's double act was as dazzling as Camilla's diamonds.

Unexpectedly, the quick change of prime minister from Liz Truss, who was in office when Queen Elizabeth died, to Rishi Sunak six weeks later, served the new King well. It was a reminder to the country that continuity and stability come from a hereditary constitutional monarch and not the country's elected rulers in Westminster.

Over the border in Scotland, however, politics remain tricky for the new King.

The death of the Queen in Balmoral and her epic last journey back to Edinburgh for her final flight to London said much about the strength of the ties between the late monarch and the Scottish people. But is there the same affection for Charles?

The question of Scottish independence, which would see Scotland splitting from the United Kingdom and perhaps also casting off the monarchy, is what keeps Charles awake at night, according to a close friend.

At the time of writing, the Scottish National Party (SNP), which governs Scotland, has just had a change at the top with its once popular, powerful, and charismatic leader Nicola Sturgeon stepping down ahead of an investigation into missing party funds. Humza Yousaf, who served as both health secretary and justice secretary in the Sturgeon government, has taken over.

Worryingly for the royal family, Yousaf has never hidden his republican tendencies. Just three days after Prince Edward was granted the Dukedom of Edinburgh in March 2023, Scotland's political leader declared his country could ditch the monarchy and choose an elected head of state within five years of independence.

"I don't know why we should be shy about that; I don't think we should be," he told the *National*, a pro-independence newspaper. "I've been very clear, I'm a republican. That's never been anything I've hidden," he said, adding he considered himself a "citizen not a subject."

Right now the popularity of the SNP is waning and with it the imminent prospect of independence. A YouGov poll for the *Sunday Times* newspaper showed support for a yes vote declining from 53 percent in December 2022 to 47 percent in February 2023, so for now Yousaf's republicanism poses an ideological threat rather than a real one.

Arguably the greater danger to the stability of Charles III's reign comes from the splintering of the Commonwealth as Britain's former colonies seek to sever their links with the UK.

One such country is Jamaica, where Prime Minister Andrew Holness has made clear his island plans to become an "independent, developed, prosperous country." Back in 2021 he said there was "no question" that Jamaica would one day ditch the British monarch as its head of state and become a republic. St. Lucia and St. Vincent and the Grenadines may all follow suit.

"I imagine it is important to Charles that the Commonwealth won't die with him," notes historian Alastair Bruce. "No one wants to be holding the institution when a significant part of its profile is taken away."

The hammer blow to his global reach will be if Australia jettisons the monarchy. The republican-leaning Anthony Albanese, who became Australia's prime minister in May 2022, has indicated he will let the matter rest in his first term. However, he does not appear to have ruled out a referendum on constitutional change if his Labor Party wins a second term in office.

Royal historian Ed Owens, honorary research associate at the Centre for the Study of Modern Monarchy, recognizes the devastating blow this would deal to what he calls "Elizabeth II's imperial monarchy."

He says: "What the British monarchy wanted to do and what the British state wanted to do was hold on to this image of international power and prestige, so empire was reformulated as something called the Commonwealth.

"The monarchy had to be the glue holding the Commonwealth together and they readily embraced this role—being the symbolic center of the Commonwealth—because it gave them power at a global level, which of course they enjoyed when they were the glue in the empire too.

"It's another string to monarchy's bow, helping justify the Crown's survival into the second half of the twentieth century."

The empire, he added, had always been the royals' "private playground," but now—it's faced with modern countries with no desire to stay stuck in the colonial past. The consequence of this can only be a lessening of the new King's power.

The royals were dispatched on multiple Commonwealth visits throughout Queen Elizabeth's Platinum Jubilee celebrations in 2022—unfortunately, not all of them ended well. The catastrophe of the new Prince and Princess of Wales's visit to the Bahamas, Jamaica, and Belize will be examined by historians for decades to come.

First, a spontaneous and jolly handshake through a wire fence with a crowd watching football looked, in the words of BBC royal correspondent Jonny Dymond, like "some sort of white savior parody." Then, what was meant to be a touching homage to the Queen and the Duke of Edinburgh went badly wrong too. In a snapshot which will haunt the couple forever, they stood in the back of the open-top Land Rover used by Queen Elizabeth and the Duke of Edinburgh on their trip to Jamaica in 1953. William was in his tropical dress uniform. Kate was in white lace and a fussy hat. It was outdated and patronizing. It made the royal family look racist at worst and guilty of unconscious bias at best—just as the Duke and Duchess of Sussex had alleged in their Oprah Winfrey interview.

Charles had hoped his mother's funeral in September 2022 would pave the way for a reconciliation with his youngest son, but Harry and Meghan returned to California without calling a truce. Those left in London were suspicious about the Sussexes' six-part documentary series set to be broadcast globally on Netflix in December 2022 and the upcoming January 2023 publication of Harry's autobiography, *Spare*.

There were hard feelings on Harry's part too. While he had been allowed to wear his military uniform to keep vigil over his grandmother's coffin during her lying in state in Westminster Hall at the Houses of Parliament, the Queen's initials had been removed from his epaulettes, leaving him devastated.

Additionally, he and Meghan were told to vacate their Frogmore home on the Windsor estate, gifted to them by the late Queen. It came as part of a wider shake-up of royal properties, signaling a tightening of the King's purse strings, but it was humbling for the Sussexes to be left without a British home of their own.

The turbulence between Windsor HQ and Harry and Meghan's freelance court in Montecito, California, reached all the way down to the new King's grandchildren, Archie and Lilibet Mountbatten-Windsor. As of March 2023, they are styled as the Prince and Princess of Sussex in the line of succession on the monarchy's official website. However, according to one source: "The titles are there, but they come with a caveat. The King needs to know that the values of the institution will be upheld if a title is going to be used."

Given these very public rows over houses, titles, and status, Harry and Meghan did not hold back in promoting their Sussex brand and protecting their personal reputation.

First they wooed the world with the inside story of their courtship in their Netflix documentary. The program put the adorable Archie on show for the first time with stunning images of his first birthday party, bird-watching with his father, and reading with his mother.

And then came *Spare*.

The King's PR team scrambled to keep up as the book accidentally went on sale in Spain five days ahead of schedule. The reveals were breathtaking. Harry admitted to doing drugs, to losing his virginity in a field behind a pub, to killing twenty-five people in Afghanistan, and to a fistfight with William which saw Harry topple into a dog bowl.

He gave his own version of the infamous row between Meghan and Kate in the run-up to the Sussexes' wedding and accused his brother and sister-in-law of encouraging him to wear the Nazi fancy dress costume for which he'd been publicly condemned back in 2005. He said William had not been his best man, that this had been a confection, a half lie, told to a country still in love with the idea of "Diana's boys."

He said he and his brother had urged the King not to marry Camilla and that he'd re-created his mother's final moments driving through the Pont de l'Alma tunnel in Paris. Among his most private revelations were his final words to his grandmother Queen Elizabeth.

It was utterly devastating—and an instant global best-seller.

There was a united front in both Kensington Palace and Buckingham Palace—no comment. Instead Charles and Camilla and William and Kate got on with the job Harry had left behind—being working royals.

In the wake of *Spare*'s publication, the entire family's popularity slumped to its lowest level in a year, with an approval rating of 47 percent, down six points since the start of 2023. It was the lowest figure recorded by pollster Ipsos UK in the previous twelve months. Interestingly, the Sussexes were the least popular members of the family—apart from the Duke of York—but the collateral damage was immense.

The rivalry between the Sussexes and the Cambridges had been in clear view a month earlier when Harry and Meghan were nominated for the Ripple of Hope Award given by the Robert F. Kennedy Human Rights organization to social change leaders. The news came just as William and Kate were due to arrive in Sussex territory—America—for the second Earthshot Prize.

Earthshot is everything to William. Launched in 2020 in an homage to President John F. Kennedy's moon shot, it was instantly spoken of as a kind of green Nobel Prize, the most prestigious environmental prize in history. It will award five $1.2 million prizes annually for ten years to the best ideas to save the planet.

Launched by Prince William under the auspices of the Royal Foundation of the Duke and Duchess of Cambridge, the prize is funded by some very deep pockets: DP World, the Aga Khan Development Network, Bloomberg Philanthropies, Marc and Lynne Benioff, the Paul G. Allen Family Foundation, and the Jack Ma Foundation.

This was only its second year of operation, with its annual awards night in Boston. An overlap with the adoring publicity for the Sussexes' Kennedy award was not something Buckingham Palace had anticipated.

Historian Andrew Lownie compares the Sussexes and their alternative new lives in California to the post-abdication court of Edward VIII and Wallis Simpson. He is not referring to Edward and Wallis's well-established Nazi sympathies. (The Windsors visited Hitler in Bavaria after years of being courted by supporters of the Nazi regime, and, in 1941, an FBI agent claimed the duke had done a deal promising to return to London and be installed as a puppet King in the event of a German victory.)

What Lownie means is that there are again tensions playing out between one couple free-styling their royalty abroad and another dutifully toeing the line at home.

For the duration of George VI's reign, while Edward was alive, there was a tension between the two brothers, explains Lownie. "In Britain the Windsors were seen as a sad couple in exile but in America they were celebrated; huge crowds came out to see them. They were always vying for attention. The Windsors announced their wedding date on the eve of George VI's coronation. There was always a play for the headlines and we see that again today."

Added to which, another race row was about to make for more troubling headlines for the royal family.

Royal aide Lady Susan Hussey was a Lady of the Household to the King, a title which reflects her decades of royal service. She was on duty at a royal reception hosted by Queen Camilla in Buckingham Palace when things took a devastating turn.

I was covering the event for *Vanity Fair* and said hello to Lady Hussey, who was by the Queen's side and seemed in high spirits and in good form. One of her jobs was to chat with guests and put them at ease, and I watched as Lady Susan cheerfully circulated the room. However, when she introduced herself to Ngozi Fulani, founder of a domestic violence charity which offers specialist services to women of African and Caribbean heritage, their conversation misfired.

The headlines focused on an uncomfortable exchange in which Lady Susan repeatedly asked Ms. Fulani where she was "really" from. Ms. Fulani posted her record of the exchange online shortly after the event, and a heated row broke out on social media and got increasingly ugly, with commentators leaping to the defense of both sides.

The palace was quick to issue a statement about the "unacceptable and deeply regrettable comments." Separately, Prince William was moved to declare, "Racism has no place in our society." It was a zero-tolerance approach which declared that even though Lady Hussey was loyal and loved—and William's godmother—she had to go.

"We had to act swiftly because it would have been disastrous otherwise," I was told by a senior courtier. The situation would be amicably resolved some months down the line when the two women met to discuss what had happened, but there is no denying that it blighted the opening weeks of Charles's reign, and for some, the episode gave further oxygen to Harry and Meghan's claims that the royal family needed to deal with its unconscious bias.

In the face of such criticism, Charles has leaned on his Queen and on the Prince and Princess of Wales for support. A powerful image of the fab four—Charles, Camilla, William, and Kate photographed on the eve of the Queen's funeral—was intended to convey an image of togetherness and familial serenity.

Similarly, Charles is open about the help he receives from the industrious Princess Anne, the princess royal, and has rewarded the loyalty of his youngest brother, Prince Edward, and his sister-in-law Sophie Wessex with the cherished titles of the Duke and Duchess of Edinburgh.

But it is William who is truly operating as the King's wingman, while mapping out his own plans for the future. His new status was underscored when he visited Poland in March 2023 to thank British and Polish soldiers supporting Ukraine in the war against Russia. It was a secret, low-key trip which made headlines around the world.

Given his own military service in the Household Cavalry (Blues and Royals) and his later attachments to the Royal Air Force and the Royal Navy before he became a full-time royal, William was the right man for this job. Speaking in the Polish capital, Warsaw, he said, "Our nations have strong ties. Through our cooperation in support of the people of Ukraine and their freedom, which are also our freedoms and yours, these ties are further strengthened. I'm here because I want to personally thank the Polish and British troops working in close and crucial partnership." They were statesmanlike words designed to be heard not just in Warsaw and London, but in Washington, DC, and Moscow too, and a clear signal of the kind of Prince of Wales we can expect William to be.

William has said he wants to be his own man and, when asked about the influence of his father in a 2016 BBC interview, said, "There are so many things I admire about my father: his work ethic, his passions, all that sort of side of things are absolutely crucial to how he's been such a successful Prince of Wales and an amazing father. But I want to be . . . personally, I want to be my own man, and take my own style, my own passions, and my own interests . . . and do things slightly differently. I think it's important each generation does things a little bit differently than the previous."

Patrick Harrison observes this about the two men: "Father and son are on the same page in terms of a slimmed-down, cost-effective monarchy; about the banishment from public life of Prince Andrew; and about the need for evolution not revolution in anything to do with the institution they cherish.

"Charles and William recognize that the institution has to continually justify itself in a non-deferential age. It needs to continually renew and reconnect with the public it serves. That's something they're working on together."

William is already a capable statesman, a campaigner for the environment and for mental health, and a patron whose charitable interests and learning stretch from the presidency of BAFTA (British Academy of Film and Television Arts) to mountain rescue to ornithology. He has also taken on the running of the Duchy of Cornwall, the 130,000-acre estate that generates the heir to the throne £21 million a year.

His father's accession has been a sudden significant step up for him too.

"If you're not careful, duty can wear you down an awful lot at a very early age," he said in a 2016 BBC interview ahead of his grandmother's ninetieth birthday.

It's why both his father and his late grandmother gave him their blessing to live as freely as he could in his youth.

For William and Kate that meant the "Anglesey years," which must now seem like a dreamy, easy period of their increasingly busy public lives. The couple rented a farmhouse on Anglesey between 2010 and 2013, living there as newlyweds while William was working as an RAF search and rescue helicopter pilot. It is also where they raised Prince George for the first few months of his life. They included the island on their itinerary when they made their first trip to the principality as the Prince and Princess of Wales in September 2022.

That relaxed, unbuttoned time served as a template for the way they try to live now—when they are not on duty. William and Kate have a smaller staff than the King and Queen, and while there are occasional luxury holidays to the private island of Mustique, they make a point of holidaying in Britain, often flying commercial. They enjoy bucket-and-spade breaks on the Isles of Scilly and family bike rides along the islands' picturesque lanes.

The Waleses' incarnation of British royalty looks more like today's Spanish royal family, with King Felipe and Queen Letizia on the throne, or perhaps Denmark, where Crown Prince Frederik and his

Australian-born wife, Crown Princess Mary, are poised to succeed. The appealing prospect of King William and Queen Kate with Prince George next in line may quell any rumblings of discontent in a country reigned over by a couple well past its ordinary retirement age.

The Waleses are still settling into their new life in Windsor, sharing Adelaide Cottage on the castle estate with Prince George, Princess Charlotte, and Prince Louis. Their house dates back to 1831, when it was built as a retreat for William IV's wife, Queen Adelaide of Saxe-Meiningen, and was once a favorite breakfast spot for Queen Victoria. It's historic but much smaller than their other two homes, apartment 1A in Kensington Palace and Anmer Hall in Norfolk. It is, however, convenient for the school run and close to Michael and Carole Middleton.

The Wales children are being raised by their parents in an ordinary albeit privileged way. They are aware of their positions within the royal family and the roles they will one day carry out in support of the monarchy. George knows that, like his papa, he will one day be King, while Charlotte will likely juggle the role of being the spare with a career. Louis could well be a private citizen, undertaking occasional royal duties like William's and Harry's cousins Princesses Beatrice and Eugenie and Zara and Peter Phillips.

Inevitably because he is an heir, there is more pressure on George, who at the time of writing was set to be a page at his grandfather's coronation.

Kate is said to admire the way the Duke and Duchess of Edinburgh are raising their children—Lady Louise Windsor and James, Viscount Severn—in the bosom of the royal family but prepared for life in the real world. That's why George is seen at ceremonial occasions but can also be found on playdates at friends' houses, enjoying birthday parties with his peers, and at weekend soccer lessons. (He has inherited his father's love of the game.)

In that landmark BBC interview, William also revealed he had been schooled in the art of monarchy by the Queen, whose guidance he has described as "soft, influencing, modest," with a focus on "timeless values." He admitted he's contemplated what kind of King he will be; how a millennial prince could make such an ancient role relevant to twenty-first-century Britain.

"It occupies a lot of my thinking space, about how on earth you would develop into something modern in today's world," he said. But, asked if he was confident he could achieve it, he didn't skip a beat. "Absolutely!"

He went on: "The royal family has to modernize and develop as it goes along . . . and that's the challenge for me. How do I make the royal family relevant in the next twenty years' time, or it could be forty years' time, or sixty years' time."

One former aide told me, "Prince William above all prizes stability. He would have looked at the Queen's household and seen [that] the one thing about the Queen's household was that it was a happy place to be. The people there tended to [have] a great sense of humor, a great sense of perspective, a great humility, and all of that created a really stable working environment which supported the Queen and Prince Philip really well over the decades.

"He would want to create the same with his own household, with his own team. Stability's a big thing for William, and if you were to put one adjective next to Queen Elizabeth it would probably be the remarkable stability she brought to the United Kingdom over decades of change."

"He will do great things for sure, and he won't be afraid to ask questions, just like his father," says someone who has worked closely with William for more than a decade. "When he does become King, I think you will see a man very similar to the man you see today, putting his own stamp on the role."

"William," says another friend, simply "has got very, very broad shoulders."

He is going to need them as the royal family picks its way through the next decade or two.

As for the Princess of Wales, she will continue her work in children's early years. "My own journey into understanding the importance of early childhood actually started with adults," Kate has explained. "I wanted to understand what more we could do to help prevent some of today's toughest social challenges, and what more we could do to help with the rising rates of poor mental health. My hope is that we can change the way we think about early childhood and transform lives for generations to come."

In June 2021 she launched the Royal Foundation Centre for Early Childhood. The center will bring together the expertise of early-years professionals from the public, private, and voluntary sectors to raise awareness of the crucial first five years of life. It was a bold move and one that signaled her vision as the future Queen, helping the children who will become adults by the time she is Queen herself.

There has been a notable shift from the sidelines into the spotlight for Kate. This was most apparent in 2022 when Kensington Palace released a trio of photographs to mark her fortieth birthday. It wouldn't be an overstatement to say they heralded a new age of Kate. Taken by Italian fashion photographer Paolo Roversi, the princess wore two Alexander McQueen frocks and jewelry from both the Queen's and Diana's collections. In the soft-white gowns, she resembled Cecil Beaton's 1940s portraits of the then princess Elizabeth and a young Princess Margaret.

In the final image she wears a rich, royally red asymmetric dress, with a hand casually in her pocket. It was a triumph and a notable contrast to her debut on *Vogue*'s cover in 2016 when she was dressed down in a brown country coat and a green fedora. Kate's decision to pose so boldly for the portraits, which will be on permanent display at the National Portrait Gallery, showed a new confidence: through the camera lens Britain could see the former Kate Middleton had come of age.

"Kate has been successful because she understands the importance of being part of a team and she has developed the ability to glow and to stand out," observes historian Robert Lacey. "She gives out a message of supportiveness to her husband, her own family, and to the wider royal family. She seems likely to be a Princess of Wales who does not detract from her prince but instead forms a unit. This was not the case with Charles and Diana, as we know. But go back in history to George V and Queen Mary, the couple who created the modern monarchy and the concept of the modern royal family. William and Kate have those same qualities; they understand the family role of the job."

It wasn't so long ago that William and Kate must have imagined themselves doing "the job" with Harry's help. But as Lacey says, "Harry soon lost interest in playing what he came to see as a subordinate role in the royal set-up."

Harry and Meghan are the same generation as William and Kate. Harry was born into the same life as William. Yet he has always challenged royal parameters while William has stayed safely inside them. As the spare, Harry has had the latitude to do so, and today the Sussexes draw their boundaries in a completely different place from the Waleses.

I spoke to an aide who knows the Sussexes well and has observed their work in the United States. "Actually the more you see about how the Sussexes are approaching these things, it is much more Californian, much closer aligned to activism and celebrity than it is to royalty," he said. "The point about royalty is it's the only institution that links together civic society, the philanthropic world, and establishment. You've got politicians, you've got the armed forces, you've got all these different institutions that matter to people and that impact people's lives, and then you have civic society, which is everyday life and businesses and so on, and then you have the philanthropic world. Royalty operates equally in all three of those areas, and is comfortable in all three. That is something unique to royalty.

"The Sussexes know they're not able to compare to them [the Prince and Princess of Wales]. The key point is that they're not even trying. What they are doing is making a difference in their politico-philanthropic world, and that's great."

But this divide, exemplified by the Waleses on one side and the Sussexes on the other, has raised fundamental questions about the responsibilities of royalty, its purpose, and its value in the modern age.

It's not so much an issue for Charles and Camilla, who are forward-thinking but still associated with a different era. It is, however, a conundrum that will have to be solved by King William and Queen

Kate. A former aide says, "William has always been very firm that his role is about duty, not celebrity, but he recognizes in today's world that he and Kate can use their global profile and that there is a huge amount of interest in them. There is always something meaningful behind a red-carpet moment."

And that is the point for William and Kate and what they hope to impress on their children. They will be much more than celebrities or philanthropists. They have a unique global platform: the monarchy is theirs to fashion in the way they see fit.

The greatest challenge for them, according to historian Anna Whitelock, is apathy. Disinterest. Boredom. A sense that by the time they reach the top of the institution, it will be insignificant in twenty-first-century Britain.

Addressing some of the biggest issues of our time, including mental health and the environment, is one way for them to combat that. Living their own "prince marries commoner" fairy-tale love story is another. Working hard and being seen to do so is one more. They're stars on social media (after appointing the Sussexes' social media team when Harry and Meghan left Britain), using their Instagram and YouTube channels to evidence the effort they make on behalf of the UK and, crucially, to connect with the younger demographic who will one day be their subjects.

What else can we expect from the eventual King William? A smaller court than his father's. More diversity reflected in his household. The future lineup of the monarchy comprises three Kings, and so he will want Kate to be his equal, not just a consort, reflecting the importance of a female presence. Over the coming months and years, the UK can expect her to carry out more solo tours and overseas visits reflecting her causes and interests, with William's full support. It will see Kate as a mirror image of the Duke of Edinburgh, who devoted his life to supporting the Queen. That's their royal ambition then: to be new Elizabethans, to reign as successfully as Queen Elizabeth II.

All that, though, is currently one step ahead. These years are for Charles to make his mark before his son takes the throne. He might be a septuagenarian monarch, but his strong work ethic will stand him in good stead. He is always at his desk before 9:00 a.m. and returns to his red box of government papers after dinner.

He has also been particular about putting his own family affairs in order. Although he is intent on trimming down the monarchy, the King has made sure no one is left out in the cold. Prince Andrew will never carry out royal engagements, but he has not been excluded from family gatherings and was with his family at Sandringham for Charles's first Christmas as king. Then there's been that shuffling of royal residences which effectively evicted Harry and Meghan. In what was nicknamed "Game of Homes," the refurbishment of Buckingham Palace continued apace with a view to more of it being open to the public and the rest of it serving as monarchy HQ. William and Kate are in Adelaide Cottage for now, but there is speculation that they will move into Windsor Castle in due course.

The Harry-and-Meghan drama is still playing out on both sides of the Atlantic, but the King has left a door open for them both, as his mother did.

There's a cash-for-honors scandal hanging over Charles's head, but he has done his best to distance himself from it by firing Michael Fawcett, the royal aide at its heart. Fawcett was the King's former valet, promoted to chief executive of the Prince's Foundation, the umbrella organization for the King's charities when he was Prince of Wales. A file was passed to Britain's Crown Prosecution Service last October. (At the time of writing, the Metropolitan Police and Buckingham Palace had both declined to comment on an ongoing inquiry.)

If there's one surprising thing about Charles's reign, it's not Charles: it's Camilla.

Once a reviled royal mistress, she has become something akin to the nation's favorite aunt who can mix a good gin and tonic, knows which horse is going to come in first, and wears fabulous hats. She has eased her way into the spotlight only to use it to redirect attention toward the issues she cares about.

Jude Kelly is the founder of the organization Women of the World, which seeks to empower women and close the gender gap. Camilla is its patron. Kelly says, "She's not someone who is trying to push herself forward, but because she sits in a place of power where the limelight is on her, she can use that to speak about other people's situations, and she does, more and more."

The issues and causes Camilla has aligned herself with are wide ranging, and some of them, for example, domestic violence and female genital mutilation, are tough. Adds Kelly, "She's comfortable calling them out, she wants to learn more about them. I often hear her ask people, 'How can I make a difference?'"

Friends say Camilla has accepted the life of duty which comes with royal marriage and is ready to work. Her friend the novelist Jilly Cooper remarks, "I think Camilla has climbed Everest in the way she has turned things around. People are now seeing her for who she is, kind, caring, and fun."

She has quietly kept Ray Mill House, the home she bought close to Highgrove after her divorce from Andrew Parker Bowles. She can be found there from time to time in her dressing gown, scrambling eggs and asking Charles to pour the tea. It remains her escape from public life.

Those closest to Camilla believe her sense of humor and tendency not to take herself too seriously have stood her in good stead. One of her friends noted that while Charles could not bring himself to watch how the hugely popular TV series *The Crown* portrayed their relationship, Camilla opened a bottle and sat down in front of the television. "Camilla watched it with a glass of red wine. Charles decided not to," says the friend of the couple. "It was all rather too close to the bone."

According to her nephew Ben Elliot: "She will always see the absurd in many things. She is very witty. She has a very close and supportive family and a close group of old friends. She adores her husband, children, and grandchildren."

Camilla's best qualification for her current job is that Queen Elizabeth trusted her completely. On New Year's Eve 2021, the then monarch made her daughter-in-law a Royal Lady of the Most Noble Order of the Garter, investing her into a seven-hundred-year-old order which recognizes great public service and is in the personal gift of the sovereign.

It's the pinnacle of the British honors system, something very rarely bestowed. "The Queen couldn't have done more than make Camilla a Lady of the Garter," says historian Hugo Vickers. "That's never happened before to a Princess of Wales or a wife of an heir to the throne. Diana wanted the garter, everyone wants the garter, but very few get it."

Camilla earned it because she showed that in loving the King for half a century or so, she is his soulmate and most ardent supporter. Together they are a partnership, and Charles depends deeply on Camilla's support. She is known to be a calming influence on the King and was unflappable when a student hurled eggs at Charles on a walkabout in York in November 2022. Those around the monarch sprang furiously to his defense, chanting, "God save the King," and "Shame on you," in furious retaliation while Camilla kept smiling and carried on with the walkabout. The student was arrested and later charged with a public offense disorder, and while the episode highlighted one lone protestor's resistance to the monarchy, for the most part Charles and Camilla have been warmly welcomed by their subjects, which must be both comforting and reassuring.

The Queen's seven decades on the throne were an extraordinary achievement, her Platinum Jubilee unmatched. Charles in contrast is unlikely to reach twenty-five years and mark his Silver Jubilee. There is speculation that he might hand the reins to William at a point in the future—before his death—when he feels he has done what he has set out to do as King. Charles is a realist and knows that to survive, the monarchy must remain current and relevant. There will inevitably be a time when the prospect of a younger King and Queen reigning over the United Kingdom is more appealing than an aging monarch and his Queen. So it's William V's reign which is the million-dollar question, and what he'll do when history is his for the shaping.

Epilogue

Coronations are a declaration of our hopes for the future.
—Prince William of Wales

The coronation of King Charles III and Queen Camilla was the first crowning of a King and Queen since 1937, and it was a truly historic moment for Great Britain.

For many, it was a once-in-a-lifetime occasion, and around the country there was a sense of excitement and intrigue about what would take place at Westminster Abbey, where monarchs have been crowned since 1066. Charles would be the fortieth monarch to be crowned at the abbey and at seventy-four, the oldest. Despite concerns that the scaled-down coronation would be short on pomp and pageantry, the coronation was a great success and attracted worldwide interest.

I was covering events over the coronation weekend for NBC's *Today Show* and *Entertainment Tonight* in the US, which, along with other major networks from around the world, sent crews to the UK.

There was great interest in how this ancient ceremony would be updated to reflect a more diverse and inclusive age and much speculation about how Charles's coronation would differ from his mother's. Charles is a traditionalist at heart, and the palace had announced that the 260-year-old Gold State Coach would transport the newly crowned King and Queen from the abbey to Buckingham Palace, where there would be a royal salute in the gardens for the very first time, followed by the famous balcony appearance and flyby.

This time Charles and Camilla would be stepping onto the balcony as King and Queen, and which family members would be joining them was a matter of much speculation.

The media had labeled it a "scaled back" coronation after the palace announced just 2,300 guests had been invited compared to the 8,000 who filled Westminster Abbey for the late Queen's coronation. The service would be televised by the BBC, but it would be just two hours rather than Queen Elizabeth's epic three-hour ceremony. The processional route had also been scaled back in order to reduce security costs.

Britain was in the midst of a cost-of-living crisis, and the cost of staging the coronation—which was estimated at between £50 and £100 million—was seen as excessive at a time when people were struggling to pay bills and nurses, doctors, and teachers were staging walkouts and national strikes. Graham Smith, head of Republic, the leading anti-monarchy group in the UK, echoed the thoughts of many people when he said, "At a cost of tens of millions of pounds, this pointless piece of theatre is a slap in the face for millions of people struggling." According to one poll, more than half of Britons did not think it was right that the government should be picking up the bill, because ultimately it would fall to the taxpayer to cover the major security costs.

Charles was mindful of the backlash and decided not only should the coronation be less expensive than previous ones, it was time to break with a number of traditions. He wanted the coronation to reflect Britain's influence on the world stage, and so handwritten invitations were sent to more than one hundred heads of state, including presidents and prime ministers.

For the first time foreign royals were also invited, including Prince Albert and Princess Charlene of Monaco, Queen Letizia of Spain, Crown Prince Frederik and Crown Princess Mary of Denmark, and Crown Prince Haakon and Crown Princess Mette-Marit of Norway, as well as the crowned heads of Bhutan, Jordan, Tonga, and Thailand, the Imperial House of Japan, and the former royal houses of Bulgaria, Romania, and Greece. In the past, royals were not invited to coronations to reduce the risk of overshadowing the monarch being crowned, but Charles saw his coronation as a chance to show off the monarchy's power and might globally while also giving the tourist industry and Britain's struggling hospitality sector a much-needed boost.

After many years of speculation, it was confirmed by Lambeth Palace that the King would follow the centuries-old tradition of taking the titles of defender of the faith and supreme governor of the Church of England. However, at the King's request other faith leaders would be included within the Anglican service in order to represent Britain's culturally diverse society, including leaders representing the Buddhist, Hindu, Jewish, Muslim, and Sikh religions.

Charles had been closely involved in every part of the service, paying particular attention to the music, which included a gospel choir and twelve new compositions as well as some of his favorite pieces of choral music. The theme of service was central to the ceremony, and rather than the usual roll call of peers traditionally invited to a coronation, 850 of the guests were community and charity representatives chosen by Charles and Camilla.

The palace had announced an action-packed weekend that included a military procession of more than 4,000 troops, 19 military bands, and 1,000 musicians. After six months of intensive planning, the armed forces were ready to stage their largest ceremonial parade in seventy years. The Big Lunch—a charity to bring communities together, of which Camilla is patron—encouraged friends, families, and neighbors to hold street parties and enjoy the newly created "coronation quiche" created by royal chef Mark Flanagan, comprising a light pastry case and delicate flavors of spinach, broad beans, and fresh tarragon. Coronation chicken, created for the late Queen's coronation, is still a staple today.

A concert at Windsor Castle was set to be the highlight of the weekend, while the Big Help Out, a voluntary program focused on serving others, was planned for the bank holiday Monday, when various members of the family, including the Waleses, Princess Anne, and the Duke and Duchess of Edinburgh, would be getting involved in community projects around the country.

It was a particularly busy itinerary for the King, who hosted a reception at Buckingham Palace for one thousand VIPs, including heads of state and dignitaries the night before the coronation. More than 203 countries would be represented, and among those who had flown in were the French president Emmanuel Macron; the president of the European Commission, Ursula von der Leyen; Canadian prime minister Justin Trudeau; Australian prime minister Anthony Albanese; New Zealand prime minister Chris Hipkins; Ukraine's first lady, Olena Zelenska; and Chinese vice president Han Zheng, who oversaw the brutal response to protests in Hong Kong. In what was seen as a major breakthrough, however, republican Sinn Féin leader Michelle O'Neill and party speaker Alex Maskey were also invited. No US president has ever attended a coronation, but the First Lady, Dr. Jill Biden, was there to represent Joe Biden, along with their granddaughter Finnegan.

There was much excitement in the capital with royal fans camping on the Mall, which was bedecked with flags from around the Commonwealth and the world. The first tents went up a week ahead of the big day, and bunting and Union Jacks sprang up in cities, towns, and villages around the UK. The weather was typically British with torrential rain on coronation day itself, but it didn't deter the crowds. I spoke to people who had come from all over the country, and farther afield, who all said that this was an important moment in history and they wanted to be a part of it.

A series of polls had been carried out in the weeks leading up to the coronation which showed that two-thirds of Britons supported the monarchy, although its popularity was waning among the under thirties. What struck me, however, was the number of young people who had turned out to see the royals. While there was not the strong republican sentiment Charles feared might taint the start of his reign, there was still the threat that the coronation could be marred by protestors who planned to demonstrate in Trafalgar Square on the day.

On the eve of the coronation Charles decided to make an impromptu walkabout with the Prince and Princess of Wales so that he could greet and shake hands with some of those gathered. "Are you nervous for tomorrow?" asked one royal fan. Charles chuckled good-naturedly and shrugged. According to one of his friends, he was nervous about the numerous robe changes during the ceremony. Charles and Camilla had also been practicing wearing crowns at the palace to get used to the weight. While Charles would only wear the magnificent five-pound St. Edward's crown for a short period of time, including the moment of being crowned, he was required to wear the Imperial State Crown for many hours. In keeping with their wishes for the coronation to be sustainable, Camilla had chosen to wear a recycled crown. The Queen Mary crown, which was made by Garrard for Queen Mary's coronation in 1911, had been redesigned and the Koh-i-Noor diamond, which India wants back, removed. In a tribute to Queen Elizabeth II the crown was reset with the Cullinan III, IV, and V diamonds, which are part of the late Queen's personal jewelry collection.

The skies were leaden on the morning of Saturday, May 6, and when the rain came it was biblical, just as it was on the day of Queen Elizabeth's coronation, and on King George VI's, so perhaps it was a good omen.

The abbey had been filling up since early that morning, and London was on lockdown as the biggest security operation in recent times was executed. As I made my way to the abbey, I was struck by the queue of guests waiting outside. There were people of all races and religions and from all walks of life, united by their service to Great Britain. There was also a smattering of celebrities, including actors Dame Emma Thompson, Dame Judi Dench, and Dame Maggie Smith, who are close friends of Charles and Camilla. Prime Minister Rishi Sunak had been asked to give a reading, and also among the VIP invitees were American singers Lionel Richie and Katy Perry, who were headlining at the coronation concert, and TV presenters Ant and Dec, who work closely with the Prince's Trust. The dress code was modern rather than the tiaras, ermine, and robes usually required for the occasion. It felt more like recent royal weddings.

The royals arrived in order of precedence with Charles's and Camilla's closest family members occupying the front pews. In order to keep numbers (and therefore costs) down, royal attendance was limited to immediate family (siblings of the King and Queen, children, and grandchildren); working royals, including the late Queen's first cousins the Duke of Kent, the Duke and Duchess of Gloucester, Prince Michael of Kent, and Princess Alexandra; and Charles's cousins, including the Earl of Snowdon and Lady Sarah Chatto.

The Middletons were seated behind the immediate royal family. It was a privilege which illustrated the importance of Kate's family within the royal hierarchy.

At 10:20 a.m. precisely the King and Queen departed Buckingham Palace in the Diamond Jubilee State Coach—a tribute to the late Queen, who was the last to ride in the carriage made to commemorate her sixtieth year on the throne. With all modern configurations, including electric windows and handrails from the Royal Yacht *Britannia*, it was a comfortable procession along the 1.3-mile route down the Mall, and Charles and Camilla arrived early, a full six minutes before the 11:00 a.m. start time.

The King appeared slightly irritated that they had to wait outside the abbey for the Wales family to arrive. "We can never be on time," Charles reportedly muttered to his wife, his irritation perhaps betraying his nerves.

No doubt he had also been worried about family politics. There had been a question mark over whether Prince Harry would attend, and he caused organizers a headache by only confirming his attendance at the eleventh hour. The coronation clashed with Archie's fourth birthday, so the Sussexes decided that Meghan would stay in California with their two children. As Harry, dressed in a Dior morning suit and his military service and jubilee medals, took his seat in the third row with his cousins Princesses Beatrice and Eugenie, their husbands, and Prince Andrew, the fifth in line to the throne could not have looked more like an outsider.

It was the first time he had seen his family since the publication of his autobiography, in which he had described his stepmother Camilla as a "villain" and revealed how he and William had begged their father not to marry her.

Hidden by his aunt Princess Anne's cocked hat (Anne was dressed in full military uniform, as she was required to ride back from the abbey to the palace behind the state coach as Gold Stick in Waiting to the King), the duke was barely visible for much of the service.

By contrast the Wales family were center stage.

The King had asked family members to wear formal robes and no tiaras. Kate wore a leaf-themed silver headdress designed by Jess Collett and Alexander McQueen, who also designed her ivory gown, which was embroidered with rose, thistle, daffodil, and shamrock, the emblems of England, Scotland, Wales, and Northern Ireland. Now the second-most senior woman in the royal family, she looked more regal than ever in her impressive Grand Cross Mantle of the Royal Victorian Order.

McQueen had also designed an ivory cape dress for Princess Charlotte, who leafed through her Order of Service with confidence and looked relaxed despite the formality of the day.

It was Prince Louis's first state occasion, and the little prince, who was dressed in a custom-made Savile Row blue tunic and black trousers, arrived hand in hand with his sister and was on his best behavior.

Prince George had been made Page of Honour to his grandfather, and in his scarlet tunic he couldn't have looked prouder as he helped carry the train of the King's robe of state.

Camilla was flanked by two attendants, her sister, Annabel Elliot, and her closest friend and Queen's Companion, the Marchioness of Lansdowne. Her children, Laura and Tom, whose names she had embroidered into her Bruce Oldfield–designed gown, and her ex-husband, Andrew Parker Bowles, were among the congregation while her teenage grandchildren Gus and Louis Lopes and Freddy Parker Bowles and her great-nephew Arthur Elliot were her Pages of Honour.

"I come not to be served but to serve," Charles said at the start of the service, echoing the vow made by his late mother on her twenty-first birthday, when she said her life "shall be devoted to your service." While there were echoes of the 1953 coronation this felt modern and progressive in comparison. There were new touches alongside the ancient rituals of the coronation. For the first time two female bishops played a role, while Penny Mordaunt, the leader of the House of Commons, bore the ceremonial Sword of State.

The moment of anointing was steeped in medieval tradition and strictly private, however, with the King dressed in the simple white colobium sindonis white linen tunic worn by his grandfather King George VI at his coronation. Shielded by a screen featuring a tree with fifty-six leaves to represent the member countries of the Commonwealth, Charles wanted the sacred and intimate moment when the archbishop anointed him with holy oil consecrated in Jerusalem to be between him and God.

The moment of crowning was perhaps the most poignant of the ceremony, and the archbishop lifted the St. Edward's crown high in the air, sparkling, so that all could see its splendor before lowering it onto Charles's head and declaring, "God save the King." Seated on St. Edward's chair, also known as the coronation chair, in the dazzling gold supertunica robe and clasping the scepter and rod in either hand, this was the moment Charles had waited his entire life for. The abbey's bells rang out as gun salutes boomed across London and around the UK like a dramatic clap of thunder.

For all the ancient ceremony and ritual, it felt like a deeply personal family affair too. As Prince of Wales it fell to William to pledge the homage of the royal blood. Kneeling before his father in his Welsh Guards uniform, and clasping his father's hands, William vowed to be his father's "liege man of life and limb."

These were the same words Prince Philip pledged to the Queen on her coronation day and the words of allegiance Charles delivered to the Queen on his investiture in 1969 at Caernarfon Castle in north Wales. Now William was promising to be his father's most loyal and faithful supporter, and the moment he kissed his father on the cheek was deeply moving and clearly affected Charles. For father and son, who have not always seen eye to eye, it was a defining moment, and as William stepped back, Charles thanked him quietly.

As William watched the ceremony it must have been with mixed emotions knowing that his coronation would be next and after his, his eldest son George's.

Conversely there was no screen for the moment Camilla was blessed and anointed. It was as though Charles wanted the world to see, and as she was crowned, he allowed himself a smile that showed his inner joy and relief. He had always insisted she would be Queen, and now, finally she was. What was unthinkable only twenty-five years ago was now a reality, and as they exited the abbey to Elgar's *Pomp and Circumstance* there were broad smiles all round.

There were cheers and cries of "God save the King!" as the newly crowned King and Queen processed from the abbey back to Buckingham Palace, this time in the resplendent but far less comfortable Gold State Coach.

The rain had not put the crowds off, and when the King and Queen appeared on the palace balcony, Charles looked overwhelmed at the sea of tens of thousands of well-wishers on the Mall. He had been stepping out onto this balcony since he was two and had always doubted whether the crowds would show up for him the way they had for his mother. "Oh my goodness," Charles exclaimed, according to lip-readers. "It's wonderful!"

Low-level clouds meant the flyby had to be reduced in size, but it didn't matter. Prince Louis waved enthusiastically and looked up in amazement at the sky. Seventy years before, a four-year-old Charles had done the very same.

Charles had invited only working royals to join him, including the Wales family; Princess Anne and Vice Admiral Sir Timothy Laurence; Edward and Sophie, the Duke and Duchess of Edinburgh, and their children James, now the Earl of Wessex, and Lady Louise Windsor; the Duke and Duchess of Gloucester; Princess Alexandra; and the Duke of Kent. The King and Queen's page boys, the Queen's sister, and the Marchioness of Lansdowne were also invited to experience the moment.

The entire day went seamlessly, although there were fifty-two arrests, which included members of the anti-monarchy group Republic. The heavy-handed police response to a seemingly peaceful protest sparked outrage in Britain, which prides itself on being a free country. The other controversy was Prince Andrew being booed by the crowds as he took part in the procession back to Buckingham Palace, but ultimately nothing detracted from the King and Queen.

It was reported that one hundred million people tuned in to watch the coronation around the world, proof that the monarchy continues to fascinate and captivate. There was less interest in New Zealand and Australia, where authorities in Sydney decided not to illuminate the Opera House sails as a mark of celebration; nonetheless, the coronation received plenty of coverage in the media.

Charles is aware of the growing tide of republicanism overseas, and now that he is crowned, there will be various royal tours to Commonwealth countries and beyond to shore up support for the monarchy. According to a poll carried out days before the coronation, citizens in six of the fourteen Commonwealth realms outside the UK where the King is head of state want to become republics. Charles has always said that it is a matter for the citizens of those countries, but he will work hard to serve them while he remains head of state and prove that the monarchy does have a purpose.

Along with his wife, Queen Camilla, he has the full support of his son William and daughter-in-law Kate, who are unswerving in their duty and devotion to the Crown. Just like the late Queen, Charles is mentoring William and George for the role that lies ahead. The greatest challenge arguably will be justifying why modern-day Britain needs a hereditary monarchy.

And what will happen to those the Queen referred to as her "substitutes"? Charles has always lobbied for a streamlined royal family, but if it is to continue carrying out the number of engagements we have come to expect of it, along with the many patronages and charities the royals represent, then Charles is going to need support not just from the Waleses but also from Princess Anne and the Duke and Duchess of Edinburgh.

There is much he has set out to achieve as monarch, and he cannot do it alone. Now after the longest wait in history for the throne he is a King in a hurry. The day after his coronation celebrations came to a close he was back at work, setting the tone for his reign. He intends to be more than a caretaker King and do what he once told an interviewer he believed was his raison d'être: "I'm determined to make the most of it and to do whatever I can to help. And I hope I leave things behind a little better than I found them."

Acknowledgments

T here are many people I must thank whose experience and insight have been so valuable in writing *The New Royals*. Not everyone is with us today, sadly, so in the first instance I would like to express my gratitude to the late Lady Elizabeth Anson, the Queen's cousin, for her many wonderful anecdotes and years of friendship.

I was fortunate to interview cameraman Philip Bonham-Carter, who died in April 2022 from a sudden illness. Philip worked on the films *The Royal Family* and *Elizabeth R* and many of the Queen's Christmas broadcasts. I am so grateful to him for his time and his wonderful recollections.

I am also grateful to the late Sir Malcolm Ross for his help over the years.

I am indebted to my good friend and colleague Sarah Oliver for her valuable contribution, input, and advice from start to finish. Sarah, thanks for being with me on this journey and going above and beyond for me.

Thank you to my brilliant team at Hachette, particularly my editor Mollie Weisenfeld and vice president and associate publisher Michelle Aielli for their support and vision. Thanks also to my literary agent at Curtis Brown, Cathryn Summerhayes, and my agent at the Hollywood Alternative, Jamie Gruttemeyer, for their stellar advice.

Embarking on a book that spans the reign of arguably the greatest monarch in history is ambitious, and I am truly grateful to the many people who agreed to speak with me. I have respected the wishes of those palace courtiers (past and present) who kindly contributed on background or asked to remain anonymous.

Many individuals agreed to be quoted and named in the manu-script and I am particularly grateful to the following for their time and assistance:

Patrick Harrison for his insight into life at Clarence House and for correcting many of the myths about our future king.

Charles Anson for reflecting on some of the key milestones of Her Majesty's reign, and Patrick Jephson for providing context on the 1990s and the Diana years.

Special thanks to Robert Lacey for the many hours you kindly spared me, Sally Bedell Smith for your brilliant books and experi-ence. And Alastair Bruce, Andrew Lownie, Andrew Morton, Pro-fessor Anna Whitelock, Dame Martina Milburn, Dr. Ed Owens, Edward Mirzoeff, Hugo Vickers, John Bridcut, Mark Bolland, Lord Peter Hennessy, Sir Trevor Phillips, Wesley Kerr, Robert Hazell, Chris Jackson, Nick Bullen, and David McClure.

Thanks to my picture researcher Nikki Sutherland, Kelly Wood-ward for her assistance with the research, and my trusted transcriber Alison Sieff.

Writing a book is always a significant undertaking, so finally a huge thank-you to my family for bearing with me and my never-ending deadlines, and for your constant love and support.

References

Bedell Smith, Sally. *Charles: The Misunderstood Prince*. London: Penguin, 2017.

————. *Elizabeth the Queen: The Woman. The Family. The Life*. London: Penguin, 2017.

Brandreth, Gyles. *Philip: The Final Portrait*. London: Hodder & Stoughton, 2021.

Brown, Tina. *The Diana Chronicles*. New York: Doubleday, 2007.

Dimbleby, Jonathan. *The Prince of Wales: A Biography*. London: William Morrow, 1994.

Hardman, Robert. *Our Queen*. London: Arrow, 2012.

————. *Queen of the World*. London: Arrow, 2019.

Jackson, Chris. *Modern Monarchy: The British Royal Family Today*. New York: Rizzoli, 2018.

Jobson, Robert. *Charles at Seventy: Thoughts, Hopes & Dreams*. London: John Blake Publishing, 2018.

Lacey, Robert. *Battle of Brothers: William, Harry and the Inside Story of a Family in Tumult*. London: William Collins, 2020.

Lloyd, Ian. *The Queen: 70 Chapters in the Life of Elizabeth II*. London: History Press, 2022.

Morton, Andrew. *Diana: Her True Story*. London: Michael O'Mara, 2017.

Nicholl, Katie. *Harry and Meghan: Life, Loss, and Love*. London: Hachette, 2019.

————. *Kate: The Future Queen*. New York: Hachette Books, 2015.

————. *The Making of a Royal Romance*. New York: Hachette Books, 2011.

————. *William and Harry*. New York: Hachette Books, 2010.

Scobie, Omid and Carolyn Durand. *Finding Freedom: Harry and Meghan and the Making of a Modern Royal Family*. London: HQ, 2020.

Seward, Ingrid. *My Husband and I: The Inside Story of 70 Years of the Royal Marriage*. London: Simon & Schuster, 2018.

Index